Economic Divergence in the European Community

THE ROYAL INSTITUTE OF INTERNATIONAL AFFAIRS is an unofficial body which promotes the scientific study of international questions and does not express opinions of its own. The opinions expressed in this publication are the responsibility of the authors.

The Institute and its Research Committee are grateful for the comments and suggestions made by Professor Stephen Holt and Peter Oppenheimer, who were asked to review the manuscript of this book.

Economic Divergence in the European Community

Edited by
Michael Hodges and William Wallace

Published for

The Royal Institute of International Affairs
by GEORGE ALLEN & UNWIN

London   Boston, Sydney

First published in 1981

The Royal Institute of International Affairs
Chatham House, 10 St James's Square, London SW1Y 4LE

George Allen & Unwin (Publishers) Ltd
Ruskin House, 40 Museum Street, London, WC1A 1LU

British Library Cataloguing in Publication Data

Economic divergence in the European Community.
  I. Hodges, Michael   II. Wallace, William
  838.91'4   HC241.2   80-42287

  ISBN 0-04-382029-8

Typeset in 10 on 11 point Times
by Typesetters (Birmingham) Limited
and printed in Great Britain
by Billing and Sons Limited, Guildford,
London and Worcester

Contents

Preface

Since the international economic upheavals of 1973–4, the terms 'convergence' and 'divergence' have become common currency in the continuing debate about the European Community's political and economic development. Very little, however, has been done to define these somewhat ambiguous terms or to examine critically the links between economic divergence or convergence and political developments within the Community as a whole. The aim of this volume is to clarify some of the assumptions behind the current debate, to identify and examine current trends in economic performance and political cohesion within the Community, and thus to contribute to a more informed debate upon the Community's future direction and to a clearer understanding of the interlocking processes of economic and political integration.

Most of the chapters which follow were originally presented as papers at a two-day conference jointly sponsored by the Royal Institute of International Affairs and the University Association for Contemporary European Studies, in the summer of 1979. These in turn drew upon the work of a Chatham House research project on 'The political implications of economic divergence for the European Community', sponsored by the Social Science Research Council. Revised and updated in the light of further research within this project and of developments within the Community in 1979–80, with an additional chapter on the debate over the European Monetary System and a concluding review of the field, they are presented here as a first full-length report of the findings of that project. A companion volume, *Economic Divergence and European Integration*, by Yao-Su Hu, will appear in some months' time.

When this project was formulated in 1977, economic and monetary co-operation was at a low point in the Community. The suggestion that a European Monetary System might provide a practicable and acceptable way forward had not yet been floated; indeed, it should be recalled that the immediate reactions to Roy Jenkins's proposals later that year were almost uniformly dismissive. The argument over the British contribution to the Community Budget, and over the future of the Budget as a whole, had not then emerged as a central issue in Community bargaining. Our intentions were to avoid, so far as we could, immediate issues, and to focus on the longer-term problems which underlay the succession of disagreements over the purposes of economic co-operation, the size of the Regional Development Fund, or the distribution of Community expenditure. Despite the welling-up of immediate issues which has accompanied our study, we have attempted to fix our attention on these longer-term problems, and to tie in our discussions of the Budget dispute of 1979–80 and of the establishment and initial operation of the EMS to this longer-term view.

We are grateful to the other participants in the conference and in other study groups connected with this project for their contributions and criticisms as this volume developed. We would like in particular to thank Yao-Su Hu, Joan Pearce and Helen Wallace, who read and commented on the manuscript at different stages, and Ann De'Ath, who carried the main burden of organising the manuscript and preparing it for the press. Errors and omissions however remain the responsibility of the editors, conscious as they are that to examine the debate about convergence and divergence is to open a Pandora's Box out of which fly most of the awkward and unresolved issues which the European Community has tried to avoid since the Treaty of Rome was drafted.

MICHAEL HODGES
WILLIAM WALLACE

List of Contributors

GEOFFREY DENTON	Director, Federal Trust for Education and Research
E. C. HALLETT	Research Department, Foreign and Commonwealth Office
MICHAEL HODGES	Professor of International Relations, Lehigh University
DANIEL T. JONES	Senior Research Fellow, Sussex European Research Centre
JOHN PINDER	Director, Policy Studies Institute
JOCELYN STATLER	Research Assistant, RIIA, 1976–80; now independent researcher
JONATHAN STORY	Professor of European Business Environment, European Institute of Business Administration (INSEAD)
LOUKAS TSOUKALIS	Fellow of St Catherine's College, Oxford; from 1980 Research Fellow, RIIA
WILLIAM WALLACE	Director of Studies, RIIA
STEPHEN WOOLCOCK	Research Associate, RIIA

List of Abbreviations

AIC	Advanced Industrial Country
AUA	Agricultural Unit of Account
BSC	British Steel Corporation
CAP	Common Agricultural Policy
EAGGF	European Agricultural Guarantee and Guidance Fund
*EC	European Community
*ECSC	European Coal and Steel Community
ECU	European Currency Unit
*EEC	European Economic Community
EFTA	European Free Trade Association
EIB	European Investment Bank
EMCF	European Monetary Co-operation Fund
EMS	European Monetary System
EMU	Economic and Monetary Union
ERDF	European Regional Development Fund
ESF	European Social Fund
EUA	European Unit of Account
FRG	Federal Republic of Germany
GATT	General Agreement on Tariffs and Trade
IMF	International Monetary Fund
MCA	Monetary Compensatory Amount
MFA	Multi-Fibre Arrangement
NATO	North Atlantic Treaty Organisation
NEDO	National Economic Development Office
NIC	Newly Industrialising Country; Nouvel Instrument Communautaire
OECD	Organisation for Economic Co-operation and Development
OMA	Orderly Marketing Agreement
OPEC	Organisation of Petroleum Exporting Countries
PPP	Purchasing Power Parity
SALT	Strategic Arms Limitation Talks
SDR	Special Drawing Rights
SPD	Sozialdemokratische Partei Deutschlands
TES	Temporary Employment Subsidy
UNCTAD	United Nations Conference on Trade and Development
VAT	Value-Added Tax

*EEC and ECSC are used when specific reference is made to those communities and treaties; EC is used to refer to the Communities since the merger of the Commissions in 1967.

1

Liberty, Equality, Divergency: The Legacy of the Treaty of Rome?

Michael Hodges

> Je refuse de faire encore des propositions en ce qui concerne
> l'Union économique. Dans chaque communiqué publié à l'issue
> d'une Conférence au Sommet, on mentionne une phrase disant:
> Nous voulons maintenant la convergence des politiques
> économiques. Ce ne sont que des vœux pieux. (*Robert Marjolin,
> 1975*)

It is undoubtedly a tribute to the resilience of the European
Community that it can withstand economic divergence for long
enough to enable a group of academics to publish a book about it.
This talent for survival may spring from the very ambiguity of the
term 'divergence'; like the common cold, divergence is a generic label
for a variety of complaints — few of them fatal. When economic
divergence surfaces in debates about the development of the European
Community, we find that at different times (and not infrequently at
the same time) it can refer to divergence of economic policies, or of
economic performance, or of economic structures.

As the chapters following will make clear, the distinctions between
these different concepts of divergence are significant. The methods of
reducing them — of promoting convergence — are correspondingly
different in kind and in degree of difficulty. Yet in the debate about
convergence and divergence which has recurred within the
Community ever since the first divergence of exchange rates in 1969
and the first ambitious attempt to promote convergence of economic
and monetary policies which followed, few participants have been
meticulous in defining their terms. The words have often served as
useful labels for imprecisely defined demands, or as a common
vocabulary for political discourse into which each participant reads
his own preferred meaning. As Roy Jenkins, the President of the
Commission, told the European Parliament on 14 November 1979,

convergence . . . may be an obfuscating rather than a clarifying word, because it can mean different things to different people. To some it means little more than the better co-ordination of economic policies. To others it is a code word for dealing with the problems of the Budget, while to others still it means the transfer of resources to produce more consistent standards of living within the Community.

Not only is economic divergence an ambiguous concept, but also the relationship between European integration and economic divergence has thus far been obscure. Clearly economic divergence is of importance because the member states of the Community are in many respects interdependent, but we do not know what relationship exists between the development of Community policies and national economic divergencies. Despite the theological disputations of the 'economists' and the 'monetarists' a decade ago in the debate about economic and monetary union,[1] we have not established a concensus on whether economic convergence is the prerequisite or the product where Community policies are concerned.

It is now generally agreed by observers of the European Community that it has reached a critical phase in its development and that some important choices will have to be made on the essential purpose of the Community in the light of its further enlargement to twelve members and of the continuing turbulence in the world economy. Progress towards European Union, as the 'Three Wise Men' noted in their recent report,[2] 'would require that the Community be able to break through the underlying economic and political restraints which currently constitute the main obstacles to advance, and thus to establish a practical consensus on the path as well as the goals for development'. In this respect the very success of the Community, in exhausting the guidelines laid down in the treaties and expanding both the scope and complexity of its activities, has made such a break-through all the more difficult and contentious.

In the current debate over the future role of the Community, the fundamental question is whether Britain or any other member state is justified in assuming that the European Community — as it was conceived and as it has evolved — has any role to play in overcoming divergencies in economic structures, policies and performance between Community members, or whether the frequent invocation of convergence is (as Robert Marjolin argued in the quotation above) an act of piety rather than a commitment to action. The Treaty of Rome's call for 'a harmonious development of economic activities' a continuous and balanced expansion, an increase in stability, an accelerated raising of the standard of living and closer relations between the States'[3] might not necessarily demand the creation of a community of equals, but rather permit the preservation of diversity in an era of economic interdependence. If the latter is the case, then it is clear that the expectation of some British policy-makers that the Community can be used to overcome economic disparities through the transfer of resources is unrealistic and unjustified, and that if the Community is to have a part to play in the promotion of economic convergence it can only be through the emergence of a new political consensus which departs from the economic and political assumptions of the EEC Treaty.

The Founding Fathers and their Working Assumptions

If we go back to the formative years of the Community, we find that neither the Treaties of Rome nor the Spaak Report on which they were based (and which was adopted by the six Foreign Ministers in Venice on 30 May 1956 after less than two hours of discussion) gave a comprehensive and unambiguous definition of what constituted a 'Common Market', except that all agreed that it included a customs union whose implementation was to proceed by a series of fairly well-defined stages. As Richard McAllister has noted, 'between that minimal state . . . and some distant peak which came to be known later as "full economic and monetary union", there was a good deal of mist and dead ground.'[5]

Nevertheless, the Spaak Report and the EEC Treaty can tell us a good deal about the working assumptions of the founding fathers as they sought 'an ever closer union'. The Spaak Report stressed growth rather than equity: 'In an expanding economy, this division of labour manifests itself less by the displacement of existing production than by an even more rapid development, in the common interest, of more economic forms of production.'[6] Although the Report did concede that in the transitional period delays and derogations from the Treaty might be necessary in certain temporary situations, and that economically undeveloped regions might need assistance from the state in order to develop the infrastructure necessary to benefit from the creation of a large market under conditions of free competition, the Spaak Report did not anticipate that long-term disruptions or imbalances would emerge from the creation of a customs union; on the contrary, all would ultimately benefit from a unified, free and competitive market.

Indeed, the Spaak Report made it clear that national economic policies might well undermine the advantages to be derived from a common market: 'The role of the state in the modern economy is also evident in the divergences which each can bring about in the levels of economic activity or prices. This cardinal point underlines both the risk and the opportunity involved in the creation of a common market.' The opportunity was to co-ordinate economic policies in order to overcome balance-of-payments problems which hindered continued expansion, while the risk was that in the absence of common rules, implemented and supervised by Community institutions, the member states would undertake actions which would undermine the common market and reinforce divergences. One of the essential aims of the institutions would be 'to obtain a convergence of efforts to maintain monetary stability, a high rate of employment and a high level of economic activity.'[7]

When we examine the Treaty of Rome, we find that its provisions for the creation of the institutions of the EEC were reminiscent of the structure which had been devised for the ECSC, with certain significant differences. In the ECSC, which had only a limited functional scope, the High Authority under Jean Monnet had been given greater decision-making power in relation to the Council of Ministers than was to be the case with the EEC Commission, which was also intended to act as the guardian of the Community interest and the only begetter of new policy initiatives. That the EEC Commission's power to act was more circumscribed was due partly to the realisation that integrating economic activity in general was more fraught with uncertainty than dealing with the coal and steel industries alone, but was also caused by the realisation that Monnet had exploited the relative independence of the High Authority to expand its competence.

The Treaty's emphasis on the virtues of the free market led it to give the Community only a secondary role in overcoming divergence, which it regarded as being largely temporary and exceptional rather than endemic, and which could be minimised by careful co-ordination of national economic policies. Indeed, the EEC Commission's inaugural report on economic conditions minimised the need for uniform macroeconomic policies:

> To maintain the balance, advances in productivity do not need to be comparable at all points. Still less is it necessary for the instruments of political economy to be applied everywhere in the same manner; on the contrary, with different situations existing in every country, the maintenance of equilibrium may call for measures which are not identical but which complement each other in the pursuit of a common objective.[8]

The EEC Treaty laid down a schedule for the initial stage of the establishment of a customs union through the elimination of internal tariffs and the erection of a common external tariff, while it also provided overall objectives and policy guidelines for a common agricultural policy. On other matters it was much less specific, so that there were no comparable guidelines for a regional policy which would ensure (in the words of the Preamble) 'harmonious development by reducing the differences existing between the various regions and the backwardness of the less favoured regions', even though many Community policies – not least the creation of the customs union itself – would have clear regional implications. As the subsequent experience of the Community was clearly to demonstrate, the process of 'negative integration', through the abolition of internal tariffs and other barriers to the movement of goods and factors of production, did not 'spill over' through the 'expansive logic of sector integration' (as Ernst Haas and other political scientists had predicted) into 'positive integration' involving the development of Community policies designed to correct the deficiencies of the free market, or at the very least to co-ordinate national economic policies in order to ensure that they moved in the same direction.

Only in the case of the common agricultural policy and commercial policy can the Community be said to have played other than a subsidiary and supplementary role, and the controversy which surrounds the CAP hardly bodes well for a departure from this pattern. The EEC's constitutional crisis of 1965–6, caused by a six-month French boycott of Community institutions (when the Commission attempted to link the financing of the CAP with the creation of direct revenue for the Community and a stronger voice for the Parliament), marked a decisive shift in the balance of power towards the Council of Ministers and away from the Commission. The 'Luxembourg compromise' which ended the crisis had the practical result of eliminating majority voting in the Council of Ministers on issues considered by any state to be vital, and the reassertion of the power of the member states was underlined by the Merger Treaty of 1965, which gave the Committee of Permanent Representatives an official role in screening proposals to be made to the Council of Ministers. This meant that the establishment of new common policies (even in transport, where the Treaty had already provided for a common policy) or the restructuring of existing policies (such as the CAP) was made much more difficult than the founding fathers had envisaged – although the durability of the CAP in spite of its mounting cost and obvious faults does serve to indicate that integration does not depend upon perpetual progress to safeguard its achievements. Indeed, the elaborate system of MCAs and 'green currencies' devised to keep the CAP functioning after the breakdown of the Bretton Woods international monetary system provides further support for the argument that the *acquis communautaire* had demonstrated its durability in the face of economic turbulence.

The Emergence of the Convergence Issue

The establishment of the common market has been accompanied by a significant increase in intra-Community trade and hence economic interdependence, so that fluctuations in the level of economic activity have tended to be transmitted between member states more rapidly than before, resulting in diminished effectiveness for national monetary and fiscal policies in regulating the level of domestic economic activity. Although the Council of Ministers recognised the need to strengthen economic policy co-ordination as long ago as 1964, when the Medium-Term Economic Policy Committee was established to draw up a series of five-year plans, the programmes emanating from the committee were very general and had no great effect upon divergent national economic policies.

As the initial phase of economic integration matured in 1968 with the establishment of a customs union and the full implementation of the CAP, the Community's member states began to be painfully aware that they had come to the area of mist and dead ground beyond which lay the fuzzy vision of European Union – federal, confederal, or other. Instability in the international monetary system (fuelled by America's expansionary domestic economic policies and high military expenditure, upward movement of raw material prices and growing militancy of union wage demands), growing doubts over the Atlantic relationship and the implications of US-Soviet détente, and the lack of progress in moving the Community beyond the basic framework provided by the Treaty of Rome all served to emphasise the vulnerability and absence of ambition of the Community. The 1969 Hague Summit opened the door to enlargement of the Community and called for plans for economic and monetary union; a year later the Werner Report's plan for progressive achievement of EMU by 1980 emphasised the need for promotion of economic *policy* convergence as a prerequisite for monetary union, but did not delve into the question of whether convergence in economic *performance* could be brought about by policy co-ordination among the Community countries alone, nor the problem of divergence in economic *structures* which an irreversible monetary union would do nothing to solve and might well aggravate in a common market.[10]

The unhappy history of EMU and the floating membership of the snake, and the intricacies of the debate between the 'monetarists' and 'economists' which followed the proposals for EMU, are discussed further in Jocelyn Statler's chapter. The demise of the Bretton Woods system, the enlargement of the Community and the changing structure of the international economy (with challenges from Japan, OPEC, Korea, etc. to be added to the American *défi*) all served to underscore the vulnerability of the Community and the failure of the *acquis communautaire* to bring about spontaneously 'a harmonious development of economic activities, a continuous and balanced expansion', and the rest. The fact was that the Community had achieved its major successes at a time when world trade and capital movements were being progressively liberalised, with the enormous economic and political power of the United States being used as both the engine and the stabilising force; the Community had been 'condemned to succeed' in its phase of negative integration because there was nothing to stop it. As it entered the period when positive integration, in the sense of common policies (or at the very least very close co-ordination of national policies), were needed, the United States's pull weakened and the web of interdependence which had been previously created faithfully transmitted the shocks created by the new situation. Although divergent national economic policies had been seen in previous years as an obstacle to further integration, the debate on the Community's regional policy served to underline the failure of the Community to achieve greater convergence by reducing regional imbalances – the Commission's 'Report on the regional problems in the enlarged Community' of May 1973 argued that 'it is clear that rapid progress towards Economic and Monetary Union would be arrested if national economies had not undergone the transformations needed to avoid excessive divergencies between the economies of Member States'.[11]

By the time the oil crisis of 1973–4 and the subsequent recession hit the Community, the initial preoccupation with policy convergence (in the sense of mutually reinforcing national economic policies) – itself a substitute for the economic convergence which a decade previously had been expected to flow automatically from the progressive implementation of the customs union – was now supplemented by concern over long-term divergences in the performance of the economies of member states. Indeed, such divergences were now seen as a prime cause of the failure of the EMU proposals to be implemented, leading the Commission to argue: 'Priority must be given to regional structural problems so as to ensure the convergence of the economies of the Member States and, thereby, the achievement of economic and monetary union.'[12] At the Paris Summit in December 1974 – a meeting notable for the agreements to establish a thrice-yearly European Council, to put into action the Regional Development Fund and to introduce direct elections to the European Parliament – the connection between the British budgetary problem and the issue of economic convergence began to emerge.

The summit resulted in a mandate to the Council of Ministers and the Commission to produce a 'corrective mechanism' which might 'avoid the possible emergence, during the process of convergence of the economies of member states, of situations unacceptable to a Member State and incompatible with the sound functioning of the Community'.[13] This was a diluted variant of a formula initially suggested by the Commission in 1971 in a memorandum to the Council when Britain was negotiating for membership, which stated:

'Should unacceptable situations arise within the present Community or an enlarged Community, the very survival of the Community would demand that the Institutions find equitable solutions.' Although Britain attempted to have this indication of good faith enshrined in the Treaty of Accession, this was strongly opposed by France, and it appeared only in the British White Paper recommending British entry on the terms negotiated.[14]

The pattern of divergence became well established by the mid-1970s, as the next chapter (by E. C. Hallett) will show. By 1978, for example, inflation rates varied from less than 3 per cent in Germany to over 12 per cent in Italy, while per capita gross domestic product as a percentage of the Community average ranged (on 1976 figures) from 141 per cent for Denmark to 47 per cent for Ireland. The pattern of income levels within the Community clearly indicates the emergence during the last decade of a two-tier Community consisting of France, Germany, Denmark and the Benelux countries on the one hand and a group of low-income countries (Ireland, Italy and the United Kingdom) on the other, with the prospect of further enlargement of the Community threatening to increase the degree of economic divergence between member states still further.

A Stratified Community?

If one reads statements by Community politicians over the last five years one finds that they fall into two major groups. One group consists of those who consider that no major progress can be made in developing Community policies until economic divergences in both policy and performance have been overcome; this group also includes some who fear that continuing divergence will lead to disintegration. The other group advocates monetary union as a means of promoting convergence and also of stimulating the development of Community regional and other policies. In fact both groups agree that economic convergence and further European integration go hand in hand, but attempts to overcome the circularity of the debate have not produced any notable result. The 1976 Tindemans Report on European Union suggested not a multi-tier but a multi-velocity approach, and on the subject of EMU argued:

> It is impossible at the present time to submit a credible programme of action if it is deemed absolutely necessary that in every case all stages should be reached by all the States at the same time. The divergence of their social and economic situations is such that, were we to insist on this, progress would be impossible and Europe would continue to crumble away . . . This does not mean 'Europe à la carte': each country will be bound by the agreement of all as to the

final objective to be achieved jointly; it is only the time-scales for achievement which vary.[15]

The political result of a multi-velocity Community was seen by some member states as the introduction of a political hierarchy, with the fastest members determining the direction and (in so far as excessive lags would be impractical) the overall rate of change. This problem is compounded by the fact that the Community remains uncertain about its future and lacks an overall long-term framework, a socio-political-economic paradigm, into which proposed initiatives can be fitted and their mutual implications assessed. For all the fears of the Balkanisation of the Community, the pious wishes for increasing co-ordination of national economic policies, and the general consensus that (in the words of the 'conclusions of the Presidency' issued after the European Council meeting in Paris in March 1979) 'the implementation of the European Monetary System . . . must be supported by increased convergence of the economic policies and performances of the Member States',[16] the problem of economic divergence has at best been treated as a surrogate for arguments about the transfer of resources from the more prosperous to the less prosperous members of the Community, rather than one which raises serious long-term questions about the political future of the Community. The debate over the introduction of the EMS in 1978–9 proved to be an unproductive parade of special interests, with the Community's laggard economies finding the quality of Franco-German mercy to be somewhat strained, an important motivation for the introduction of EMS being the desire to overcome the *immobilisme* which has beset Community policies during the last five years of international economic turbulence. As Chancellor Schmidt argued during the EMS debate, there was a danger that monetary instability might undermine the common market, such that 'five more years of monetary upheaval in the Common Market will lead us to a situation in which we are dealing with fictions, not realities'.[17]

The problem with EMS is felt to be that, along with the imposition of 'essential disciplines' on national authorities, it will reinforce the tendency of the market to concentrate capital and activity in the more competitive areas of the Community, and will deprive the less favoured nations or areas participating in it of the means to protect themselves against this imbalance in economic activity. When the weaker economies attempted to link EMS with resource transfers and budgetary questions, however, they aroused the suspicion that an open-ended commitment to resource transfers would not only cushion but probably retard economic adaptation.

Although the EMS debate and the controversy over the British net contribution to the Community Budget have illustrated the limits of political cohesion within the Community, and the first year of the EMS (in particular the decision to delay implementation of the second stage) indicated the fragility of political initiatives when confronted by adverse economic factors, it should be remembered that the Community has made some substantial political progress at a time of unprecedented economic turbulence. The establishment of the European Council has created a forum in which it has come to be expected that major problems (including that of economic divergence) are tackled amidst an atmosphere of high drama in which the Community's leaders are condemned to participate, if not succeed. The gradual advance in European Political Co-operation, which has begun to produce a distinctively European perspective on international problems (witness the proposal for the neutralisation of Afghanistan advanced in early 1980, and the evolution of the Nine's attitudes towards the Arab–Israeli conflict) has occurred at precisely the same time as economic divergence became most pronounced. Similarly, the agreement on further enlargement of the Community has been based upon political considerations rather than economic ones, which played a relatively minor role in the discussions. Not least of these political developments, of course, has been the direct election of the European Parliament in 1979; its dramatic rejection of the 1980 Community Budget provided a foretaste of its potential impact on the political life of the Community and was itself inspired by dissatisfaction with the failure of Community policies to tackle the economic problems of the member states.

The Political Consequences of Economic Interdependence

Since all this occurred at a time of increasing divergence in the economic performance of the member states of the Community, it is clear that we must examine the linkage between economic and political integration more carefully, and not assume that there is a stable relationship between them. It would be helpful if we had a theory of interdependence which could enable us to predict the political consequences of economic divergence for the European Community. It is clear that existing theories of integration are in this respect inadequate or obsolete; theories of economic integration deal almost exclusively with market integration and pay little attention to the problems of policy integration,[18] while theories of political integration are concerned almost exclusively with the incremental growth of supranational institutions in an analytical focus which has had no counterpart in reality for over a decade. Both branches of integration theory were, of course, a product of their time, and both reflected the uncertainties and ambiguities of the debate between the liberals and the *dirigistes*.

The Treaty of Rome itself was a product of this sublimated disagreement on the role of government in the modern economy; it is primarily an instrument of market integration (through the liberalisation of goods and factor movements) together with some sectoral policies, notably for agriculture, but with the exception of commercial policy it leaves all the major instruments of macroeconomic policy in the hands of the member states, and therefore the Community as originally established had no direct role in the task of promoting growth, employment, price stability and balance-of-payments equilibrium. It is clear now, and was clear in 1958, that there was no agreement to eliminate governmental intervention in the economy (let alone transferring such powers to Community institutions), nor to harmonise economic policies except where they directly affected the operation of the common market.

If there was no clear agreement on liberalisation as an overall objective, neither was there a consensus on the need for redistribution in the EEC. The EEC has been characterised as a trade-off between the German desire for a liberalised customs union for industrial goods and the French wish for a guaranteed market for agricultural produce, but this was about as far as the redistributive aspect of the Treaty of Rome went. Indeed, as R. A. McAllister has noted, 'the Treaties simply did not envisage the kind of crises we have. The gap between the world of macroeconomic management and an adequate body of doctrine, legal obligation and sanction was and is simply too wide.'[19]

In so far as Community policies have had an effect on economic divergence between member states, it has sometimes been a perverse one. Commission figures show that Germany received more aid from the European Social Fund in the period 1962–72 than Italy did (190 and 145 million units of account respectively), while there is now evidence to suggest that Germany is now responsible for much of the escalation in the costs of the Common Agricultural Policy.[20] The Community's regional policy has been of little use in reducing the gap between rich and poor member states, which widened during the 1970s; such small redistribution as the Regional Fund brings about is negated by the overall effect of the EC Budget, three-quarters of which through CAP spending redistributes resources from poor to rich countries. If the gap between rich and poor regions in most EC countries has narrowed in the last decade, the credit should not go to the Community or to national regional policies; as *The Economist* (18 August 1979) noted, 'the great leveller has not been official regional aid, but the economic slump, which has spread misery more widely'.

Whatever might be said about the perverse nature of the Community's Budget (see Geoffrey Denton's contribution in Chapter 5) – and it is indisputably regressive to have Britain, the third poorest country in the Community, make a net Budget contribution in 1980 larger than that of France and Germany combined – the Budget is unlikely to provide an adequate means of overcoming or compensating for economic divergence between member states. The MacDougall Report on Public Finance in the Community, which argued in favour of establishing an interim 'pre-federal' budget amounting to 2–2½ per cent of Community GDP (double or triple the current level), was forced to admit that even an expenditure of 10 billion units of account, concentrated heavily in the weakest states and regions, might achieve an equalisation of about one-quarter of the average equalisation occurring in *fully* integrated economies – in which disparities are rarely overcome. It observed that 'this is small in comparison with what would probably be required to render full economic and monetary integration acceptable'.[21]

In its present form, the Community Budget is capable neither of financing a wide range of policies, nor of redistributing resources and acting as an agent of economic stabilisation. Given the current vogue at the national level for advocating extensive reductions in the role of public finance, this marginal role played by the Community Budget seems likely to continue.[22] As Jonathan Story points out in his chapter, the Franco-German relationship remains the cornerstone of European integration; neither country has shown any enthusiasm for the idea of long-term resource transfers to overcome disparities in income, particularly in the absence of converging growth rates, on the grounds that such income compensation would spur inefficiency and thus perhaps even worsen divergence.

Economic divergence has in the past proved to be an obstacle to the development of effective Community policies rather than a stimulus; as Stephen Woolcock demonstrates in his chapter, divergence in national industrial structures often prevented recognition of a common problem and encouraged short-term defensive measures at the national level, which in turn precluded the development of positive industrial adjustment policies for the Community as a whole. Even if the need for a *communautaire* approach to the problems of divergence were generally accepted, it is important to remember the argument put forward by Daniel Jones in this volume that the origins of divergent economic performance lie deep in the past industrial development of the member states, and that overcoming those divergences will involve a long and pervasive modification of cultural values as well as the transfer of resources. Given these cultural differences, it is difficult to see how (for example) Britain and Germany could select – let alone attain – mutually acceptable unemployment and inflation targets to converge on. In this respect, the monetary discipline of the EMS is not likely to overcome what Giovanni Magnifico has termed differing national propensities to inflate, which he defines as 'a different ability to build up inflationary pressures and a different vulnerability to them',[23] and which are caused by such factors as the differing power of national trade union movements, the political saliency of inflation, differences in social policy, and so on.

As R. A. McAllister has noted, European integration was seen twenty years ago 'more as a "growth engine" than as an engine of distribution',[24] and as such could promise all things to all men as long as growth was sustained and imbalances in development did not become intolerable. As time went by, it became increasingly clear that the 'golden triangle' of the Community was deriving a disproportionate benefit from economic growth at the expense of the peripheral areas such as the Mezzogiorno, without a concomitant growth in the redistributive capacity of Community institutions, nor even a consensus that such discrimination in favour of the less prosperous regions or countries of the Community was a legitimate Community responsibility. The recessionary climate of the 1970s and the admission of Britain and Ireland to membership in 1973 served to accentuate the divergent interests of the member states as they wrangled over the slicing of a cake that had ceased to expand, in the absence of an agreed role for the Community or the steps to achieve it.

Divergence as a *Faux Problème*

Although much lip-service is now paid to the desirability of convergence (both in terms of policy and performance) within the Community, it is difficult to take this seriously in the absence of a more general agreement on the ultimate objectives of the Community which might clarify the sort of convergence which is needed. It is not clear that a formally recognised two-tier or multiple-velocity Community would promote convergence, and it might well introduce an element of political stratification. If, however, convergence is not necessary for the Community to function in the desired manner, then the need for a two-tier system to cope with divergence would diminish considerably. The ambiguous language of the EEC Treaty itself is of scant assistance to us in assessing the importance of divergence − the reference in Article 2 to 'harmonious development of economic activities' may be aiming for complementarity rather than equality, and the objective of 'balanced expansion' seems to apply to regions rather than whole countries.

Given the interdependence of the industrialised economies and their differing degrees of vulnerability to changes in the international economic system, the problems of divergence will remain a permanent feature of the Community and will need to be managed rather than eliminated. Divergence cannot be made to disappear at a stroke, and there is some justification for doubting the assumption that economic divergence is in all its manifestations a Bad Thing. If divergence is partly the expression of different social preferences, it might be presumptuous, time-consuming, expensive (and impossible?) to eliminate it, and it could be argued that the major political consequence of economic divergence in the Community should be the abandonment of our tendency to equate integration with homogenisation.

It is clear that diversity is unlikely to diminish in the Community and that the prospects for a detailed and realistic 'Grand Design' for Europe are no greater now than they were when the Spaak Report was written a quarter-century ago. A gradualist and non-confrontational approach to developing Community capabilities seems to provide a way out of the current impasse because it broadens the range of options open to national governments rather than drastically narrowing them. Indeed, the current operation of the EMS (with only eight of the nine Community members participating) could be seen as a step in this direction and as a rejection of the much more regimented approach to economic and monetary union of the Werner Report a decade previously. The recent development of the 'Ortoli facility' – a fund raised by the Commission on the international capital market and disbursed by the European Investment Bank in loans for productive investment according to a list of priorities drawn up by the Council – is another example of the way in which the Community can expand national policy options rather than diminish them; other examples can be found in John Pinder's discussion of the 'extra-national' method later in this volume.

Provided that such measures are planned and discussed by all member states, that they do not undermine the benefits available to all from the creation of a unified market and that non-participants retain an option to join in at a later date, such an approach might prevent the Community from stagnating and yet avoid the issue of political stratification. The cohesion of the European Community may rest less on the promotion of convergence than on the maintenance of the belief on the part of member states that the benefits of increased economic interdependence within the Common Market outweigh the costs, and that the combined political weight of the Community affords them a greater measure of protection against external disturbances than they could obtain elsewhere. Since the Community cannot justly be accused of causing economic divergence, and can do little to overcome its results in the foreseeable future, it might be advisable to concentrate on developing particular policies to deal with specific problems rather than agonising over impossible questions of equity and the long-term destiny of the Community. Jean Monnet, who argued that politics was the art of making possible tomorrow what might seem impossible today, would doubtless have approved.

Notes: Chapter 1

1 L. Tsoukalis, *The Politics and Economics of European Monetary Integration* (Allen & Unwin, London, 1977).
2 B. Biesheuvel, E. Dell and R. Marjolin, *Report on European Institutions* (European Council, Brussels, October 1979), p. 2.
3 *Treaty of Rome*, Article 2.
4 P.-H. Spaak, *Comité Intergouvernemental créé par la Conférence de Messine: Rapport des chefs de délégation aux ministres des affaires étrangères* (Secretariat of the Committee, Brussels, April 1956).
5 R. A. McAllister, 'The EEC dimension: intended and unintended consequences', in James Cornford (cd.), *The Failure of the State* (Croom Helm, London, 1975), p. 180.
6 Spaak, op. cit., p. 13.
7 ibid., pp. 17, 23.
8 *Report on the Economic Situation in the Countries of the Community* (Commission of the European Communities, Brussels, 1958), p. 164.
9 E. Haas, *The Uniting of Europe* (Stevens, London, 1958).
10 'Report to the Council and the Commission on the realisation by stages of "economic and monetary union" in the Community' (Werner Report), *Bulletin of the European Communities*, Supplement 1/70, Brussels, 1970.
11 *Report on the Regional Problems in the Enlarged Community* (Thomson Report) COM(73)550 (Commission of the European Communities, Brussels, 1973).
12 'The realisation of Economic and Monetary Union', *Bulletin of the European Communities*, 5/73, Brussels, 1973, p. 9.
13 Quoted in M. R. Emerson and T. W. K. Scott, 'The financial mechanism in the Budget of the European Community: the hard core of the British "renegotiations" of 1974–5', *Common Market Law Review*, vol. 14, 1977, pp. 209–29.
14 *The United Kingdom and the European Communities*, Cmnd 4715 (HMSO, London, July 1971), para. 96; and *Sunday Times*, 25 November 1979.
15 L. Tindemans, 'European Union', *Bulletin of the European Communities*, Supplement 1/76, Brussels, 1976.
16 *Agence Europe*, no. 2637, 14 March 1979.
17 *Financial Times*, 8 December 1978.
18 J. Pelkmans, 'Economic theory and the impact of the customs union and the common market', unpublished paper, Tilburg University European-American Seminar, June 1979.
19 R. A. McAllister, 'Ends and means revisited: some conundra of the Fourth Medium-Term Economic Policy Programme', *Common Market Law Review*, vol. 16, 1979, p. 74.
20 Y. S. Hu, 'German agricultural power: the impact on France and Britain', *The World Today*, vol. 35, no. 11, November 1979.
21 *Report of the Study Group on the Role of Public Finance in European Integration* (MacDougall Report) (Commission of the European Communities, Brussels, 1977).
22 H. Wallace, *Budgetary Politics: The Finances of the European Communities* (Allen & Unwin, London, 1980), ch. 5.
23 G. Magnifico, *European Monetary Unification* (Macmillan, London, 1973), p. 62.
24 McAllister (1975), op. cit., pp. 194–5.

2

Economic Convergence and Divergence in the European Community: A Survey of the Evidence

E. C. Hallett

The term economic convergence has been used in a number of different ways ranging from an approximation of economic policies to convergence of economic performance. This chapter is concerned exclusively with convergence and divergence of economic performance. The analysis is at a macroeconomic level and is confined to inter-country comparisons. There is no examination of regional or sectoral disparities within countries.

Even if one concentrates on economic performance a number of different definitions of convergence are possible. It could mean an increasing similarity in rates of growth and inflation, changes in exchange rates or balance-of-payments positions. It could also mean a narrowing of income disparities between countries. It is clear that simultaneous convergence in terms of all these indicators of economic performance is not possible. It is obvious, for example, that convergence of growth rates is not compatible with convergence of income levels and that convergence of inflation rates could result in very different rates of growth and levels of unemployment. This chapter therefore examines a number of different indicators of economic performance under two broad headings, similarity of economic trends and disparities in income levels, with a view to determining the degree of convergence shown by each of them, without attempting to arrive at any aggregate assessment of the degree of convergence achieved within the Community.

Although the Treaty of Rome contained no precise commitment to the achievement of economic convergence it was generally anticipated that it would come about as a result of a combination of what might be called 'autonomous integration' (i.e. increased interdependence between the economies of the member states as a result of the removal of barriers to trade and factor mobility) and of 'institutional integration' (i.e. the establishment of procedures for the progressive approximation of economic policies).[1]

Autonomous Integration

It is clear that since the establishment of the Community intra-Community trade has increased at a significantly faster rate than member countries' trade with the rest of the world. (This is shown clearly by Tables 2.1 and 2.2.) The extent to which this has been due to the establishment of the Community itself cannot be determined with any certainty, but there can be little doubt that the removal of tariff and other barriers to trade between member states has been a significant contributory factor. There has, in effect, been an increase in each member country's average and marginal propensities to import from its Community partners. This has produced a significant increase in economic interdependence, with the consequence that fluctuations in the level of economic activity tend to be transmitted more rapidly than before between member countries. It also means that national monetary and fiscal policies operating in isolation will tend to be less effective in regulating the level of domestic economic activity.[2] This increased sensitivity of member countries' economies to changes in the level of economic activity elsewhere within the Community might be expected to contribute to an increasing synchronisation of the cyclical fluctuations experienced by the member states. It also provides a strong incentive for the effective co-ordination of economic and monetary policies.

Institutional Integration: Co-ordination of Economic and Monetary Policies

The need for co-ordination of economic and monetary policies was recognised in the Treaty of Rome and over the years the Community has established an elaborate institutional and procedural framework designed to promote such co-ordination. The history of these efforts is well known and it is not necessary to examine them here. There is considerable scepticism within the Community, however, as to whether the existence of this framework has in fact made the effective co-ordination of economic policies possible, still less whether it provides the means for achieving convergence of economic performance.

Indicators of Economic Convergence and Divergence

The following sections examine whether the interaction of

'autonomous' and 'institutional' integration has in fact led to convergence of economic performance in terms of an increasing similarity of economic trends and a narrowing of income disparities.

Inflation Rates
The degree of disparity in rates of inflation is probably the most widely used indicator of convergence in terms of economic trends. Table 2.3 shows the annual rates of change in consumer prices for each member state for the years 1959–80. This shows clearly that there was a marked increase in the degree of disparity in inflation rates from

Table 2.1   *Intra-Community imports (goods only) in GDP 1958–79 percentage share (current prices)*

	DK	D	F	IRL	I	NL	BLEU	UK	EC
1958	15·8	4·4	2·5	23·7	3·1	19·1	15·9	3·3	5·0
1959	17·2	5·2	2·9	22·7	3·5	20·6	17·4	3·3	5·5
1960	17·1	5·5	3·7	23·9	5·0	23·2	20·0	3·9	6·3
1961	16·3	5·5	4·0	26·6	5·2	25·8	21·3	3·8	6·5
1962	15·8	5·8	4·3	26·4	5·8	25·4	21·9	3·8	6·8
1963	14·5	5·9	4·8	28·0	6·6	26·7	23·6	3·8	7·2
1964	15·3	6·2	5·2	27·9	5·7	27·0	24·5	4·2	7·4
1965	14·5	7·3	5·0	27·7	5·0	25·9	24·7	4·1	7·6
1966	13·9	7·1	5·6	26·1	5·5	25·6	26·5	4·2	7·8
1967	12·8	6·8	5·6	25·2	6·0	24·2	24·4	4·5	7·7
1958–67	15·3	6·0	4·4	25·8	5·1	24·4	22·0	3·9	6·8
1968	12·2	7·3	6·1	28·3	5·8	23·8	25·4	4·9	8·1
1969	12·8	8·3	7·2	29·3	6·7	25·2	28·1	4·8	9·0
1970	13·3	8·2	7·4	29·5	7·6	27·0	28·8	4·9	9·4
1971	11·6	8·6	7·4	27·2	7·4	25·2	30·5	5·1	9·4
1972	10·7	8·4	7·7	26·3	8·0	23·6	30·2	5·6	9·6
1973	12·3	8·2	8·2	30·4	9·6	24·6	33·1	7·2	10·5
1974	14·2	8·7	9·5	33·3	11·1	26·9	35·7	8·5	11·9
1975	12·7	8·8	7·8	32·2	8·6	24·1	32·4	7·6	10·6
1976	14·2	9·6	9·1	36·1	10·2	24·6	34·7	8·2	11·8
1977	13·6	9·5	9·1	39·0	9·5	23·4	33·3	9·7	12·0
1968–77	12·8	8·6	8·0	31·2	8·5	24·8	31·3	6·7	10·2
1978	13·1	9·3	8·9	40·8	9·7	23·2	33·2	9·9	11·8
(1979)	13·8	10·1	7·9	43·6	9·8	24·9	34·1	11·0	12·2

Key: Denmark (DK), Germany (D), France (F), Ireland (IRL), Italy (I), Netherlands (NL), Belgium–Luxembourg Economic Union (BLEU), United Kingdom (UK), European Communities (EC).
Source: EC Commission, *European Economy*, November 1979.

Table 2.2   *Extra-Community imports (goods only) in GDP 1958–79, percentage shares (current prices)*

	DK	D	F	IRL	I	NL	BLEU	UK	EC
1958	11·0	8·8	7·0	11·1	7·5	19·1	13·2	12·9	10·0
1959	11·8	8·8	6·3	11·6	6·8	18·4	13·6	13·1	9·9
1960	12·9	9·2	7·3	13·9	9·5	20·3	15·9	15·0	11·3
1961	14·0	8·7	6·9	14·4	9·3	19·4	15·0	13·4	10·5
1962	14·8	8·8	6·7	13·3	9·2	18·2	14·9	13·1	10·2
1963	14·2	8·7	6·5	13·6	9·7	18·1	14·9	13·2	10·2
1964	15·7	8·6	6·7	13·6	8·6	18·0	15·3	14·2	10·4
1965	15·2	9·0	6·2	13·7	8·5	16·7	14·7	13·2	10·0
1966	14·9	8·7	6·4	13·3	9·0	16·4	14·9	12·6	9·9
1967	14·7	8·1	5·9	14·8	9·0	14·8	14·1	12·6	9·6
1958–67	13·9	8·7	6·6	13·3	8·7	17·9	14·7	13·3	10·2
1968	14·2	8·2	5·5	14·4	8·3	14·8	14·9	13·9	9·5
1969	14·3	8·5	5·8	14·4	8·7	14·8	15·1	13·6	9·7
1970	14·9	8·3	6·3	13·2	8·9	16·3	15·3	13·2	9·8
1971	14·0	8·0	6·0	13·5	8·3	16·0	13·2	12·1	9·2
1972	12·6	7·2	6·0	11·6	8·3	14·3	12·3	12·1	8·8
1973	14·6	7·5	6·6	12·0	10·1	15·7	13·7	14·7	9·8
1974	17·0	9·4	10·4	17·6	15·1	20·0	18·3	19·7	13·4
1975	15·0	9·0	8·2	14·3	11·5	18·3	15·8	15·8	11·4
1976	15·9	10·3	9·3	16·0	13·3	19·9	16·6	17·3	12·6
1977	15·0	10·2	9·4	18·3	12·6	19·3	15·9	9·7	12·2
1968–77	14·8	8·7	7·3	14·5	10·5	16·9	15·1	14·2	10·6
1978	13·4	9·7	8·4	17·4	12·0	17·2	14·9	9·9	11·5
(1979)	13·5	10·9	7·5	19·2	13·7	18·8	15·9	11·0	11·4

Key: Denmark (DK), Germany (D), France (F), Ireland (IRL), Italy (I), Netherlands (NL), Belgium–Luxembourg Economic Union (BLEU), United Kingdom (UK), European Communities (EC).

Source: EC Commission, *European Economy*, November 1979.

Table 2.3   EEC countries: annual rates of change in consumer prices 1959–78 (%)

	Belgium	Denmark	France	Germany	Ireland	Italy	Netherlands	United Kingdom	EEC Average	Standard Deviation
1959	1·2	1·8	5·7	1·0	0·0	0·5	0·9	0·6	1·8	2·220
1960	0·3	1·2	4·1	1·2	0·4	2·4	2·5	1·0	2·1	1·290
1961	0·9	3·5	2·4	2·5	2·8	2·1	1·6	3·4	2·5	0·604
1962	1·5	7·3	5·2	3·0	4·3	4·6	1·9	4·3	3·9	1·267
1963	2·1	6·2	5·2	2·9	2·5	7·5	3·8	1·9	4·0	1·833
1964	4·2	3·1	3·1	2·4	6·7	5·9	5·5	3·3	3·5	1·224
1965	4·1	6·5	2·5	3·4	5·0	4·6	4·0	4·8	3·7	0·959
1966	4·2	6·7	2·7	3·5	3·0	2·3	5·8	3·9	3·5	0·996
1967	2·9	6·9	2·7	1·4	3·2	3·2	3·5	2·5	2·5	1·022
1968	2·7	8·6	4·5	2·6	4·7	1·4	3·7	4·7	3·5	1·428
1969	3·8	4·2	6·4	1·9	7·4	2·6	7·4	5·5	4·2	2·035
1970	3·9	5·8	5·2	3·4	8·2	5·0	3·7	6·4	4·8	1·153
1971	4·3	5·8	5·5	5·3	8·9	4·8	7·5	9·4	6·1	1·634
1972	5·5	6·6	5·9	5·5	8·7	5·7	7·8	7·1	6·1	0·746
1973	7·0	9·3	7·3	6·9	11·4	10·8	8·0	9·2	8·1	1·381
1974	12·7	15·3	13·7	7·0	17·0	19·1	9·6	16·0	12·7	4·299
1975	12·8	9·6	11·7	6·0	20·9	17·0	10·2	24·2	12·9	6·335
1976	9·4	9·0	9·6	4·5	18·0	16·8	8·8	16·5	10·3	4·779
1977	7·1	11·1	9·8	3·9	13·6	17·0	6·4	15·9	9·9	4·959
1978	9·4	9·9	9·1	2·4	7·6	12·1	4·1	8·3	6·6	3·456
1979	4·5	9·8	10·7	5·0	13·3	14·8	4·2	13·4	10·0	4·094
1980 (est.)	6·9	12·5	12·1	5·0	15·3	17·1	6·8	18·9	11·3	5·374

Source: Compiled from various issues of OECD, Main Economic Indicators (monthly publication).

1973 onwards in comparison with earlier years. In 1961, for example, inflation rates among the present nine member states ranged from 0·9 per cent (Belgium) to 3·4 per cent (UK) (among the Six the range was only 0·9–2·5 per cent). In 1965 the range was from 2·5 per cent (France) to 6·5 per cent (Denmark) (2·5–4·6 per cent for the Six). By 1975 the range had widened from 6·0 per cent (Germany) to 24·2 per cent (UK). After a peak in 1975 the degree of disparity tended to diminish slightly but the trend now appears to be upwards again. In

Table 2.4   *Balance of payments: current balance in GDP, 1958–79, percentage shares*

	DK	D	F	IRL	I	NL	BLEU	UK	EC
1958	2·9	2·5	−0·4	−1·6	2·0	4·5	3·9	1·7	1·7
1959	0·4	1·6	1·5	−6·4	2·5	4·8	0·7	0·7	1·5
1960	−1·6	1·6	1·5	−0·2	0·9	3·2	0·7	−1·1	0·7
1961	−2·0	1·0	1·1	0·2	1·3	1·4	0·2	−0·0	0·7
1962	−3·4	−0·1	1·0	−1·8	0·7	1·0	0·7	0·3	0·4
1963	0·1	0·2	0·4	−2·8	−1·5	0·7	−0·5	0·3	−0·0
1964	−2·4	0·2	−0·3	−3·5	1·2	−1·1	0·2	−1·3	−0·3
1965	−1·8	−1·3	0·8	−4·4	3·8	0·2	0·6	−0·2	0·3
1966	−1·9	0·3	0·1	−1·6	3·4	−1·0	−0·1	0·1	0·5
1967	−2·4	2·2	0·0	1·4	2·4	−0·3	1·2	−1·0	0·7
1958–67	−1·1	0·7	0·7	−2·8	1·7	2·4	0·7	0·1	0·7
1968	−1·6	2·3	−0·5	−1·3	3·6	0·3	1·4	−0·8	0·9
1969	−2·8	1·4	−1·1	−4·8	2·9	0·3	1·8	0·7	0·7
1970	−3·5	0·6	0·1	−4·0	1·3	−1·5	3·2	1·2	0·5
1971	−2·4	0·4	0·6	−3·8	1·9	−0·4	2·4	1·7	0·9
1972	−0·3	0·4	0·5	−2·2	1·7	3·0	4·2	−0·0	0·8
1973	−1·7	1·3	−0·2	−3·1	−1·9	4·0	3·3	−2·1	0·1
1974	−3·0	2·6	−2·3	−9·6	−5·1	3·2	2·1	−5·2	−1·0
1975	−1·5	1·0	−0·0	−0·1	−0·3	2·5	1·2	−2·4	0·0
1976	−4·8	0·8	−1·8	−3·1	−1·5	3·2	0·9	−1·8	−0·6
1977	−3·7	0·9	−0·9	−2·8	1·1	0·9	−1·5	0·2	0·1
1968–77	−2·5	1·2	−0·6	−3·5	0·4	1·6	1·9	−0·9	0·2
1978	−2·6	1·5	0·8	−2·6	2·4	−0·7	−1·5	0·6	−0·9
(1979)	−3·7	−0·2	0·1	−8·3	1·5	−0·3	−1·8	−0·8	−0·2

Key: Denmark (DK), Germany (D), France (F), Ireland (IRL), Italy (I), Netherlands (NL), Belgium–Luxembourg Economic Union (BLEU), United Kingdom (UK), European Communities (EC).

Source: EC Commission, *European Economy*, November 1979.

1979 the range was from 4·2 per cent (Netherlands) to 14·8 per cent (Italy). In 1980 it is likely to be from 5·1 per cent (Germany) to 18·9 per cent (UK).

The tendency towards increased disparity in inflation rates in the 1970s is clearly shown by the weighted standard deviation of member countries' rates of inflation from the EC average.[3] The standard deviation fluctuated over the period 1959–72 but no consistent upward or downward trend was apparent. From 1973 onwards the standard deviation increased significantly, reaching a peak in 1975, then declining somewhat until 1978 and moving upwards again thereafter.[4] The EC Commission has also carried out an analysis of the standard deviation of inflation rates with broadly similar results to those set out above.[5]

Exchange Rates
The divergence in inflation rates and the wide differences in member states' current account balance-of-payments positions (see Table 2.4) have been associated with a marked degree of divergence in member states' exchange rate movements. Table 2.5 shows percentage changes in effective exchange rates for member countries for each half-year from 1973 to 1979 in comparison with the first quarter of 1970. By the second half of 1979, exchange rate changes within the Community ranged from an appreciation of 49·8 per cent in the case of Germany to a depreciation of 50·1 per cent in the case of Italy in comparison with the 1970 position.

Rates of Growth
The degree of disparity in member states' rates of growth in gross domestic product may also be used as an indicator of convergence of economic trends. Table 2.6 shows the annual percentage changes in real GDP for each member country for the years 1962–80. The weighted standard deviation for the EC countries has fluctuated considerably over the period without showing any consistent rising or falling trend. There was a continuous downward trend from 1974 to 1978, reflecting both a lower degree of disparity and a general fall in absolute rates of growth, but there is an upward trend in disparity from 1979 onwards. (The implications of divergent growth rates for the reduction of income disparities are considered below.)

Synchronisation of Cyclical Fluctuations
It was suggested above that increasing economic interdependence might lead to an increasing degree of synchronisation of the cyclical fluctuations experienced by member countries. The following procedure was adopted in order to determine whether this had in fact occurred within the Community. Quarterly figures were collected for

Table 2.5 EC countries: effective exchange rate changes, 1973–9, percentage changes from 1st quarter 1970

	1973 II	1974 I	1974 II	1975 I	1975 II	1976 I	1976 II	1977 I	1977 II	1978 I	1978 II	1979 I	1979 II
Belgium	+ 2·0	+ 2·5	+ 4·0	+ 5·4	+ 2·6	+ 3·6	+ 6·7	+10·2	+10·1	+12·1	+11·3	+12·3	+12·3
Denmark	+ 6·5	+ 4·0	+ 6·0	+ 8·8	+ 8·0	+ 8·7	+11·3	+ 8·6	+ 7·7	+ 9·2	+ 9·0	+ 9·7	+ 6·9
France	+ 1·5	− 6·5	− 4·5	+ 0·9	+ 3·7	+ 1·3	− 6·5	− 8·6	− 9·4	−12·6	−11·7	−12·6	−12·6
Germany	+22·0	+22·0	+21·5	+23·9	+20·7	+24·9	+30·4	+37·4	+38·4	+42·0	+42·1	+46·6	+49·8
Ireland	−10·5	−10·1	−11·0	−13·3	−16·4	−20·2	−25·7	−25·0	−24·7	−26·6	−25·1	−25·1	
Italy	−15·5	−19·5	−23·5	−25·8	−25·1	−36·7	−40·2	−44·1	−44·7	−47·3	−49·1	−50·2	−50·1
Netherlands	+ 6·5	+ 8·5	+11·0	+ 2·4	+10·9	+11·5	+15·4	+17·7	+17·5	+19·5	+18·4	+20·3	+19·3
United Kingdom	−18·0	−18·0	−18·5	−22·4	−26·9	−32·0	−39·1	−39·0	−36·0	−37·9	−39·4	−36·6	−33·5

Source: Compiled from various issues of OECD, *Economic Outlook.*

Table 2.6 EC countries: annual percentage changes in GDP (volume), 1962–80

	Belgium	Denmark	France	Germany	Ireland	Italy	Luxembourg	Netherlands	UK	EC Average	EC Standard Deviation
1962	5·3	5·6	6·7	4·0	3·2	6·2	1·7	4·3	0·8	4·2	2·099
1963	4·4	0·8	5·7	3·4	4·7	5·4	1·8	3·3	4·1	4·4	1·144
1964	7·0	9·3	6·3	6·8	4·1	2·6	7·2	8·6	5·8	6·0	1·572
1965	3·7	4·6	5·9	5·6	2·1	3·2	1·8	5·3	2·2	4·4	1·461
1966	3·0	2·7	4·0	2·9	1·3	5·8	1·7	2·8	1·9	3·3	1·167
1967	4·0	4·2	4·8	-0·2	5·3	7·0	0·2	5·3	2·5	3·1	2·522
1968	4·3	3·8	4·7	7·1	7·4	6·3	4·1	6·7	3·4	5·4	1·436
1969	6·6	8·6	7·0	8·2	6·9	5·7	8·3	6·8	1·1	5·9	2·479
1970	6·3	2·7	5·9	5·9	2·9	5·0	2·3	6·9	2·2	5·0	1·502
1971	4·1	3·4	5·4	2·9	3·5	1·6	2·5	4·4	2·5	3·3	1·356
1972	5·7	4·6	5·6	3·4	4·7	3·1	4·4	3·9	2·6	3·9	1·154
1973	6·3	3·3	5·6	5·1	5·4	6·3	7·1	4·3	5·5	5·4	0·612
1974	3·9	0·5	3·9	0·6	0·4	3·4	3·4	3·3	0·8	2·1	1·530
1975	-1·9	-1·1	0·1	-3·2	-0·5	-3·5	-7·7	-1·1	-1·8	-1·9	1·411
1976	5·5	5·4	4·6	5·7	2·4	5·7	3·1	4·6	2·3	4·8	1·197
1977	1·8	1·9	3·0	2·4	5·0	1·7	1·3	2·3	0·7	2·2	0·633
1978	2·6	0·9	3·3	3·2	6·1	2·6	4·5	2·4	3·3	3·0	0·545
1979	3·0	3·1	3·4	4·4	3·2	4·9	2·7	2·3	0·2	3·3	1·519
1980 (est.)	1·9	-0·3	2·1	2·1	1·4	2·0	1·8	1·0	-2·5	1·2	1·675

Source: OECD, national accounts of OECD countries.

consumer prices and industrial production for Belgium, France, Germany, Italy, the Netherlands, the UK and Denmark, and for comparative purposes for certain other OECD countries (Canada, the United States, Japan, Norway and Sweden, Greece, Portugal and Spain), for the periods 1958–65 and 1971–8. (Figures for industrial production for Denmark, Greece, Portugal and Spain were not available for 1958–65.) The selection of the time-periods was arbitrary and not related to particular economic events. Within each of the time-periods the deviations from trend were calculated for each country for both variables in order to provide an indication of cyclical fluctuations. The deviations from trend were then correlated for each pair of countries for each variable in order to provide an indication of the degree of interrelationship. The resulting correlation coefficients for the succeeding time-periods were then compared to see whether there was an increase. Such an increase would indicate increasing synchronisation of cyclical fluctuations.

The comparisons for consumer prices indicate some increase in synchronisation (the correlation coefficients for 1971–8 are higher than those for 1958–65 in 69 out of 105 cases), but the results are not conclusive. For industrial production, however, there is clear evidence of an increase in synchronisation (the correlation coefficients are higher in 46 out of the 55 cases where comparison is possible). This increase appears to have been experienced among all the countries under consideration, however, and there is no evidence that it has been greater among EC member countries.

The main conclusion which can be drawn from this exercise is that the increase in synchronisation of cyclical fluctuations which has occurred has been brought about primarily by factors other than EC membership.

Income Disparities

If economic convergence is defined as a process of narrowing income disparities in member states, the most appropriate indicator is probably gross domestic product per capita. Tables 2.7 and 2.8 show the levels of GDP per head for each member country as a percentage of the EC average for the years 1960–79 at current prices and exchange rates and at purchasing power parities. Taking the percentages based on current prices and exchange rates, the figures for Belgium, Denmark, Germany and the Netherlands show a steadily rising trend, France a slightly rising one (though it has fallen back slightly since 1977), and Luxembourg and the UK show a sharply falling trend (the latter declining from 117·1 per cent of the EC average in 1960 to 76·6 per cent in 1979). Italy, after showing a steadily rising trend throughout the 1960s, has fallen back again during the 1970s, while Ireland's position has remained relatively

Table 2.7   EC countries: GDP per capita as a percentage of EC average (current prices and exchange rates)

	1960	1961	1962	1963	1964	1965	1966	1967	1968	1969	1970	1971	1972	1973	1974	1975	1976	1977	1978	1979
Belgium	106·4	103·2	102·4	101·3	103·0	104·1	104·0	106·0	107·7	108·3	108·2	107·0	110·8	113·6	121·8	121·6	125·2	130·2	131·1	123·6
Luxembourg	140·5	156·7	121·9	117·8	123·3	118·5	114·5	110·5	115·2	120·9	127·3	116·6	118·9	129·6	137·1	117·5	117·4	121·0	124·2	125·6
Denmark	111·1	112·0	116·2	113·9	118·1	122·8	125·7	128·7	126·2	130·2	127·8	125·3	126·8	132·2	133·5	134·2	141·7	139·6	142·9	140·0
France	113·5	113·1	115·1	117·1	117·1	115·9	116·9	119·0	122·6	121·1	112·7	110·8	114·2	116·6	112·8	121·9	122·3	117·4	117·1	115·9
Germany	112·7	116·4	116·1	114·1	113·8	114·4	113·3	109·1	113·2	116·5	125·6	128·1	128·8	136·3	138·5	131·6	135·2	138·4	138·3	134·8
Ireland	54·1	53·5	53·6	53·0	54·8	54·2	53·6	54·5	51·1	53·6	53·3	54·7	55·7	52·1	48·4	47·5	46·8	47·6	50·2	49·9
Italy	59·7	60·6	62·8	66·2	65·4	65·2	65·8	69·0	80·7	70·1	69·6	67·7	66·1	62·4	61·4	59·1	56·7	56·7	55·6	61·1
Netherlands	83·1	82·3	81·7	81·2	86·2	88·8	89·2	92·7	97·0	98·9	98·3	100·8	104·1	108·8	114·5	113·9	121·3	125·6	123·6	118·3
United Kingdom	117·1	113·4	109·4	107·2	106·1	105·7	105·1	103·4	93·0	90·3	88·5	89·1	85·1	76·3	75·9	77·8	73·1	72·6	73·4	76·6
Greece	36·2	37·1	36·3	40·2	38·4	40·6	42·1	42·9	48·9	45·9	45·8	44·7	43·0	44·5	47·2	44·2	44·9	45·9	45·4	43·8
Portugal	24·2	23·6	23·2	23·2	23·1	24·1	24·8	26·6	28·3	28·7	28·7	29·1	30·2	32·3	33·3	29·6	30·3	28·8	24·3	22·5
Spain	33·2	34·3	36·5	39·6	40·5	44·2	47·3	48·4	44·5	44·7	44·2	44·2	46·9	49·8	54·6	54·9	53·9	52·1	51·4	58·2

stable at around 50 per cent of the EC average. The overall range between the lowest and highest income countries has remained more or less constant (from around 50 per cent of the EC average to around 140 per cent) though Germany and Denmark have replaced Luxembourg at the upper end of the range. Within this overall range, however, there is clear evidence of a steadily converging trend among the group of countries consisting of Belgium, France, Germany, the Netherlands, Denmark and Luxembourg (i.e. the original Six minus Italy and plus Denmark). The degree of disparity in GDP per capita among these countries has markedly narrowed during the period under consideration. This has led in effect to the emergence of a two-tier Community as far as income levels are concerned, with the upper tier consisting of the countries listed above and the lower tier consist-ing of Ireland, Italy and the UK. The gap between the upper and lower tiers appears to be widening.

The Commission has produced figures for GDP per capita as a per-centage of the Community average for certain years based on purchas-ing power parities.[6] These show a smaller degree of disparity with less change in the relative positions of member states than do the figures based on market exchange rates. A two-tier Community with conver-gence within the upper tier still emerges, however.

Table 2.8   *EC countries: GDP per capita as percentage of EC average (purchasing power parities)*

	1960	1970	1976	1977	1979 (est.)
Belgium	99	102	109	109	108
Denmark	113	121	112	119	116
France	100	106	113	113	112
Germany	118	116	118	119	118
Ireland	59	61	61	62	61
Italy	69	76	73	72	77
Luxembourg	—	127	—	110	111
Netherlands	104	107	107	108	103
United Kingdom	112	97	93	92	91

Sources: EC Commission, *European Economy*, November 1978 and November 1979.

Differences in growth rates between member countries clearly have important implications for the reduction of income disparities. If the latter are to be progressively reduced, it is necessary for low income countries to experience consistently higher rates of growth than high income countries over a considerable period. To see whether this had in fact been happening within the EC, member countries were ranked according to GDP per head and according to annual rates of growth for each year during the period under consideration. For convergence to come about it would be necessary for the countries which ranked lowest according to GDP per head to be ranked highest according to rates of growth. These rankings are set out in Tables 2.9 to 2.11.[7] These show that the pattern of growth rates has to only a limited extent been consistent with promoting convergence of income levels. Italy ranked relatively high in the growth table in most years during the 1960s, though it has done less well in recent years, while Ireland, which has generally had a poor growth record, was the fastest growing member country in 1977 and 1978. The UK has traditionally come out at or near the bottom of the growth table. Of the higher income countries only Luxembourg has tended to come out at the lower end of the growth table. The pattern of growth rates has, however, been such as to promote convergence of income levels between France, Belgium, the Netherlands, Luxembourg, Denmark and Germany.

Enlargement and Economic Convergence

The accession of the three applicant countries, Greece, Portugal and Spain, will tend to make it more difficult to achieve convergence of

Table 2.9   *EC countries: ranking according to annual rates of growth in GDP (volume), 1962–80*

	1	2	3	4	5	6	7	8	9
1962	F	It	D	B	N	G	Ir	L	UK
1963	F	It	Ir	B	UK	G	N	L	D
1964	D	N	L	B	G	F	UK	Ir	It
1965	F	G	N	D	B	It	UK	Ir	L
1966	It	F	B	G	N	D	UK	L	Ir
1967	It	Ir =	N	F	D	B	UK	L	G
1968	Ir	G	N	It	F	B	L	D	UK
1969	D	L	G	F	Ir	N	B	It	UK
1970	N	B	F =	G	It	Ir	D	L	UK
1971	F	N	B	Ir	D	G	UK =	L	It
1972	B	F	Ir	D	L	N	G	It	UK
1973	L	B	It	F	UK	Ir	G	N	D
1974	B =	F	It =	L	N	UK	G	D	Ir
1975	F	Ir	D =	N	UK	B	G	It	L
1976	G =	It	B	D	N =	F	L	Ir	UK
1977	Ir	F	G	N	D	B	It	L	UK
1978	Ir	L	F =	UK	G	B =	It	N	D
1979	It	G	F	Ir	D	B	L	N	UK
1980 (est.)	F =	G	It	B	L	Ir	N	D	UK

Note: = denotes equal ranking.
Key: Belgium (B), Denmark (D), France (F), Germany (G), Ireland (Ir), Italy (It), Luxembourg (L), Netherlands (N), United Kingdom (UK).

economic performance within the European Community. All three countries are relatively backward in economic terms in comparison with the existing member states and all have a level of GDP per capita well below the Community average. They have a relatively narrow industrial base, serious problems of industrial and regional imbalance, a large and relatively backward agricultural sector and a labour surplus problem. They have also tended to experience higher rates of inflation than the existing member countries. On the other hand all three have tended to experience rates of growth well above those achieved by the existing members (though it is doubtful whether this has continued to be the case with Portugal in recent years). This suggests that the degree of divergence may diminish in the longer term, as income levels in the applicant countries 'catch up' with those of the existing members. This has already been happening in the case of Greece and Spain. Table 2.7 shows that as a percentage of the Community average the GDP per capita of Greece and Spain rose from 36·0 and 33·2 respectively in 1960 to 43·8 and 58·2 in 1979. Portugal's GDP per capita as a percentage of Community average rose steadily from 1960 to 1974 but has fallen back since then.

Table 2.10   *EC countries: ranking according to GDP per capita (current prices and exchange rates), 1960–79*

	1	2	3	4	5	6	7	8	9
1960	L	UK	F	G	D	B	N	It	Ir
1961	L	G	UK	F	D	B	N	It	Ir
1962	L	D	G	F	UK	B	N	It	Ir
1963	L	F	G	B	UK	B	N	It	Ir
1964	L	D	F	G	UK	B	N	It	Ir
1965	D	L	F	G	UK	B	N	it	Ir
1966	D	F	L	G	UK	B	N	It	Ir
1967	D	F	L	G	B	UK	N	It	Ir
1968	D	F	L	G	B	N	UK	It	Ir
1969	D	F	L	G	B	N	UK	It	Ir
1970	D	L	G	F	B	N	UK	It	Ir
1971	G	D	L	F	B	N	UK	It	Ir
1972	G	D	L	F	B	N	UK	It	Ir
1973	G	D	L	F	B	N	UK	It	Ir
1974	G	L	D	B	N	F	UK	It	Ir
1975	D	G	F	B	L	N	UK	It	Ir
1976	D	G	B	F	N	L	UK	It	Ir
1977	D	G	B	N	L	F	UK	It	Ir
1978	D	G	B	L	N	F	UK	It	Ir
1979	D	G	L	B	N	F	UK	It	Ir

Key: Belgium (B), Denmark (D), France (F), Germany (G), Ireland (Ir), Italy (It), Luxembourg (L), Netherlands (N), United Kingdom (UK).

Table 2.11   *EC countries: ranking according to GDP per capita (purchasing power parities), 1960–79*

	1	2	3	4	5	6	7	8	9
1960	L	G	D	UK	N	F	B	It	Ir
1970	L	D	G	N	F	B	UK	It	Ir
1977	D =	G	F	L	B	N	UK	It	Ir
1979 (est.)	G	D	F	L	B	N	UK	It	Ir

Note: = denotes equal ranking.
Key: Belgium (B), Denmark (D), France (F), Germany (G), Ireland (Ir), Italy (It), Luxembourg (L), Netherlands (N), United Kingdom (UK).

Conclusions

Viewed in terms of economic trends, the member states of the Community have experienced a marked increase during the 1970s in the degree of divergence in terms of inflation rates and exchange rates, in comparison with earlier years. There is, however, no evidence of increased disparity in growth rates; in fact there is some evidence of convergence towards low rates of growth in recent years. There is some evidence of increased synchronisation of cyclical fluctuations, though this experience has been shared by other OECD countries.

The trend in income disparities has, however, been towards the emergence of a two-tier Community, caused by a steady convergence within one group of countries, and with current prices and exchange rates apparently forcing a wedge further between the upper and lower tiers.

Notes: Chapter 2

1   The terms 'autonomous' and 'institutional' integration do not correspond exactly with the terms 'negative' and 'positive' integration which John Pinder has used (e.g. in ch. 5 of G. R. Denton (ed.), *Economic Integration in Europe*, Weidenfeld & Nicolson, London, 1969). 'Negative' integration, as defined by Pinder, relates to 'the removal of discrimination between the economic agents of the member countries', whereas 'autonomous' integration relates to the *effects* of the removal of discrimination. 'Positive' integration relates to 'the formation and application of co-ordinated and common policies' whereas 'institutional' integration relates only to 'procedures designed to promote macroeconomic policy co-ordination'.
2   This is the case under fixed exchange rates. It may be less true under floating rates.
3   In calculating the standard deviations, member countries' divergences from the EC average were weighted according to their share of Community GDP.
4   The increase in standard deviation from 1973 onwards reflects the increase in absolute rates of inflation as well as the increase in disparity between countries. Use of an alternative indicator of dispersion such as the coefficient of variation (i.e. the standard deviation divided by the mean) indicates a lower degree of disparity, though one which is still somewhat higher than during the 1960s.

5   *European Economy*, November 1978 and November 1979.
6   ibid.
7   It will be noticed that, for GDP per capita, the rankings based on purchasing power parities are often different from those based on market exchange rates.

3

Industrial Development and Economic Divergence

Daniel T. Jones

Introduction

Economic divergence has become one of the most important factors underlying current economic problems and policy choices at every level of decision-making. The divergent economic performance of individual countries strongly influences the locational decisions of large transnational companies. Many of the crucial national policy debates, such as the current argument in Britain about resorting to some form of protectionism, are about divergent performance and how to respond to it, in this case to Britain's persistently poor industrial performance in relation to its main competitors. Furthermore in the European Community two important issues, how to resolve the increasingly regressive nature of the national contributions to the Community Budget and the survival of the European Monetary System, have achieved such prominence because of the divergent economic performance of the member states. At the international level we appear to have come to the end of the period when the United States provided the necessary leadership of the international economic system. Apart from the domestic political changes in the United States and the impact of its large oil deficit, the growing importance of the German and Japanese economies, with their huge surpluses, in the international trading and monetary systems has undermined the dominant position of the United States. Again this is the result of divergent economic performance. We shall consider some of these developments further below.

The analysis that follows will concentrate on the contribution of the industrial sector to divergent economic performance. The industrial sector has been the most dynamic sector in all of the advanced industrialised countries (AICs) and its relative performance has to a large degree determined the economic fortunes of each country. Moreover all of these countries rely on exporting manufactured goods to pay for raw material imports and the relative international competitiveness of this sector is therefore a critical performance indicator. Much of the debate in recent years has concentrated on the more macroeconomic, demand-side issues; witness the discussion of the so-called locomotive theory of growth amongst the AICs. This contribution sets out to complement such an analysis with a consideration of the structural, supply-side factors contributing to divergent performance. It also argues that these structural differences are deep-seated and of long standing.

In trying to analyse the relative economic performance of different countries it is important to focus attention not only on the different rates of growth of output, living standards, productivity, and so on, but also on the changing absolute differences between countries. One of the most useful performance indicators in this regard is labour productivity; with the help of this and other measures I outline some of the main facts of divergent performance in the next section. The following sections analyse more closely the possible reasons for differential industrial performance. A further section argues that the fundamentally altered circumstances of the world economy since the early 1970s and the growing pressures for structural adjustment will probably intensify the political pressures resulting from divergent performance. Finally I consider the implications at a national, Community and international level of these developments and suggest some priorities for further consideration.

Divergence and Growth

One of the most obvious manifestations of the problem arising from divergent economic performance in the European Community is the growing gap between the UK and the six original member countries. By 1976 standards of living were already 20–30 per cent higher in all the other member states; only in central and southern Italy and Ireland were living standards lower than in the UK (see Table 3.1).[1] In terms of labour productivity in industry the differences were even greater; Irish productivity was still lower than the UK, but in Italy productivity was about 15 per cent higher and in the rest of the member states between 70 and 90 per cent higher. The UK is thus next after Ireland (now at the bottom of the league) in terms of industrial productivity within the European Community. This is a quite staggering situation if one considers that in the early 1950s Britain produced more per man in industry than in all of these countries.

At the time the Community was formed there was little cause to worry about differences in industrial performance amongst the member states, with the exception of Italy. Italy was then the only

Table 3.1   *Relative living standards and industrial productivity in selected countries (UK = 100)[1]*

	GDP per capita			Industrial output per person employed[4]		
	OER 1976	PPP 1976	OER 1960	OER 1976	PPP 1960	PPP 1976
USA	229	165	268	268	259	259
Japan	103	111	72	147	78	160
Sweden	193	140	155	192	—	—
West Germany	149	131	143	197	125	173
France	144	130	134	187	127	177
Netherlands	121	118	158	226	130	187
Belgium	140	131	131	211	108	173
Italy	82	81	76	111	79	115
Denmark	151	121	143	180	—	—
UK	100	100	100	100	100	100
Ireland	63	70	76	82	—	—
Spain	58	73	48	77	—	—
Greece	62	73	47	74[3]	—	—
Portugal	35	47	43	67	—	—
Argentina	48	66	73	97[3]	—	—
Mexico	30	41	69	76	—	—
Brazil	32	52	42	62[3]	—	—
Singapore	59	71	37	74	—	—
South Korea	18	30	29[2]	36	28[2]	34
Philippines	10	21	26	30	27	32
India	4	10	8	10[3]	10	11[3]

Notes: 1 At 1970 official exchange rates and purchasing power parity exchange rates, extrapolated to 1960 and 1976 in real terms.

2 1963.

3 1970.

4 GDP of industry (mining and quarrying, manufacturing and electricity, gas and water) per person employed in industry. Purchasing power parities for industrial goods were estimated for the categories clothing and footwear, furniture and appliances, transport equipment and producers durables from the first Kravis reference below, pp. 174–95.

Sources: Base period estimates of GDP per capita in 1970 at official exchange rates obtained from the *UN Yearbook of National Accounts Statistics* and the World Bank, *World Tables 1976* and at purchasing power parity exchange rates from Irving B. Kravis *et al., International Comparisons of Real Product and Purchasing Power* (Johns Hopkins University Press, Baltimore, Md, 1978), pp. 8 and 10, and Irving B. Kravis *et al.,* 'Real GDP per capita for more than one hundred countries', *The Economic Journal,* vol. 88 (June 1978), pp. 232–7. Extrapolations to 1960 and 1976 of GDP per capita and data on the contribution of industry to GDP and on industrial

member of a second tier of countries that has now grown to include the UK and Ireland and may soon encompass Spain, Greece and Portugal. It would seem from Tables 3.1 and 3.2 that all the mainland countries of Western Europe shared in the particularly rapid growth associated with the general lowering of tariff barriers and the integration of the European economies throughout the period. To avoid sounding too pessimistic about the relative performance of the UK, it should be noted that this was a time when Britain's productivity growth was also particularly rapid by historical standards (see Table 3.2). I have shown elsewhere that industrial productivity in the UK accelerated until 1973, though this was not sufficient to offset the faster growth elsewhere, and indeed was due more to a fall in the number employed than to faster output growth.[2] This development was partly the result of a labour shake-out as UK industry had to become more competitive in a more open trading system. With the near-stagnation of output and productivity after 1973 (see Table 3.2) and the constantly falling share of trade in manufactured goods (see Table 3.3) it would seem that this was a defensive rather than an offensive reaction.

Perhaps the most dramatic way to illustrate the slower growth of UK productivity and the growing gap between the UK and the other European countries is in Figure 3.1, which refers to the whole economy and not just to the industrial sector. From this figure it is clear that the slower rate of productivity growth of the UK as compared with its main competitor, Germany, has not just been a feature of the postwar period; indeed it has been evident for at least a century (the graph has been drawn on a semi-logarithmic scale so that a constant rate of growth appears as a straight line). Caution of course is in order in reading precise figures from such international comparisons, particularly over such a long time. However, our results are in broad agreement with other investigations. In terms of manufacturing productivity, Germany probably overtook the UK in the early 1950s, but it had already done so once before in the mid-1930s, and indeed it is likely that German manufacturing productivity was only slightly lower than the UK already in 1913.[3] Data for the United States would seem to indicate that the United States overtook the UK in manufacturing productivity somewhat earlier in the last century than for total productivity as shown in Figure 3.1.[4]

From Table 3.2 and Figure 3.1 it is clear that, whilst the sustained period of rapid growth of output and productivity in the postwar period in Europe was exceptional by historical standards, the under-

employment were taken from the above UN and World Bank sources and from *OECD National Accounts Statistics, OECD Labour Force Statistics* and the *ILO Yearbook of Labour Statistics.*

Table 3.2 Growth rates of GDP and GDP per person employed, 1870–1978 (annual average rates of change, percentage per annum)

	1870–1913[3]	1922–29[4]	1932–38[5]	1950–59	1959–73	1913–22[4]	1929–32[5]	1938–50	1973–78
a. GDP per person employed									
USA	1·9	2·1	3·9	2·2	2·0	2·1	− 3·5	2·3	0·2
Japan	3·4	4·1	3·7	6·1	9·1	2·8	5·9	− 2·3	4·0
Sweden	2·2	3·3	4·4	2·8	3·2	− 1·6	− 1·8	2·4	0·0
Denmark	2·1	2·0	0·2	1·8	3·7	− 0·2	3·0	1·5	1·3
France[2]	1·4	5·8	1·1	3·6	5·3	− 1·2	− 1·9	1·4	2·4
Germany[1]	1·6	4·8	4·0	4·5	4·8	− 1·8	0·0	0·1	3·2
Netherlands	0·7	2·0	1·7	3·4	4·6	1·4	− 1·6	0·2	2·6
Italy[2]	0·8	2·2	2·2	4·7	5·9	1·1	5·4	0·0	1·1
UK	1·1	1·6	1·9	1·7	2·6	− 1·0	0·5	0·4	0·5

b. GDP

USA	4·3	4·8	6·7	3·4	4·0	2·6	−10·0	5·1	2·4
Japan[2]	4·4	5·0	4·8	8·6	10·6	3·4	4·7	−1·2	4·6
Sweden	3·0	4·0	5·8	3·3	3·9	−0·3	−3·8	3·2	1·2
Denmark	3·2	3·7	2·4	2·6	5·0	0·4	1·5	2·4	1·7
France[2]	1·6	5·8	1·1	4·1	6·1	−1·4	−2·8	1·0	2·5
Germany[1]	2·9	4·1	9·0	7·4	5·0	−0·8	−6·7	0·4	1·9
Netherlands	2·2	4·0	3·5	4·6	5·6	2·8	−2·5	2·1	2·5
Italy[2]	1·4	2·3	2·6	5·7	5·1	1·4	−7·9	0·4	2·0
UK	2·2	2·7	4·0	2·2	3·0	−1·4	−1·9	1·3	0·5

Notes: 1 Germany comprises the territory of the present Federal Republic after 1925 and the series throughout has been adjusted for territorial changes.

2 Prior to 1950 no unemployment statistics were available for France, Italy, or Japan, and statistics of the labour force were used instead, therefore cyclical variations before then may to an extent be understated.

3 The USA and Germany 1871, Japan 1880 and the Netherlands 1900.

4 Sweden 1923 and Germany 1925.

5 The extent of the depression is indicated, subject to note 2 above, by the choice of trough years in each country: Italy 1930, the USA and Japan 1933, the Netherlands 1934 and France 1936.

Sources: Deborah C. Paige *et al.*, 'Economic growth: the last hundred years', *National Institute Economic Review*, no. 16, July 1961, pp. 48–9, and Angus Maddison, *Economic Growth in the West* (Allen & Unwin, London, 1964), pp. 201 and 231, updated to 1978 using OECD and national sources.

Table 3.3   *Manufactured exports and patents for selected European countries and Japan, 1899–1975*

	1899	1913	1937	1965	1975
a. Shares of manufactured exports from these countries[1]					
Germany[2]	26·2	31·6	29·5	25·6	26·0
UK	38·8	35·9	28·3	18·0	11·9
France	16·8	14·4	7·9	11·8	13·1
Italy	4·2	3·9	4·5	9·0	9·5
Benelux[3]	6·5	5·9	13·0	14·3	13·7
Sweden	1·1	1·6	3·5	4·4	4·5
Switzerland	4·7	3·7	3·8	4·3	3·9
Japan	1·8	2·8	3·4	12·5	17·3
Total[3]	100·0	100·0	100·0	100·0	100·0
b. Shares of patents registered by these countries in the USA					
Germany[2]	34·7	47·2	44·0	30·8	27·4
UK	45·2	30·8	25·7	24·1	14·0
France	11·5	10·9	11·7	12·7	10·8
Italy	0·9	1·7	1·8	3·9	3·5
Benelux[3]	3·0	2·1	6·2	6·6	4·0
Sweden	1·7	2·7	3·9	5·2	4·5
Switzerland	2·9	4·1	5·2	8·1	6·6
Japan	0·1	0·5	1·4	8·7	29·2
Total	100·0	100·0	100·0	100·0	100·0

Notes: 1 Manufactured goods comprise ISIC groups 5–8. Most patents relate to manufactured goods, so the two sections are broadly comparable. The USA has also been excluded for comparability.

   2 West Germany only after 1945; excluding exports from West to East Germany after that date.

   3 No trade data are available for the Netherlands in 1899 and 1913. Export shares for the Benelux include intra-Benelux trade.

Sources: Patent shares estimated from calculations by Keith Pavitt and Luc Soete of the Science Policy Research Unit at the University of Sussex from information supplied by the Office of Technology Assessment and Forecast, US Department of Commerce, Washington, DC, unpublished, 1977. Export shares estimated from Alfred Maizels, *Industrial Growth and World Trade* (Cambridge University Press, Cambridge, 1965), p. 434, and updated using *OECD Statistics of Foreign Trade*.

lying differences in the dynamism of the main economies, particularly the UK and Germany, have existed for a much longer time. Each time that Germany was about to overtake the UK in industrial productivity in the past the process was interrupted by war or by depression. Germany suffered more serious disruption from each of these events

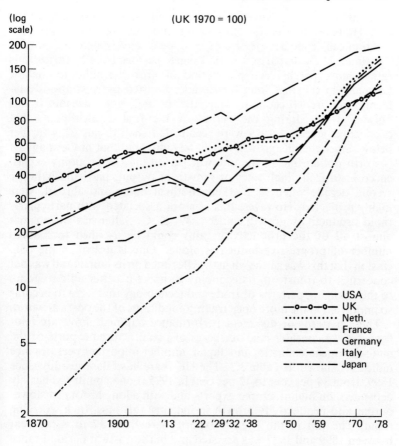

(log scale)

(UK 1970 = 100)

Figure 3.1 *GDP Per Person Employed, 1870–1978.*

Notes: 1 Germany comprises the territory of the present Federal Republic after 1925. The series throughout has been adjusted for territorial changes.
2 Prior to 1950 no unemployment statistics were available for France, Italy, or Japan, and statistics of the labour force were used instead, therefore cyclical variations before then may to an extent be understated.
3 The extent of the depression is indicated, subject to note 2 above, by the choice of trough years in each country; otherwise the same years were chosen, except for the USA and Germany in 1871, Japan in 1878 and Germany in 1925.

Sources: Base period estimates of relative GDP per capita in 1970 at purchasing power parities obtained from Irving B. Kravis *et al., International Comparisons of Real Product and Purchasing Power* (Johns Hopkins University Press, Baltimore, Md, 1978), p. 10, adjusted to GDP per person employed using the *OECD Labour Force Statistics* 1965–76. Extrapolations to 1959 and 1978 using series from OECD and national sources, for years between

in terms of border changes, unemployment, and so on, than did the UK. However it was able to recover and improve on its previous position each time irrespective of the type of government in power at the time. The comparison with French performance historically is rather more patchy. After a period of growth similar to that of Germany in the first interwar decade, boosted by reparations payments, the French economy stagnated in the second decade. It was only in 1951, during the period of the first French plan, that production levels of 1929 were regained. I shall discuss this further below. Since then its growth has closely mirrored that of Germany. It is worth noting that in the interwar period the UK economy experienced historically high rates of growth of output, particularly in the second decade when its markets, both at home and abroad, were highly protected. However, this was not associated with particularly rapid productivity growth; indeed, W. E. G. Salter has shown that almost all of the productivity gains could be ascribed to a small number of progressive industries alone.[5] One is drawn to the conclusion that this was a time when the UK rested on its laurels and was not concerned to transform its economy to make it better able to adapt to the changing patterns of trade and technology that were to become so important in the more open trading conditions of the postwar world.

These patterns of divergent performance outlined above are reinforced if we consider relative shares of manufactured exports of the main European countries and Japan, another important performance indicator, shown in Table 3.3. The UK share has fallen steadily since 1899, from 39 per cent to 12 per cent in 1975. For a country as heavily dependent on manufactured exports and with a long history of slower output and productivity growth in industry this must be a worrying trend. The fall in the French export share from 17 to 8 per cent between 1899 and 1937 was arrested and in the postwar period France improved its export position in line with its domestic output growth and the growth of world trade. Germany managed to maintain its dominant export position throughout this century, accounting for about a quarter of manufactured exports of these countries throughout the period. Italy too has improved its position in the postwar period, while Japan continued its dramatic rise to join the forefront of the ranks of the industrialised countries. It is quite conceivable that Japan will soon replace Germany as the leading exporter of manu-

Figure 3.1   *Sources continued*

> 1913 and 1959 using the growth rates in Deborah C. Paige *et al.*, 'Economic growth: the last hundred years', *National Institute Economic Review*, no. 16, July 1961, pp. 37 and 48–9, and from 1870 to 1913 the series in Angus Maddison, *Economic Growth in the West* (Allen & Unwin, London, 1964), p. 231, and Kazushi Ohkawa, *The Growth Rate of the Japanese Economy since 1878* (Kinokuniya, Tokyo, 1957), p. 250.

factures in the world. A crude extrapolation of the post-1973 productivity growth rates in Figure 3.1 would indicate that the leading European countries would attain US productivity levels in about 1985 and Japan a few years thereafter. The UK would of course be left with a productivity just over one-half that of all these countries by that time. Whether events will turn out like this will of course depend on many factors, some of which will be discussed below.

The Origins of Divergence

In discussing the factors that have been responsible for the divergent performance outlined above I shall primarily focus on the differences between Germany and the UK, the two major European economies with the best and worst performance respectively, while also considering France and other countries where relevant. This bias reflects the interest of this particular author, though in almost ignoring Italy I am unfortunately following a practice common amongst economic historians. The greater attention paid to the problems of the UK is justified in that the UK has been the odd man out amongst the European countries for a greater part of the period under review.

The very persistence of the divergent growth of Germany and the UK over such a long time-period makes one suspicious of explanations that focus on purely demand-side macroeconomic factors. Our attention is then drawn to consider differences in the response of industry to successive challenges or to the lack of them, that is, to more microeconomic supply-side questions. As we shall see, it will also be necessary to stray into areas that are rightly the preserve of the industrial sociologist or political scientist. One is ill-equipped to discuss the origins of divergent performance without a consideration of the social and institutional factors. Any study that tried to do so would be incomplete and would miss key factors that play an important part in explaining divergence. I shall follow Ingvar Svennilson in looking at growth as not only a quantitative increase in output and productivity but also as being inextricably bound up with the process of transforming the structure of the economy.[6] Transformation is closely connected with the process of new capital investment which is in turn one of the main determinants of the level of employment and hence also of the level of output. Transformation involves the introduction of new products and new production methods utilising different input combinations and human skills, a redistribution of resources from one industry to another and the adaptation to changing trade patterns. Social and institutional factors play a key role in this transformation process. It goes without saying that such transformations only take place over a number of years, and do not concern short-term cyclical or other changes in the economy.

Over a long time-period it is difficult to assess the extent to which particular factors are a cause or are themselves the resulting symptoms of divergent performance. Unravelling economic, social and political relationships over time is an extremely complex business, with no easy answers. It is impossible in this short chapter to do more than give a brief summary of the main factors involved. Those who wish for a greater understanding of these issues and to examine the evidence for what I have to say more closely should directly consult the works on which I have drawn in my own analysis.[7] Fortunately in such a fascinating and perennial subject the literature abounds with studies written throughout the last century or so and many common themes can be traced back in time through these studies.

Britain's early industrialisation gave it the advantages and disadvantages of a pioneer. While others were able to introduce capital equipment embodying the latest techniques, the existing capital stock of the pioneer may well inhibit its own replacement. This was certainly the case in a number of British industries such as steel, and later chemicals. However this drawback does not of course apply to the establishment of new industries in which Britain also lagged behind. Being a pioneer did mean that Britain had the advantages of an extensively developed infrastructure and trading links. As we shall see below the timing of industrialisation was more important in determining the pattern of social relationships and institutions in each country.

The most durable feature of Britain's pioneering role was a sense of superiority which has remained until long after it was justified. Many commentators were warning of the serious shortcomings of British industry in relation to the United States and Germany well before the First World War, but little heed was taken of their warnings. In a few industries there were signs of a response to intensified competition, though this did not include the major industries such as steel, chemicals, or textiles.[8] Britain was not again subjected to the full force of international competition until the early 1960s with the tariff liberalisation of the successive GATT rounds. The 1920s were largely taken up with reconstruction in Euorope; Svennilson estimates that the First World War caused at least an eight-year delay in the growth of European industry. The impact of the depression and the collapse of the international financial and trading systems were felt less severely in Britain as it was able to insulate itself from these developments. Its trade was already largely directed to its empire markets, around which it developed a protective wall, and its balance of payments remained in surplus due to the substantial invisible earnings on its investments overseas. Table 3.4 shows that it was not until the mid-1960s that the fundamental shift from empire to European markets took place. Indeed it was not until 1973 that over half of Britain's exports went to the rest of Europe. Even though Britain was challenged in these empire markets in its staple export products such as textiles and switched its exports to newer industries during the 1930s, exports from these newer industries were also largely directed towards empire markets (see Table 3.4). It was not until the Second World War that Britain's overseas investments were substantially liquidated, though it still continues to earn a surplus on invisible trade such as insurance and shipping to this day. Once Britain was again exposed to the effects of international competition the fundamental weaknesses observed in the pre-First World War period began to re-emerge. The appreciation of these has unfortunately been slower to materialise and the main response of industry has been of a defensive nature.

In contrast to Britain, Germany was fully exposed to all the major shocks of the twentieth century and has consistently sold its products in more competitive markets. Over two-thirds of its exports have always been to other European countries and a larger proportion of these consisted of products of the newer industries, such as machinery and chemicals, as well as basic metals. Thus in addition to being the under-dog initially, in itself an important stimulus to improve performance, Germany was constantly faced with strong pressures to achieve an improved industrial performance. Moreover its industries proved themselves capable of meeting these challenges time and time again.

We now turn to a more detailed consideration of the factors that have been responsible for the positive reaction of German industry and the more defensive tradition of UK industry. With the advance of industrialisation and the increasing complexity of industrial processes, the quality, as well as the quantity, of the inputs available, particularly the technological sophistication of the capital investment and the skill base of the workforce and the efficiency with which these inputs were combined by management, are the most crucial factors. We shall consider these in turn.

Technical Change

Britain has long been thought of as a country with an impressive record of invention and scientific achievement. Although such images are coloured by the particular national viewpoints from which they are observed, it is still the case that in terms of Nobel prizes in relation to the size of population Britain is one of the leading countries. If we turn, however, to her success at applying these discoveries the record is far less impressive. It is this introduction of new products on to the market that is most expensive and time-consuming and the available evidence suggests that, apart from a few exceptions, Britain has not devoted as many resources to technological innovations as have its main competitors. Germany's early lead in key industries such as

Table 3.4   *Destination and composition of UK, German and French exports, 1913–77 (%)*

a. Destination[1]

		Big Three	Other Europe	USA	Other Countries	Total Exports ($b.) Current Prices	Constant Prices[2]
UK	1913	12·8	20·0	5·4	61·9	2·6	16·7
	1938	7·6	24·5	4·4	63·5	2·3	14·4
	1960	7·0	26·2	9·2	57·6	9·9	23·0
	1977	14·1	43·3	9·4	33·2	57·4	57·4
Germany[1]	1913	22·1	44·0	7·1	26·9	2·4	17·7
	1938	10·6	54·6	2·8	32·1	2·2	10·6
	1960	12·9	53·1	7·7	26·3	11·4	29·5
	1977	18·0	55·7	6·8	19·5	117·9	117·9
France	1913	33·8	32·7	6·2	27·3	1·3	7·6
	1938	17·7	36·5	5·6	40·2	0·9	4·4
	1960	18·8	30·6	5·8	44·8	6·9	17·1
	1977	23·7	46·4	5·2	24·7	63·4	63·4

b. Composition[3]

		Raw Materials and Food	Metals	Machinery	Transport Equipment	Chemicals	Textiles	Other
UK	1913	21·0	12·7	7·7	4·7	4·0	37·0	13·0
	1938	21·6	11·5	15·2	8·8	4·6	21·7	16·6
	1960	12·9	13·8	26·7	16·3	9·0	6·1	15·2
	1977	15·9	8·7	26·1	11·4	11·8	3·5	22·6
Germany[1]	1913	29·2	15·9	9·7	2·3	7·9	13·0	23·0
	1938	13·4	19·5	19·9	8·3	12·6	8·3	18·0
	1960	10·8	18·0	27·1	16·2	11·0	3·5	13·4
	1977	9·6	11·1	30·9	17·1	15·7	3·5	15·7
France	1913	33·3	5·1	1·8	4·0	3·9	22·6	29·3
	1938	35·4	13·4	4·5	4·1	7·4	14·8	20·4
	1960	25·4	17·9	12·0	12·7	8·6	6·9	16·5
	1977	21·5	11·8	20·9	16·5	11·3	3·6	14·4

Notes: 1 The Big Three countries comprise the UK, Germany and France. After 1945 West Germany only, and exports from West to East Germany are excluded. Other European countries include the CMEA countries after 1945.

2 Adjusted to 1977 prices.

3 The following ISIC groups were used: raw materials and food 0–4, metals 67–9, machinery 71–2, transport equipment 73, chemicals 5, textiles 65 and other 61–4 and 8–9.

Sources: Ingvar Svennilson, *Growth and Stagnation in the European Economy* (UNECE, Geneva, 1954), pp. 293, 303 and 314, updated using the *UN Yearbook of International Trade Statistics* and the *OECD Statistics of Foreign Trade*, Series B. Constant price series from Alfred Maizels, *Industrial Growth and World Trade* (Cambridge University Press,

chemicals, electricity generation and advanced machinery of all kinds was in large part due to its success at exploiting its scientific and technical skills. The United States, on the other hand, was more successful at developing mass market products which required standardisation and interchangeability of parts. The achievements of Henry Ford, for instance, in introducing mass production brought the motor car within reach of a majority of the population. These different emphases, well described in Marshall, can still be seen today in the kind of products in which each country has a comparative advantage.[9] Neither of these important developments seems to have had such an influence on British industrialisation.

A recent study of the role of technological progress in Britain's industrial performance, edited by Keith Pavitt, showed amongst other things the close parallels between the resources devoted to technological effort and success in export markets, particularly in the capital goods industries.[10] The close relationship between export shares and the share of patents registered by foreigners in the United States by country can be seen in Table 3.3. The United States is the obvious country in which new patents are registered after the domestic market, and despite the shortcomings of patent statistics it gives a useful picture of the pattern of innovative activity in different countries. Britain's technological effort has been highly concentrated in the aerospace, nuclear and defence industries, to the detriment of the more bread-and-butter industries of international trade, such as mechanical and electrical engineering and vehicles. Only 40 per cent of British industrial research and development (R & D) is devoted to these industries, compared with one-half in the other countries shown in Table 3.5. It has been argued that the scarce and best talents available to British industry were pre-empted by the aerospace, nuclear and defence industries, which apart from the latter have not in retrospect been particularly successful in world markets.[11] A more worrying phenomenon, despite the current rush to subsidise microelectronics, is the decline in Britain's R & D effort while others are increasing theirs. Furthermore, this decline in R & D effort has been particularly sharp in the important mechanical engineering industry, where R & D actually fell by 37 per cent between 1967 and 1975. The chemical industry always emerges as the exception, increasing R & D by 27 per cent.

One of the consequences of this tendency to pay less attention to technological considerations in Britain has been that the sophistication of the products it is exporting has fallen down the value-added spectrum. Christopher Saunders has shown that unit values of engineering exports were broadly comparable between France,

Cambridge, 1965), p. 428, and the above *UN Yearbook* and *OECD Statistics*, Series A.

Table 3.5   *Research and development expenditures in manufacturing industry, 1975 (%)*

	West Germany	France	UK	USA	Japan
Chemicals	29·4	19·3	20·5	15·2	21·7
Basic metals	3·1	4·0	4·0	3·1	9·3
Machinery	13·1	4·8	11·1	13·3	10·9
Electrical	}30·1	5·4	4·2	9·4	10·7
Electronic		26·6	16·2	15·8	15·1
Aerospace	9·6	20·4	24·7	26·1	0·5
Vehicles and ships	11·7	11·1	8·8	10·8	18·1
Other manufacturing	3·0	8·4	10·5	6·3	13·7
Total manufacturing	100·0	100·0	100·0	100·0	100·0
State-financed (%)	13·4	26·4	33·4	34·8	1·8
Total ($b.)[1]	5·4	3·4	2·7	23·4	5·2

Industry-financed R & D as % of manufactured product					
1967	2·2	n.a.	3·3	3·5	2·4
1975	2·7	n.a.	2·7	4·2	3·1

Industry-financed R & D per capita (UK 1967 = 100)[2]					
1967	101	61	100	128	61
1975	134	78	90	142	104

Notes: 1   Current exchange rates.
   2   At 1970 prices and adjusted R & D exchange rates.
Sources: The distribution of R & D expenditure was estimated from OECD, *Trends in Industrial R & D in Selected OECD Countries, 1967–75* (mimeo, Paris, 1978) and shares of manufacturing product taken from Keith Pavitt and Luc Soete, 'Innovative activities and export shares: some comparisons between industries and countries', in Keith Pavitt (ed.), *Technical Innovation and British Economic Performance* (Macmillan, London, 1980), Table 3.11, which also drew on OECD sources.

Germany and the UK in the early 1960s, whereas by 1975 German and French unit values were about 60 and 40 per cent higher respectively.[12] In some product lines Britain is now exporting products of a similar sophistication to those exported by some of the leading newly industrialising countries (NICs).

   The second worrying consequence, also the result of successive devaluations of sterling between 1967 and 1977, is the perverse pattern of specialisation of British trade. The Maldague Report shows that the UK is becoming more, and not less, involved in trade in products with a low skilled labour content, and is losing its position in more sophisticated goods with a higher skill content.[13]

Management and Training

An essential complement to technological progressiveness is managerial competence. Almost all the studies mentioned above concluded that in many respects British management was deficient. The nature of the education system, dominated by Oxbridge and the public schools, together with Britain's preoccupations with other questions such as the Commonwealth and acting as the world's banker, have starved British industry of the best talent available. Whereas a career in management was the accepted route to higher status and reward in Germany and the USA, this was and is still not true today in Britain. While 80 per cent of German chief executives and 90 per cent of French executives have degrees, often from technical universities or *grandes écoles*, a majority of the British have risen from the shop floor, only 40 per cent having been to university.[14] This anti-industry bias in the education system and the prevailing attitudes of the elite have not only weakened the ability of British management to respond to the increasingly complex demands being made on management but have also actively inhibited changes in technical and management education. The development of any form of rigorous, professional education for engineers or managers took place very late in Britain's industrialisation, and indeed the practical men with no formal training who were managing British industry were hostile to newcomers with their professional training. The disregard for training in the industrial arts in Britain can be observed throughout the whole of Britain's industrialisation. The early development of high-quality training in such institutions as the *Technische Hochschulen* in Germany not only established an early appreciation of the need for such training within industry itself but ensured that such professions achieved a greater recognition and status in society than would otherwise have been the case. In Germany, for instance, there were ten technical universities with 14,000 students in 1908, whereas Britain only had a few technical schools of a far inferior standard with only 3,000 students. Austin Albu has described the half-hearted efforts of Britain to catch up in this regard since then; it still has a long way to go to match the standard, not the best, practice in all the other European countries, the United States and Japan.[15]

The pervasive hostility to training in Britain can be seen most clearly in regard to vocational training of the bulk of the workforce. Any visitor to British factories inquiring about this will be told that the typical operative on the shop floor needs no more than to be briefly shown how to work the machines. This was and is not the typical response abroad. Well before Germany became a major industrial

power it had created a comprehensive primary and secondary education system that included extensive post-school vocational training for
young workers. Report after report from Commission after Commission called for the introduction of a similar system in this country.[16]
However, apart from the education system of a small elite, the main-
stream education system was developed after Britain industrialised
and not before as in Germany, France and Japan. Gradually a
national education system was developed in Britain in the first half of
this century. The response was, however, too slow in coming and too
grudgingly undertaken to make a major impact on British industrial
performance. For instance, there were no state secondary schools in
England until after 1902 and in the 1920s only 12 per cent of children
went on to secondary or tertiary education. This was far fewer than in
most other continental European countries. Although one of the main
recommendations of the 1944 Education Act in Britain was to set up a
comprehensive post-school vocational training system, this was never
carried out. To this day Britain has nothing to match the compulsory
day-release training schemes for 16–18-year-olds that have existed in
many continental countries for the best part of a century. In Germany
the schemes are run jointly by the employers, trade unions and
educationalists. In Britain efforts to start such schemes have faced
great hostility from industry. The situation today has been
summarised by Sir Dennis Barnes, the chairman of the Manpower
Services Commission, who said: 'of all the young people who finish
full-time education at 16 or 17 in this country, only about 40% get
some kind of effective and useful training compared with about 80%
in countries like Germany and Sweden'.[17]

Another indication of the effects of managerial weakness in Britain
is the inability to exploit the economies of scale in industries where this
has involved very large production units. S. J. Prais has shown that
organisational dis-economies of scale become important at relatively
small plant sizes in Britain, and preliminary evidence tends to confirm
that this is a particularly British phenomenon.[18] This is one reason
why British plants in industries such as motor vehicles and steel have
remained much smaller in this country and their performance has been
particularly disappointing.[19]

Industrial Relations
Given the far less paternalistic attitude towards shop-floor employees
in this country than elsewhere in Europe and the persistence of the
idea, typified above in relation to training, of an employee as simply a
unit of labour power, it is perhaps not surprising that industrial
relations take on a different aspect in Britain. A majority of the
British industrial workforce left the land much earlier than in Europe
and went into far worse conditions, as any visitor to parts of

Liverpool, Manchester, Newcastle and Glasgow can still see. A great number of people did not leave the land in Europe until the postwar period. For these reasons trade unions in Britain are very conscious of their craft origins and the denial of any useful training and involvement leads to their becoming a powerful force for technological conservatism. This was of course doubly reinforced by the slower growth of living standards in Britain.

Many of the problems of running large plants and of introducing new technology stem from the problems of the interaction of poor managerial competence and a hostile and fragmented trade union structure. Ronald Dore concluded a massive study of industrial relations in Britain and Japan by emphasising again the

scars and stiffnesses that come from the searing experience of having made the first, most long drawn out industrial revolution. The slowness of the process gave time for the classes gradually to draw apart and over generations to develop their own quite separate cultures before the elite awoke to a realisation of what was happening to the cohesion of their society and began grudgingly to accept a new collectivism. That is a feature underlying many features of modern Britain, like the antique inflexibility of her trade union institutions.[20]

The particular evolution of industrial relations in Britain has always emphasised established 'custom and practice', that are recognised and negotiated at plant level. A recent study by David Marsden shows quite clearly that employers in Germany and France have been quite successful in conducting a greater part of the discussions of the more contentious issues through more formalised channels at a higher level.[21] Similarly the systems of industrial democracy in these two countries each in their own way act to diffuse efforts to organise collectively at the work place. There is no doubt that these developments have led to greater order in industrial relations in Germany and, in between periodic crises such as 1968, in France also. Neither country has such a fragmented shop steward bargaining system as does Britain, often conducted on a highly *ad hoc* basis. Not only does this lead to greater unpredictability in British industrial relations, it also means that bargaining over issues such as the introduction of new technology can reach right down to the workgroup level. These features place British management at a severe disadvantage compared to their continental counterparts.

The Development of an Industrial Consensus

The final factor that will be considered is the area of inter-firm and firm—government relationships. One of the very significant findings of a perceptive analysis by Andrew Shonfield of the way the German economy works was 'that the Germans are equipped with both the business habits and institutions which would allow them to make an easy transition to a planned economy', while in Britain 'commercial customs and national history both argue against the process of central planning'.[22] Given the non-intervention rhetoric of postwar Germany and its industrial success it has not been necessary to resort to any form of government planning. However, the existence of the powerful industrial associations, providing an essential clearing house for information and forecasts as well as a forum for developing industry-wide solutions to particular problems, and the close involvement of the banks in business, to a degree unimaginable in Britain, provides a good proxy for the planning process. Indeed it is arguable that it fulfils this task far more efficiently. The influence of the banks in Germany through acting as proxies for small shareholders and occupying seats on the boards of most larger companies is not perhaps sufficiently appreciated in this country. These factors of German industry have been at the core of German industrial success throughout its industrialisation, strengthened of course during the Nazi period. In earlier times government was more closely involved, for instance, the highly successful rationalisation movement of the 1920s was largely government-sponsored, though implemented by the industrial associations. Since the war the banks have been delegated the responsibility for administering various state subsidies and regional grants, a job normally undertaken by the state itself elsewhere.

Much of the effort devoted to industrial policy in France and Britain has been in trying to create a substitute for these methods of developing an industrial consensus. Two particular decisions taken by France in the early postwar years helped to reverse her dismal performance in the 1930s. The first was the development of the planning process under Jean Monnet in 1946 and the second was the decision to join forces with, rather than to compete against or protect French industry from, German competition in the signing of the European Coal and Steel Community Treaty in 1951, again inspired by Jean Monnet. There seems little doubt that this latter decision, which was a break with past traditions, meant that France shared in the dynamism associated with German economy. It was only able to do so because of the fundamental change in business attitudes engendered by participating in the early planning process. Jean Monnet was able to set targets and identify particular industries that were the key to greater industrial success and moreover he was able to direct a large part of the funds available for industrial investment at the time, including the counterpart funds of the Marshall Plan. This early stimulus was crucial and although this particular function of the plan has become far less effective and important in recent years the French government's predilection for selecting and actively promoting particular industrial sectors has not.

Britain on the other hand had neither the attitudes nor the institutional interrelationships necessary for developing such German-style consensus within industry, nor was it able to pursue an industrial policy capable of providing such a consensus. So far all of the efforts to introduce some form of planning in Britain have been dismal failures. The Labour government of 1945 had all the institutions and conditions, plus the same counterpart funds, available, but failed to develop a coherent plan. The National Plan of 1965 was likewise a failure. Other attempts such as the creation of NEDO and the Industrial Strategy of 1975 have proved more durable though so far only marginally effective. The failure realistically to conceive and carry out policies designed to achieve a greater industrial consensus in this country stems in part from the hostility of British industry to any form of state intervention and a prevailing belief that there was little wrong with British industry. In part it also stems from the non-discriminatory predisposition of the British civil service. For instance, although large parts of British industry are in state ownership there has been little attempt to use these, as Jean Monnet did, as an essential part of any national strategy. Even the Labour government of 1945 refused to conceive of their development within the planning framework.[23]

British banks have also been unable and unwilling to perform many of the functions of German banks. Traditionally they were more pre-occupied with international lending, particularly to foreign governments, and domestic industry came well down the list of priorities. Because they are not nearly so involved in the operations of their industrial clients they do not share the same longer-term strategic thinking necessary in many industries. German banks are more able to take such long-term lending decisions as they often have an influential position in many of the interrelated firms in question, and can hence minimise the risks attached to uncertainty about competitors' or suppliers' reactions to a particular investment decision. Critics of the foreign preoccupation of the British banking system often blame this for the lower investment in British industry. However, given the much lower efficiency with which new capital investment is utilised in Britain it is natural that capital should have been attracted elsewhere.

This survey of the factors underlying the differential performance of Britain, France and Germany is inevitably incomplete and selective. In making the survey I have necessarily focused on the differences between these countries rather than on the similar trend towards a more concentrated ownership of industry, for instance. However, I was concerned to establish factors individual to each country that have had a lasting effect on their industrial performance. From the discussion it is clear that in Britain

> low investment and productivity, the burden of public spending and rising imports are the symptoms of a more general failure to adjust to a new international order and to the emergence of more efficient business practices, or rather to adjust fast enough to keep pace with rapid changes occurring elsewhere in the world economy.[24]

Popular diagnoses based on a short-term time-horizon such as the squeeze of industry by the public sector in the capital and labour markets are rightly dismissed as failing to grasp the underlying issues.[25] If the solutions to these problems were so easy or clear-cut then they would have been solved long ago. Until such an understanding emerges, proposed solutions will have only a marginal effect on Britain's performance.

Adjustment Pressures and the Changing International Context

From the earlier analysis of this chapter it is evident that the postwar period of sustained and particularly rapid growth was quite exceptional by historical standards, at least within the last century or so. It is also clear that since the early 1970s the situation has changed considerably and in many respects is more typical of the experience of the earlier part of this century. Although opinions still differ as to whether or not this is simply a prolonged recession which can eventually be overcome by international demand management, there seem to be a number of factors of growing importance that will ensure that a return to rapid and sustained growth becomes increasingly unlikely.

One thing that has certainly had a significant impact on the international context in which this divergent economic performance is taking place is the breakdown of many of the assumptions on which the international economic system was based since 1945. Charles P. Kindleberger has argued that

> the international economy is harmonised not by free trade and capital movements . . . but by the ability and willingness of a leading power to 'underwrite' it. This leadership consists of four elements: maintaining an open market for imports, providing counter-cyclical lending, co-ordinating macroeconomic policies and discounting in crisis.[26]

Britain fulfilled this role up to the First World War, and the United

States for twenty-five years after the Second. But no one country could provide such leadership in the interwar period, with catastrophic results, and since 1971 with the collapse of the Bretton Woods system the world has found itself in a similar predicament. The United States is for various reasons unable and unwilling to continue to do so and some form of collective leadership will have to be sought as a replacement. This is a much more difficult task that requires more and not less willingness to co-operate at an international level. This co-operation will be subjected to growing pressures in the future.

The events of 1973 and the subsequent pressure on resources, and in particular on oil, have reinforced the downturn in world economic performance that was already becoming evident at that time and further undermined the US dominance of the system. It also seems clear that the main focus of economic growth in the rest of this century is likely to shift from the AICs to the countries of South-East Asia and possibly Latin America, and within Europe to the countries of the southern European periphery. These countries, commonly grouped together as the NICs, are likely to play an increasingly important role in world trade. Although a number of recent studies have estimated that the effects of this development on the AICs will be minimal, this may underestimate the growing political impact that it will undoubtedly generate.[27] As I have shown earlier, it is countries such as Britain that will be hit first by such trade as it produces less sophisticated goods than most other AICs. In such price-sensitive mature products, lower wage rates obviously give the NICs an advantage in this kind of trade.

The other major development that will undoubtedly require major structural changes in European industry is the impact of new electronics technology. Whether this will eventually prove to be a net creator or destroyer of jobs, it will certainly involve substantial changes in the distribution of resources between industries. Countries that are most able to adapt to these changes for social and institutional reasons as well as for economic reasons will be better placed to maintain or improve their relative industrial performance. In this connection Germany had traditionally been the most technologically advanced and adaptive economy in Europe. Indeed, in many areas it has been second only to the technological leader, the United States. However, the very dramatic rise of Japan, and in particular its trans-formation from an essentially imitative economy to one that might well be the technological leader worldwide in a number of important industries in a few years, puts this situation in a different light. Japan has set itself the goal of overtaking the United States in the key area of electronics technology, and looks like succeeding. It is already beginning to export successfully the most sophisticated products in a number of fields, such as advanced computer-controlled machine tools. Whether the German engineering industry with its very strong mechanical and electrical engineering skills can catch up with Japanese electronics technology is a vital question for Japan's future performance. So far it has dominated world exports of these sophisticated high-value-added products.

From the above discussion the curious situation seems to be emerging of European countries squeezed at the top end of the value-added spectrum by the technological leaders, such as Japan, and at the bottom end by the NICs. Britain's position in this divergence squeeze is particularly acute in that its performance in those middle-range industries, such as motor vehicles, heavy electrical engineering, standardised machine tools and other machinery, is already weak for the reasons outlined above. It is precisely in these industries that Britain has to maintain a comparative advantage in order to survive in world markets, without suffering politically unacceptable low levels of income. This also has an important implication for industrial policy. It is no longer probably the right strategy to aim to beat the technological leaders in the most advanced products; this is simply beyond the realistic capabilities of the UK economy. The French are, however, identifying and supporting precisely some of these middle- to upper-middle-range industries.

Implications and Responses

For Britain the problems of adjusting to these new circumstances and reversing its long-term relative decline are particularly daunting. However, there are signs that British industry and society have begun to respond to increased openness and the competition on world markets. So far these responses have been of a rather defensive nature. The ability to translate these into more positive responses will depend on a full realisation of the fundamental problems underlying the British situation. A continuing preoccupation with short-term solutions simply distracts attention from the problems that will eventually have to be tackled and makes the problems themselves more intractable. It is also important for Britain, as well as for Europe, that its partners in the Community also understand the nature of the task facing Britain.

At the opposite end of the divergence spectrum a number of new questions are emerging for Germany. Germany is under growing pressure to assume the increased responsibilities associated with its extremely strong currency and trading position. It will undoubtedly have a major role to play in any new international monetary arrangements. As discussed above, Germany may also increasingly face a technological challenge from the Japanese electronics industry in many of the advanced engineering products on which its strong trading performance has been based.

For the European Community the continuation and possible intensification of divergent economic performance amongst the member states will pose very considerable problems. The recent Maldague Report even concluded that the EC could break up because of it.[28] It is important to remember that the origins of this divergence pre-date the formation of the European Community by many decades. Therefore although Community politicians stress the need for the Community itself to pursue policies to promote a greater convergence among the member states it is unlikely that the Community alone can bring this about. Solutions to many of the problems outlined above will also involve a combination of action at an international level and within individual countries. The degree to which these problems create growing tensions within the Community will depend on a number of factors. The first is to find a new way of reconstructing the international economic system – an aim to which the European Monetary System could contribute if it were to be part of a wider monetary arrangement. The second is the degree to which the European economies are able to adjust to a period of slower growth, with a greater emphasis on tackling social and environmental questions and in coping with the transformation of life-styles and industrial structure implied by the adjustment pressures outlined above. The third is whether the European institutions can develop sufficient flexibility to accommodate different and divergent standards of living and performance amongst the member states. The European Community is now in a fundamentally different situation from that envisaged at its inception. The fourth is whether the political will can be mobilised to overcome the inevitable protectionist and nationalistic pressures that will emerge during more difficult economic conditions.

Notes: Chapter 3

This study was written in the context of a larger research project at the Sussex European Research Centre into government intervention and structural adjustment in European industry, supported by the Anglo-German Foundation for the Study of Industrial Society and the Volkswagen Foundation. The author would like to thank many colleagues at the University of Sussex for their helpful comments on an earlier draft.

1 Living standards in northern Italy were almost identical with the UK in 1976 while in central Italy they were about 20 per cent lower and in southern Italy they were just over one-half that of the UK.

2 See Daniel T. Jones, 'Output, employment and labour productivity in Europe since 1955', *National Institute Economic Review*, no. 77, August 1976.

3 The study by L. Rostas, *Comparative Productivity in British and American Industry* (Cambridge University Press, Cambridge, 1948) shows that German manufacturing productivity was between 4 and 11 per cent higher in 1936 depend-

ing on the method of estimation; see pp. 28 and 40. Data on p. 67 of E. H. Phelps Brown's 'Levels and movements of industrial productivity and real wages internationally compared, 1860–1970', *The Economic Journal*, vol. 83, March 1973, indicate that German industrial productivity was only 7 per cent lower than the UK in 1913.

4   See the results of a number of studies summarised in Irving B. Kravis, 'A survey of international comparisons of productivity', *The Economic Journal*, vol. 86, March 1976, p. 34.

5   See W. E. G. Salter, *Productivity and Technical Change*, 2nd ed (Cambridge University Press, Cambridge, 1969), p. 154.

6   Readers who are interested in a detailed treatment of these issues, and in particular as they relate to the experience of the interwar period, should consult Ingvar Svennilson, *Growth and Stagnation in the European Economy* (UNECE, Geneva, 1954).

7   Apart from the Svennilson study referred to in note 6, the following studies can be highly recommended: Alfred Marshall, *Industry and Trade* (Macmillan, London, 1919); E. J. Hobsbawm, *Industry and Empire* (Penguin, Harmondsworth, 1968); David S. Landes, *The Unbound Prometheus* (Cambridge University Press, Cambridge, 1969); and Correlli Barnett, *The Collapse of British Power* (Eyre Methuen, London, 1972). For those with less time, William Walker, 'Britain's industrial performance 1850–1950: a failure to adjust', in Keith Pavitt (ed.), *Technical Innovation and British Economic Performance* (Macmillan, London, 1980); G. C. Allen, *The British Disease* (Institute of Economic Affairs, London, 1976); Correlli Barnett, 'The hundred years' sickness', *Industrial and Commercial Training: Management of Human Resources*, vol. 8, no. 6, June 1977; and E. H. Phelps Brown, 'What is the British predicament?', *The Three Banks Review*, no. 116, December 1977, provide very useful distillations of the main issues.

8   See S. B. Saul, 'The mechanical engineering industries in Britain, 1860–1914', *Economic History Review*, vol. XX, 1967.

9   Two contemporary studies that illustrate the continuing influence of these different paths of industrialisation are those by William Walker and J. Gardner, 'Innovation and competitiveness in portable power tools', in Pavitt, op. cit., and Daniel T. Jones, *Plant Size and Efficiency in the Production of Metalworking Machine Tools* (National Institute Discussion Paper 19, NIESR, London, mimeo., 1978).

10 Keith Pavitt and Luc Soete, 'Innovative activities and export shares: some comparisons between industries and countries', in Pavitt, op. cit.

11 See Mary Kaldor, 'Technical change in the defence industry', in Pavitt, op. cit.

12 See Christopher Saunders, *Engineering in Britain, West Germany and France: Some Statistical Comparisons* (Sussex European Paper No. 3, Sussex European Research Centre, Brighton, 1978), p. 67.

13 Report of a Group of Experts on Sectoral Analyses, *Changes in the Industrial Structure in the European Economies Since the Oil Crisis* (Maldague Report) (Commission of the European Communities, Brussels, July 1979), pp. 67–79.

14 Quoted in Barnett (1977), op. cit., p. 241.

15 See Austen Albu, 'British attitudes to engineering education: an historical perspective', in Pavitt, op. cit.

16 See Barnett (1977), op. cit., p. 243.

17 Quoted in ibid., p. 244.

18 S. J. Prais, 'The strike proneness of large plants in Britain', *Journal of the Royal Statistical Society*, series A, vol. 141, 1978.

19 See Daniel T. Jones and S. J. Prais, 'Plant size and productivity in the motor industry: some international comparisons', *Oxford Bulletin of Economics and Statistics*, vol. 40, May 1978.

20 Ronald Dore, *British Factory Japanese Factory* (Allen & Unwin, London, 1973), pp. 419–20.

21 David Marsden, *Industrial Democracy and Industrial Control in West Germany, France and Great Britain* (Department of Employment Research Paper No. 4, Department of Employment, London, 1978).

22 Andrew Shonfield, *Modern Capitalism* (Oxford University Press/RIIA, London, 1969), pp. 260–1.

23 A full account of the failures of British industrial intervention can be found in Alan Budd, *The Politics of Economic Planning* (Fontana, London, 1978), and in Peter Mottershead, 'Industrial policy', in Frank T. Blackaby (ed.), *British Economic Policy 1960–1974* (Cambridge University Press, Cambridge, 1978).

24 William Walker, 'Britain's industrial performance 1850–1950: a failure to adjust', in Pavitt, op. cit.

25 These arguments were discussed and dismissed in F. Blackaby (ed.), *De-Industrialisation* (Heinemann/NIESR, London, 1979).

26 Charles P. Kindleberger, 'Systems of international organisation', in David P. Calleo *et al.*, *Money and the Coming World Order* (New York University Press, New York, 1976), p. 32, quoted by Robert Skidelsley in 'Keynes and the reconstruction of liberalism', *Encounter*, April 1979, p. 39.

27 The so-called Hayes Report, whose full title is *The Newly Industrialising Countries and the Adjustment Problem* (Government Economic Service Working Paper No. 18, Foreign and Commonwealth Office, London, 1979).

28 Maldague Report, op. cit., p. 147.

4

Industrial Adjustment: The Community Dimension

Stephen Woolcock

Introduction

Industrial adjustment can mean many things to many people. To the industrialist striving to cope with increased competition during a period of slow growth it will mean improving productivity and developing new products which promise higher demand. For workers employed in industries especially hard hit by falling demand or import competition it will mean loss of job security and concern about future employment prospects. At the national level it poses difficult questions for policy-makers. For example, should the speed of change be slowed in order to mitigate the social and political costs of adjustment during slower growth? If so, how can one ensure that such defensive policies do not lead to an ossification of unproductive industrial activities, and what policies, if any, are needed to help ensure that adjustment takes place?

Industrial adjustment thus poses problems of allocating the costs of adjustment to change. At a Community level there is the added problem of how to accommodate divergent national responses to these issues, whilst ensuring that unilateral national actions do not undermine the cohesion of the Community. Different national responses will not only make the formulation of common policies more difficult, but will also exacerbate the problems of divergence. As member states intervene to slow the speed of change and thus influence the allocation of the costs of adjustment, they effectively determine to what extent economic resources are tied into relatively unproductive industrial activities. No matter how justified such action is in social and political terms it will make the industry concerned relatively less competitive. There is then a distinct possibility that further measures will be required to compensate for the loss in competitiveness, which result in a further decline in productivity and divergence in economic performance. When this occurs in a number of industries, such micro level interventions will have an impact on the macroeconomic performance of the economy concerned. Failure to adjust or a relative slowing of the speed of adjustment in one member state compared to others can thus exacerbate economic divergence.

This, however, is only one side of the coin. Divergent economic performance can itself cause divergent national responses. When general economic performance is relatively poor there will be fewer alternative job opportunities for those affected by closures in declining industries. There will also be fewer alternative investment opportunities in more dynamic sectors, so that the propensity of governments to intervene to slow the speed of adjustment will increase with a decline in industrial performance. One has, therefore, a situation in which adjustment and industrial, or indeed general, economic performance, are intrinsically linked.

This chapter will discuss the interdependence between the capacity of industry to adjust and industrial performance. It will look at the Community dimension by considering the extent to which different national responses are accommodated, and assess the effectiveness of policies designed to promote the balanced adjustment of industrial structures throughout the Community.

The Issues

There are various causes of the need for industrial adjustment. In the field of international trade, industrial adjustment can be understood as the shifting of resources from activities, in which advanced industrialised countries (AICs) of the Community are facing growing competition from the developing world, into more sophisticated products. This form of adjustment to changes in the international division of labour involves intra- and inter-industry relocation of resources from labour-intensive products, such as clothing, into more skill-intensive, higher value-added activities. It also involves the more capital-intensive but standard technology products, such as standard consumer electronics, in which the newly industrialising countries (NICs) are becoming increasingly competitive.[1] Such imports are counterbalanced by exports from other sectors, so that the case for liberal trade policies based on long-run economic benefits is justified. On the other hand, increased trade specialisation inevitably requires adjustment. During a period of slow growth, adjustment to changes in the pattern of trade are more difficult.

There has, therefore, been increasing pressure on national governments and Community institutions to regulate trade in certain sectors. The case for trade regulation is generally put in terms of the need to provide 'temporary protection' in order to enable industries to adapt at a socially acceptable speed. The problem with trade regulation such as the Multi-Fibre Arrangement (MFA) in textiles and clothing, or orderly marketing agreements (OMAs), is that they can, and have, become permanent forms of protection. Experience in various sectors shows that some form of import restraint is inevitable for what are largely political reasons. The objective therefore must be to ensure that this regulation of trade is genuinely temporary. With its competences in the formulation and implementation of trade policy, the Community plays a central role in determining the length of such 'breathing spaces'.

Whilst slower growth increases the pressure to adjust in general terms, some industries have been affected by both short-term cyclical and longer-term structural effects. In industries such as iron and steel the income elasticity of demand has slipped below unity, so that the industry has been especially hard hit by the decline in general growth rates. Future economic growth is also unlikely to be steel-intensive, as a wide range of steel consuming industries such as consumer durables are now facing a progressive saturation of demand. In other industries the ratio of GDP growth to industrial demand has also changed disadvantageously. In base petrochemicals, for example, it is around unity, compared to the positive relationship which existed up to the early 1970s, and future dynamic growth will have to be sought in higher value-added specialised products. Changes in the world energy market have also affected shipbuilding and, despite a revival in 1976–7, the automobile industry.

In the case of shipbuilding, trade protection was inoperable as a means of easing the process of adjustment to the rapid changes in demand owing to the nature of the shipping industry. Consequently, national governments intervened by providing subsidies to the ship-yards in order to slow the speed of adjustment to socially acceptable rates and retain a potential in the industry. Such national aid to an industry in the form of subsidies, however, threatens to shift the burden of adjustment on to other producers unless it is controlled and co-ordinated. The regulation of national aid programmes is therefore a further dimension to Community industrial adjustment.

In capital-intensive industries such as the steel industry, import regulation alone does not ensure that the funds needed for investment in the restructuring are generated and adjustment to lower levels of demand takes place. For this reason the steel producers in the Community and the United States sought to raise prices and regulate competition.[2] In the case of the iron and steel industry the Commission has powers to influence prices directly, but in other industries this is not the case. The role of governments and the Community in providing trade protection and subsidies is real, but much adjustment goes on without any public intervention. Faced with declining demand and falling prices, producers may well seek to ensure that cut-throat competition is avoided. The extent to which producers will seek to reduce competition during a recession depends on the structure of the companies concerned. In large diversified companies, such as the General Trading Companies in Japan, much adjustment can be facilitated internally. If only one part of a company's activities is adversely affected, resources can be transferred from other parts of the company to help sustain production potential until demand improves. This is indeed one reason why the relatively undiversified steel producers, such as the British Steel Corporation, have been harder hit than, for example, many of the German producers.

In the case of synthetic fibres, most of the European producers are well-diversified chemical companies. However, the decline in demand, combined with continued investment in new capacity by some producers, meant that the losses incurred by the fibre manufacturers was too great to be carried for very long. As a result the eleven fibre manufacturers in the Community sought to conclude an anti-crisis cartel agreement in 1977. In the case of such agreements the Community has a role to play in the form of competition policy. In the specific case of the synthetic fibre crisis cartel, the Commission, after much agonising, finally asked the producers to dissolve the agreement, which had been tacitly supported by the Commission, in December 1979. This was done on the grounds that it did not comply with the EEC Treaty provisions on competition policy. This is but one example of how private sector responses to the need to adjust and rationalise production impinge on competition. Another case is that of the German steel industry, where the privately controlled regional rationalisation groups have existed for many years.[3] A third dimension to industrial adjustment in the Community is therefore the regulation of restrictive practices, an area in which the Commission has real powers by virtue of Articles 85–90 EEC and Articles 65–7 ECSC.

There are two further Community dimensions to industrial adjustment which are more directly related to the present economic climate. First, the problems of inflation have meant that the use of demand management has been severely curtailed. Governments are not prepared to expand demand which would ease the frictions caused by adjustment during a period of slow growth. In order to control inflation many governments are also restricting the money supply and reducing public expenditure. All this makes it harder for industry to get the funds it needs to rationalise existing production facilities and develop new products. Any source of finance for industry, or finance which helps to mitigate the costs of adjustment, is therefore important. In this respect the funds provided by the various Community financial instruments are limited, but when effectively co-ordinated they can be of some significance given the shortage of investment capital in some industries. There is evidence that the Community financial instruments have been of some significance in the iron and steel industry.

The second issue is the co-ordination of national responses to the problem of increasing imbalance in the labour market. Industrial employment is on the decline throughout the Community.[4] With little expansion of public sector services, private sector services may not be able to absorb the extra labour. This was in fact the case from 1973 to 1977. Such an imbalance in the employment market makes workers less prepared to move and thus reduces the ability of industries or economies to adjust. This is particularly true when industries threatened by closures are located in areas which do not offer sufficient alternative employment. In an effort to reduce the supply of labour and thus re–establish a balanced employment market, an increasing number of Western European trade unions are calling for a reduction in the working week and various other forms of work-sharing. It need hardly be stressed that unilateral action by one country or one national industry in this field will worsen its competitiveness. If there are to be real adjustments on the labour market, therefore, employment market policies will add a further Community dimension to industrial adjustment.

Economic Divergence and Industrial Adjustment

There are two issues here of relevance to economic divergence within the European Community. On the one hand, differences in the capacity of the national industries to adjust will tend to lead to greater economic divergence. On the other hand, divergence itself makes the formulation of common approaches to industrial adjustment more difficult.

On the first point it is difficult to prove a direct causality between general economic performance and the ability to adjust to changes in trade and demand patterns. This is due to the complex nature of the factors which have to be considered in any empirical work. For this reason, proponents of positive adjustment policies[5] within the OECD have called for a shift to more positive policies based on *a priori* arguments.

There is an important issue here. During the debate within the OECD the stronger economies argued that negative, defensive policies should be given up in order to promote economic growth in the weaker economies. Those countries suffering from slow growth, however, said they could not remove defensive policies until growth improved, so that the stronger countries (this was at the time when the locomotive theories were being discussed) should inflate their economies.

There is generally verbal support for the need to accommodate changes in industrial structure without recourse to permanent defensive policies. In practice, however, some countries show a greater propensity to accept arguments, put forward by industrialists or trade unionists, that temporary protection or aid is required to re-establish international competitiveness. Other countries, with the Germans to the fore, argue that such measures lead to an ossification of unproductive industrial structures. But even the most liberal countries have intervened when the social costs of change become unacceptable.

Just what is and what is not socially acceptable depends on the political balance in any country at a given time. What is important for the Community dimension to industrial adjustment is the differences in the propensity of national governments to follow defensive policies. If a given member state of the Community defends employment or markets in activities of declining demand more than others, one can reasonably expect this to reduce the productivity in that sector. When there is recourse to such defensive policies for an increasing number of sectors, the slowing of adjustment at this micro level can then be expected to have a detrimental effect on the macroeconomic performance of the country concerned.

Some empirical work has been done which suggests that the ability to adjust industrial structures improves economic performance.[6] This work measures positive adjustment in terms of an increase in production over domestic consumption in industries which exhibit an above-average growth rate in world demand. A surplus of domestic production over consumption in declining industries was considered to indicate a reduced capacity to adjust to changes in the pattern of demand or negative adjustment. The results suggest that, over the period 1960–74, Japan showed the greatest dynamism, followed by the Federal Republic of Germany (FRG) and the Netherlands. France and Italy kept more or less abreast of changes in demand, whilst the UK became increasingly dependent on declining industries. On this measure of adjustment capacity there was some correlation between adjustment and growth but it tells us little about the causality.[7]

In more recent work[8] it was found that economies which performed better during the 1960s exhibited a greater ability to adjust to the problems caused by slower growth during the 1970s. This suggests that the capacity to adjust is determined by characteristics which are long term in nature. In many respects the findings of the work commissioned by Brussels coincides with the earlier work discussed. It is found that the UK is more dependent on industries in which the NICs are becoming increasingly competitive, owing in part to a poor investment record. Italy is also dependent on such industries due to greater concentration on consumption rather than investment, but has been successful in exporting such products as clothing and footwear to other Community countries. France has strengthened its position in important export sectors such as equipment goods, but still has a great deal of adjustment to do in the labour-intensive sectors, such as textiles and clothing. Germany and the Netherlands have adjusted out of these industries relatively quickly, with employment in clothing, for example, declining rapidly in both cases. The report concludes that some member states of the Community have still a great deal of adjustment to do, and that 'much thought will therefore be needed at European level to find a consistent line for European and national sectoral industrial policy'.

In summary, therefore, it is evident that the ability of the member states to adjust differs. This inevitably introduces frictions which might undermine attempts to establish common policies, for example, the European Monetary System. It is not possible to establish the causality between the capacity to adjust and economic performance as the two are intrinsically linked. However, greater recourse to selective measures to slow the speed of adjustment in a range of industries can be expected to influence macroeconomic performance. There is therefore an *a priori* argument for policies which help to promote industrial adjustment.

The Community Dimension to Industrial Adjustment

Trade and Commercial Policy
The case for temporary trade protection or the regulation of trade is generally couched in terms of the need to provide a breathing space which the industry concerned can use to restructure and re-establish its international competitiveness; in short, to adjust to changes in the pattern of trade. With its responsibility for negotiating multilateral and bilateral trading agreements the Community determines the provision of such breathing spaces. This is not to say that the Commission determines policy, although it may have some influence. The mandate in trade negotiations is decided by the Council, so that the Community policy represents a compromise between the protectionist and liberal forces in the Council at any one time.

The Community, and specifically the Commission, is explicitly committed to a liberal trade policy. In negotiations with other trading partners the Commission comes under pressure to liberalise Community trade restrictions. Furthermore, as a major trading bloc heavily dependent on international trade, the Community cannot afford to be protectionist. On the other hand, the Commission and the Community in general is under pressure from some national governments, and most industrial lobbies in the sectors concerned, to regulate the speed of adjustment to changes in the international division of labour. The Community must seek to avert unilateral recourse to trade restrictions on the part of national governments, which undermine the customs union but also risk throwing the Community and international trade in general into a spiral of even more restrictive beggar-thy-neighbour national actions. The Community's role in trade policy is therefore to seek a balance between the need to mitigate the social and political impact of adjustment, and the maintenance of a sufficient degree of external competition to ensure that unproductive industrial activities are forced to adjust.

There are some important related issues on this point. Experience in the textile and steel sectors suggests that there might well be a danger that internal competition is traded off against external competition in the formulation of Community trade policy. The more liberal trading nations of the Community such as West Germany would like to ensure internal competition, meaning no restrictions on intra-industry trade and no excessive use of public assistance to private industry,[9] as well as external competition in the form of a liberal trade policy. However, the real problems of adjustment in some specific industries, such as textiles and steel, have meant that national governments have come under strong political pressure from politically important constituencies to slow the speed of adjustment. In the cases of steel and textiles, strong pressure from the French and British meant that more restrictive Community policies had to be adopted if unilateral measures were to be averted. Faced with the prospect of restrictions on intra-Community trade, the more liberal member states yielded on the external front in order to avoid restrictions being placed on exports to their most important market, the Community itself.

The main cause of concern here is selective quantitative restrictions on trade as in the Multi-Fibre Arrangement (MFA). As some countries are less able to adjust their industrial structures than others, there is a danger that the requisite adjustment within the Community will be determined by the speed with which the slowest adjusts. If the Community is to avoid unilateral national actions but at the same time speed up the process of adjustment to changes in the international division of labour, it is essential that some leverage is brought to bear which promotes industrial adjustment in these specific industries. By pressing for a liberalisation of selective import controls and minimising recourse to new measures the Community can exercise such leverage.

The Control of National Aid Programmes

Experience in a range of industries has shown that *all* governments have found it necessary to intervene when the social or economic costs of rapid changes in demand or patterns of trade become unacceptable. For example, even the FRG has provided assistance to its shipbuilding industry. One is not considering an idealised liberal trading system but one in which social and political factors play an important part. In industries in which trade protection is a non-starter, such as shipbuilding, national governments have provided substantial public assistance. As in the case of 'temporary' trade restrictions, the issue here is how one ensures that such public assistance is used to promote adjustment to the changes in demand and not to merely subsidise existing production capacity.

In the steel industry national governments have provided assistance in the form of financial aid. In this sector the main problems in the industry were caused by a decline in demand. This resulted in surplus capacity (capacity utilisation in 1975 was as low as 60 per cent) and a fall in prices. Under such conditions many steel producers were unable to invest in more productive plant or the necessary rationalisation of production which would re-establish a balance between supply and demand. Some of the more diversified steel producers could transfer resources from other activities to their steel operations, but others were obliged to call for public aid. Such calls for public aid are all the more likely in capital-intensive industries such as steel, in which the high fixed capital costs of large-scale coastal plants make rapid adjustments in output difficult. The ability of the various steel producers to adjust output and thus minimise costs is also influenced by the mobility of labour. In the FRG, for example, 11 per cent of those in the steel industry in 1977 were foreign guest-workers who can be expected to be more mobile than steel workers in Wales or Lorraine. Furthermore, national insurance funds were used to compensate workers affected by a reduction in the number of hours worked in Germany. In comparison the existence of an agreement on a guaranteed working week between the unions and the British Steel Corporation (BSC) further reduced the ability of the BSC to adjust output. This is reflected in the number of man-hours lost in production. In November 1975, for example, there was a reduction of 2·3 million man-hours in the German steel industry compared to only 85,000 in the British industry. Industries less able to adjust output to match demand cannot reduce operating losses. The resultant drain on financial resources during a period of recession has been only too apparent in the steel industry. This helps to explain why some member states have made greater use of public aid than others. It also illustrates some of the reasons why adjustment to changes in demand are harder in some countries than others. Two further factors which make it harder for some industries to adust than others are differences in the general growth rates and the severity of regional employment problems. We shall return to this latter factor.

In the case of the steel industry all member states have provided either direct or indirect assistance. The scale of public aid has been largely determined by the severity of structural problems in the industry and the extent to which the industry has adjusted over the longer term. In addition to the UK, France and Belgium have also provided extensive public aid to the industry and have increased public ownership of the industry by converting public debt into equity. Despite the greater capacity for adjustment in Germany, the state has also intervened, indirectly, by providing extensive loan guarantees to facilitate the restructuring of the steel industry in the Saar. Here the structural problems of the industry were similar to those in other member states in the sense that timely adjustment had not taken place. Consequently a DM900m. loan guarantee was provided in 1978 in order to mitigate the social consequences of large-scale closures along with regional aid for reconversion of the areas affected.

Public aid has also been provided for more labour-intensive industries. For example, 50 per cent of the aid provided under the Temporary Employment Subsidy (TES) in the UK went to maintain employment in the textiles and clothing industry, even though this scheme was designed as a general employment subsidy.

The Community dimension on these issues is twofold. First, national aid programmes will tend to shift the burden of adjustment on to other producers in the Community. The provision of public sectoral aid to an industry in one or a few member states is also likely to stimulate calls from competitors in other countries for compensatory aid from their governments. The German shipbuilding industry was one case in which the federal government was obliged to provide substantial production subsidies to the industry, despite its firm opposition to any form of public intervention. These subsidies were provided because the German shipyards made a convincing case that they could no longer compete with other European shipyards receiving public aid. If such a chain reaction were allowed to develop unchecked, there would be a real danger that whole industries in the Community will become progressively less efficient.

The Commission has extensive powers in this field under Articles 92–3 EEC. It has developed effective criteria for the application of these powers,[10] and intervened to reduce or modify numerous national aid programmes. The ability of the Commission to control national sectoral aids rigorously, however, is limited by the need to take account of the social and political implications of bankruptcies, or the large-scale closures, which would happen in the absence of assistance. For this reason the Commission has essentially conducted a holding operation, in which the worst excesses of public aid have been attacked in order to minimise distortions in intra-Community trade. This is exemplified by the fact that the powers to impose a total ban on state aid to the steel industry (Article 4 ECSC) were not used. In the course of the steel recession of the 1970s, therefore, a more liberal code has been devised.[11] This code allows for emergency aid to be granted to rescue companies pending a definitive solution to the problems of the company. But such aid is only given the necessary prior approval of the Commission when restructuring programmes are provided and when there are acute social problems.

In addition to the function of damage limitation, Community policy on sectoral aids also has a more positive function in promoting industrial adjustment. This is done by requiring national governments to justify sectoral aid programmes. In sectors for which specific measures have been taken, such as steel and shipbuilding,[12] national aid must be consistent with objectives on restructuring which are laid down by the Community. In the case of steel this is done by means of the General Objectives[13] which contain indicative guidelines on future supply and demand. Backed by a consensus within the Community on the need to adjust to lower demand, the Community's steel policy has prevented national policies shifting the burden of adjustment on to others. At the same time the Community's anti-crisis measures have been liberal enough to bring leverage to bear on inefficient producers to adjust. In the case of shipbuilding the Commission has been less successful. In its policy document in 1977[14] the Commission estimated that Community demand for shipbuilding would fall by 40 per cent below the 1975 level by 1980. Such a radical adjustment was considered unacceptable by the industry and national governments, so that Community policy in this sector has consisted of merely co-ordinating the continued high levels of national subsidies. The positive link between policies on sectoral aid and more active policies to promote adjustment and re-establish a balance between supply and demand has not been made in the case of shipbuilding.

The case of shipbuilding, therefore, illustrates the limitations of mere holding operations. In such cases more active policies, such as the proposed scrap and build scheme,[15] appear to be necessary as a complement to sectoral aid policy, in order to promote the balanced adjustment of the industry. The Community dimension must not be overstressed. In the case of the steel industry a major reason why the British, and to a lesser extent the French, adopted more radical retrenchment policies was quite simply the burden on public expenditure of continuing to maintain excess capacity. In steel and shipbuilding excess capacity is a Community-wide, indeed worldwide, problem. Therefore any industry forced to make radical retrenchments in the face of a declining global market has an interest in ensuring that competitors are not given unreasonable assistance by their governments.

Competition

The Community dimension to industrial adjustment does not only involve public policies in the field of trade or public sectoral aid. Most adjustment takes place without any form of public intervention. This is particularly the case when industries are not undergoing severe difficulties. By definition, adjustment also involves the more dynamic sectors of industry in which demand is growing. One such area is electronics. This is a diverse sector which exhibits far greater dynamism than industries such as steel or clothing. At one end there is computers and micro-chip technology in which governments have shown a propensity to intervene. At the other end, however, is the consumer electronics sector in which public sector involvement is virtually non-existent. Adjustment in the consumer electronics field during the 1960s and early 1970s caused few adjustment problems, despite relatively rapid change. The production of radios, for example, has more or less completely shifted to countries like Japan in the first instance, and then on to Hong Kong and Taiwan and the other Asian NICs. This process took place without major adjustment problems partly because manufacturers in Europe shifted resources into televisions and audio equipment.

There are now further dynamic forces at work in this industry which may require greater co-operation or mergers between the various European producers. After striking success in televisions and stereo equipment the Japanese have been able to make substantial investment in new technologies such as video-discs. There is also increasing competition from South Korea and Taiwan in standard consumer electronic products, which will begin to affect the European market when the PAL patents, which have provided a degree of protection for the European producers, begin to run out in the early 1980s. The European producers are thus faced with increasing competition in this sector on two fronts; from the Japanese and Americans in the more advanced products, which include various commercial and domestic applications of micro-chip technology, and from the NICs in the standard products. In order to improve productivity and invest in research and development of the new products which will provide secure employment in the 1980s, substantial investment in basic research is needed. Such research and development efforts are beyond the scope of the smaller European producers, Philips being a notable exception. In the future, therefore, there may well be a greater need for corporate adjustment on a Community basis. Such arguments have been made for some time,[16] but there are signs that the need for a consolidation of the European producers in this and other sectors has grown with a decline in domestic growth rates and increased dynamic competition from outside.[17]

A further example of how a relatively fragmented industrial

structure in Europe can influence competitiveness is synthetic fibres. Due in part to the resistance of national governments to the rationalisation and closure of plants, the average output per plant in polyester filament in Europe is only half the US average.[18] Trade in polyester fibres has led to transatlantic tensions in 1979–80 the European producers claiming that the US producers have 'unfairly' benefited from lower feed-stock prices due to US energy pricing policies. Whilst US feed-stock prices are one factor, the lack of Community-wide adjustment in the form of rationalising production facilities has contributed substantially to the tensions. This is just one example of how a failure to adjust at a Community level can reduce international competitiveness and thus add to existing tensions in trading relations.

Corporate adjustment at a Community level will, however, inevitably influence competition and thus adds a further Community dimension to industrial adjustment. This is the whole area of how such mergers and specialisation agreements are to be regulated. This is necessary if restrictive practices are not to eliminate effective competition.

In some parts of the electronics sector national governments in all the major Community countries have provided substantial assistance to their national industries. They have done so by means of public funds for research and development, public procurement policies and domestic standards and specifications. Such public support has proved necessary because of the relatively fragmented nature of the electronics industry in Europe. Furthermore, national governments have felt that a national potential is essential because of the impact microelectronics is expected to have on the competitiveness of a large number of industrial activities. However, the Commission has argued that such national policies will be more expensive than a co-ordinated Community approach, and will not produce internationally competitive industries.[19]

The Provision of Community Assistance

It has been shown that the effective control of national sectoral aid is constrained by the need to mitigate acute social problems. The Community does provide assistance in its own right to help mitigate these problems and remove protectionist pressures. There is a range of Community financial instruments, such as the European Regional Fund (ERDF), the European Social Fund (ESF), the European Investment Bank (EIB) and the recently introduced Ortoli facility (the New Community Instrument).[20] However, none of these instruments was designed with industrial adjustment specifically in mind. In some cases they have been modified to accommodate the problems of industrial adjustment. For example, Article 4 of the revised ESF provides for assistance in the form of retraining to textile workers affected by reduced output or new technologies, and is thus intended to help facilitate the adjustment process.[21] But the funds available for this reconversion assistance for workers are extremely limited.

The Community's regional policy has also attempted to accommodate the problems caused by industrial adjustment. Recent regional policy objectives now include the promotion of economic activity in areas affected by changes in the international division of labour.[22] Furthermore, the *ex quota* section of the ERDF, under which the allocation of resources is not constrained by national quotas, will provide assistance to areas affected by the problems of the steel and shipbuilding industries. Once again, however, such funds are very limited.

The EIB provided over 10·5b. EUA in loans up to the end of 1979, much of which has been for regional policy objectives. (For example, 74 per cent of loans in 1978 went to problem regions.) These loans are made mainly for infrastructural projects. But some loans have been made to industry. For example, the British Steel Corporation (BSC) received over 300m. EUA between 1973 and 1979. Indeed, it is in the steel industry that Community assistance has been most significant. By virtue of the powers of the Commission to borrow on capital markets and redirect this capital to the steel industry the Commission has been far more active in this industry. In 1978 about 700m. EUA was provided to help facilitate adjustment in the steel industry. The main components of this aid were 370m. EUA in loans for the modernisation of steel plants under Article 54 ECSC; 113m. EUA to promote alternative employment in areas affected by closures or rationalisation (a further 44m. EUA was spent on retraining and other benefits for workers affected by closures) under Article 56 ECSC; and finally some 100m. EUA was provided in loans from the EIB for modernisation and reconversion.

Recent proposals by the Commission have attempted to extend the provision of such adjustment assistance to industries other than steel and coalmining. The Ortoli facility, which was finally approved by the Council in October 1978,[23] was however limited in scope. (A maximum of 1b. EUA can be loaned.) The first allocations of these loans have gone mainly to energy and infrastructure projects, and future loans can be expected to concentrate on energy projects.

A further Commission proposal on aid for industrial restructuring[24] for the shipbuilding, man-made fibre and refining industries has not progressed very far owing to opposition, mainly from the FRG. German opposition to the proposal is based on the view that any 'adjustment assistance', no matter what the source, is more likely to be used to maintain existing unproductive industrial activities than to adjust, and will thus constitute a distortion of competition. Other countries which have still a great deal of adjusting to do tend to favour the proposals, although there is little enthusiasm from Britain, despite the fact that Britain could be expected to be one of the main beneficiaries of such a scheme.

Problems Facing the Development of a Common Community Response

The differences which have hindered the development of more active Community policies on industrial adjustment raise some fundamental questions. The first of these involves the level at which decisions concerning the speed of adjustment are taken and the degree of interest representation. Should, for example, the responsibility for industrial adjustment rest solely with companies, or should the social implications of adjustment be accounted for by state or even trade union representation? The national norms pertaining to this question will inevitably differ. In the FRG, for example, the private sector retains effective control over the process of industrial adjustment in the vast majority of cases. The degree of public control exercised by the state is generally greater in other Community countries.

The case of the steel industry provides a useful example. In the FRG the adjustment in the steel industry has been orchestrated by the private sector. This does not mean that the federal state and Länder have not provided some indirect assistance in the form of loan guarantees and reconversion aid, but the state has been at pains to avoid assuming direct control of the restructuring process. In Belgium and France, public ownership, but more important public control of the industry, had increased during the recession. In Belgium there is a tripartite body, which also includes the Commission of the European Communities as an observer. In France and Britain tripartite consultations are less institutionalised and it is essentially a bilateral process between government and industry. Public ownership in the steel industry has also increased further during the recession so that the German steel industry is the only major European industry still in predominantly private ownership.

With increased public and trade union participation there has been a greater propensity for governments to use social and political criteria when assessing investment decisions. The steel industries under public control are thus more likely to carry social as well as economic costs. Under such conditions it is difficult to devise common policies at a Community level owing to the differences in the way member states balance economic costs, against the social and political disruption caused by adjustment such as in the form of plant closures.

The problem of who should control the speed of adjustment is not limited to the declining industries. In advanced technology industries also, such as microelectronics, national governments, producers and trade unions are all at pains to ensure that their interests are represented. For example, in connection with the Community's efforts to develop a co-ordinated approach[25] to the changes which are about to take place due to microelectronics, the trade unions have made it clear that whilst they support technological advances these must go hand in hand with more consultation and more active labour market policies. The European producers, however, argue that new technology can only be implemented effectively if they maintain their investment autonomy.

A second factor which raises fundamental issues for the Community is the fact that the impact of adjustment, in the form of plant closures or other reductions in employment, differs from member state to member state. Once again this can be clearly illustrated by the steel industry which to a large extent reflects issues common to many industries. The impact of closures in areas such as Wales and Lorraine is greater than in the steel areas in Germany. In both Wales and Lorraine the steel industry accounted for around 20 per cent of industrial employment in the worst-hit communities in 1977. In Germany, where more jobs were lost in the industry than in any other Community country over the 1974–7 period, nearly half of the jobs were lost in and around Düsseldorf. Despite this concentration the steel industry in the area accounted for no more than 7 per cent of industrial employment. At the same time, unemployment was only 3·4 per cent in North Rhine–Westphalia in 1977 compared with 5·2 per cent in the steel areas in Belgium, 4·3 per cent in France and 5·0 per cent in the UK.[26] Furthermore, in the areas in the UK in which the steel closures were an issue in 1977 and which are now going ahead, the industry accounts for, for example, 30 per cent of local industrial employment in Clwyd and 25 per cent in Gwent. The impact and thus the social and political implications of adjustment therefore differ from member state to member state. So that, depending on the given political situation in the member states concerned, the desire to slow adjustment in some will be greater than in others.

If there is to be a balanced adjustment across the Community, therefore, Community assistance will be needed to ease the process of adjustment in the member states hardest hit. This raises the question of resource transfer and thus the Community Budget. Owing to the opposition to direct Community assistance for companies in difficulties, Community aid is more likely to take the form of reconversion assistance for the workers or regions affected. This opposition comes from competing producers in other member states, who oppose direct subsidies on the ground that they distort competition. As we have seen, however, the provision of Community aid in the form of the ESF and the ERDF is severely constrained by lack of funds. The

Regional Fund, furthermore, is based on arduously negotiated national quotas which will be difficult to change overnight. The ex-quota sector represents an advance but is so far very limited. In the case of the Social Fund Community rules require that Community assistance is linked to national aid. So that in the case of the UK, for example, where expenditure on such aid is being cut, the ability of the Community to finance reconversion schemes remains limited. Unless there is an increase in the size of the Community Budget, extra assistance via the Social and Regional Funds will have to be at the expense of agricultural spending. Such a structural reform of the Community Budget would potentially benefit the UK and Italy, but would reduce the employment-maintaining support for French and German agriculture. The reallocation of Community resources to the countries especially hard hit by industrial problems would thus be against French and German interests. In the long term, however, such costs must be balanced against the costs of restrictions on intra-Community trade, which may well be the result of a failure to achieve a balanced adjustment throughout the Community.

Finally, there is the question of the impact of enlargement on Community policies.[27] As discussed earlier there is always a danger that internal competition will be maintained at the expense of external competition. The enlargement of the Community will increase this danger unless more active policies are developed to cope with the problems in industrial adjustment resulting from enlargement. Greece and Portugal both have important textile and clothing industries. Spain has an important shipbuilding industry and will, on accession, add a further 10 per cent to the Community's steel capacity. If the integration of the applicant economies is not to be at the expense of increased protection against imports from outside the Community, with all this implies for the world trading environment, the Community dimension to industrial adjustment will therefore have to be strengthened.

What Form of Community Policy?

There is no quick and easy route to the attainment of the objective of containing divergent national responses and promoting balanced adjustment. Indeed, any Community approach must account for the fact that differences in the capacity of national industries to adjust are caused by long-term characteristics of the respective national economies. (See Chapter 3 on Industrial Development and Economic Divergence.) Nevertheless, there are immediate problems in certain industries, such as steel and shipbuilding, which have to be tackled if the longer-term objective of balanced adjustment is not to be under-mined by the progressive divergence of national policies. The

Community response must therefore take a differentiated form. In the case of industries suffering from acute structural problems in the majority of member states, Community policies will need to be more active. In the majority of sectors, however, adjustment can best be promoted by general policies designed to improve the framework within which corporate adjustment occurs under market forces.

In the crisis industries policy-makers would do well to concentrate on how the existing, *de facto*, intervention can be used in such a way as to promote adjustment, rather than considering whether or not there should have been intervention in the first place. At the Community level much of what is needed by way of instruments is already in place. It is a question of improving further on the existing co-ordination of the various Community instruments. This means using trade policy and the control of national aids to maintain the pressure for adjustment. In sectors undergoing rapid change Community aid will be needed if the costs of this adjustment are to be balanced across the Community. At all times, however, there is a need for a positive link between the provision of assistance in any form, namely, temporary trade regulation, national or Community aid and clearly defined adjustment objectives.

Experience with the anti-crisis measures in steel shows that such an approach is not impossible. It does, however, mean that there must be a broad consensus of objectives, which in turn requires the provision of extensive information on employment and market trends. In the case of the steel industry this has taken the form of the General Objectives and information on the social implications of the steel policy.[28] In other sectors, as we have seen, the Commission has been less successful in reaching a consensus on what has to be done, but is developing the provision of sectoral information in shipbuilding.[29] Such information on the prospects for European industry is an essential element of a more active Community policy.[30] On the one hand it will help private and public sectors to formulate more forward-looking strategies rather than reacting to problems as they occur. Experience has shown that if nothing is done until a company or industry faces a crisis, protection or anti-crisis measures become inevitable. Once established it then becomes very difficult to phase out such defensive mechanisms.[31]

The provision of information as an indicator for possible future trends can also reduce the risks of unjustifiably optimistic demand projections leading to the creation of surplus capacity. There is some evidence that this happened in at least one Community country in the synthetic fibre industry. The investment in new capacity in Italy appears to be a case in which some of the present problems of surplus capacity might have been avoided, had there been interchange of ideas at European level on the likely level of future demand for the industry.

Finally, information on the likely impact of Community trade policy or on the provision of national aid will enable a more objective evaluation of the claims of sectoral lobbies. In many cases calls for protection and countervailing duties have to be dealt with without the benefit of detailed information on the impact of alternative policies on the sectors concerned as well as other industries.

The means for providing Community aid are severely limited. There is little prospect of an immediate increase in the size of the Social and Regional Funds. The provision of Community loans backed up by interest rebates is therefore the most feasible approach. Such a policy would enable the maximum leverage with the minimum expense. The case of the Community steel policy once again serves to illustrate that, provided Community funds are properly co-ordinated, they can be of some significance. There is a strong case for extending such loan facilities to help adjustment in other industries such as shipbuilding and textiles. But support for a Community policy along the lines of the Commission's proposals will depend on whether the measures taken in the steel sector have, and are seen to have, a positive effect on adjustment.

From the point of view of those working and of communities directly affected by rapid change, national and Community assistance will also have to be visible if it is to be considered as a real alternative to defending existing jobs. For this reason selective action to ease problems of communities affected by closures or by decline in a particular industry is more effective as an alternative to protection than thinly spread general aid schemes. Provided such selective aid were provided in such a way that it promoted adjustment, for example, by creating alternative employment and improving industrial infrastructure, there is no reason to suppose that this would prop up unproductive industries.

In the majority of cases, in which adjustment takes place under market conditions and in which public intervention or restrictive business practices are not widespread throughout the Community, Community policies will continue to be aimed at creating a suitable framework for adjustment on a Community level. This framework consists of the progressive establishment of a common market, competition policy, and so on.

In the field of advanced technology sectors this will involve co-ordination of national policies, in such a way that national public procurement policies and standards do not result in a fragmentation of the Community markets along national lines. For without the ability to make full use of the larger market, European companies in such sectors as microelectronics, or more generally telematics, will not be able to withstand US and Japanese competition.

The Community's policy in the field of industrial adjustment cannot be seen in isolation from general economic and monetary policy. For example the establishment of the European Monetary Systems (EMS) will have far-reaching implications on industrial adjustment. In the case of countries such as the FRG and the Netherlands, the stabilising effect of the EMS would reduce the pressure of excessive currency appreciation on industries such as clothing, in which competition is highly price-sensitive. For example, the clothing industries in Holland and the FRG lost more than 50 and 30 per cent respectively of their labour forces between 1970 and 1977. In countries with weak currencies such as Italy and until recently the UK, the shift out of such labour-intensive, price-competitive industries has been much slower.[32] For these countries the EMS would create a further incentive for carrying out the adjustment required to improve competitiveness by imposing monetary discipline. Perhaps most important of all, however, the EMS would help reduce the instability in exchange rates which is making the task of industrial adjustment especially difficult.

Conclusions

It has been shown that there is a link between the capacity of economies to adjust their industrial structures and industrial performance. It is not possible, however, to determine the causality of this link. What is clear, however, is that the stronger economies such as West Germany and the Netherlands have found it easier to adjust during the period of slower growth which started in the mid-1970s. The greater availability of alternative employment and investment opportunities has meant that adjustment has been easier; there has therefore been less recourse to defensive policies to slow the speed of change. Countries which started the recession with weaker economies, such as Britain and Italy, have found adjustment more painful and have thus made greater use of defensive policies. The relatively poor economic performance of such countries may well be due to lack of adjustment in the past, and it seems clear that the divergent economic performances are long term in nature.

In terms of the current problems of divergent responses to the need to adjust, the weaker economies have argued that growth must improve before defensive policies can be eased. On the other hand the stronger economies have tended to stress the need to desist from taking defensive actions which jeopardise the attainment of non-inflationary growth objectives. Divergent economic performance has therefore clearly been a significant factor in determining national responses to issues such as trade protection and the provision of public assistance to industries. The balance that is struck between the social costs of rapid adjustment and the economic costs of long-term assistance is, however, also dependent on the political situation in any given country at any given time.

Different national responses to the need to adjust also contribute to the problems of economic divergence. When there is recourse to defensive policies for an increasing number of industries, such micro level policies have an increasing impact on macroeconomic performance objectives. Thus failure to adjust or permanent delay of adjustment in some countries results in *greater* economic divergence. In the context of economic divergence, therefore, the Community has two principal functions. It must accommodate or contain divergent national responses, which are caused by long-term characteristics of the different national economies. But in addition it must promote a balanced adjustment of industries across the Community in order to avoid greater economic divergence.

Notes: Chapter 4

1   Louis Turner *et al.*, *Living with the Newly Industrialising Countries* (Chatham House Paper No. 7, Royal Institute of International Affairs, London, 1980).

2   Ingo Walter, 'Protection of industries in trouble: the case of iron and steel', *World Economy*, vol. 2, no. 2, 1979.

3   Herbert Köhler, 'Kartel der Vernüft', *Der Volkswirt*, no. 44, 30 October 1964.

4   Report of a Group of Experts on Sectoral Analyses, *Changes in the Industrial Structure in the European Economies since the Oil Crisis* (Maldague Report) (Commission of the European Communities, Brussels, July 1979), p. 100.

5   The nearest the OECD has come to defining positive adjustment is to suggest that what matters is 'whether over the long run the policies concerned facilitate movement of labour and capital from the production of goods and services in declining demand to those where demand is increasing, from less to more efficient forms of location and production, and from production in which other countries are gaining a comparative advantage to new competitive lines of production'; OECD, *Positive Adjustment Policies: Some General Issues* (Note by the Secretary General, Paris, 14 June 1979), CES/79.10, p. 9.

6   Groupe d'études prospectives internationales, *Croissance mondiale et stratégie de spécialisation* (Centre français du commerce extérieur, Paris, April 1976).

7   Such studies can only be considered as rough guides to the differing abilities of economies to adjust. They seek to measure statistically what are in fact complex social, cultural and political issues.

8   Maldague Report, op. cit.

9   See German Memorandum on 'Community policy in the field of industrial structural policy', *Europe Documents*, no. 1002, 18 May 1978.

10   *Commission Policy on Sectoral Aid Schemes*, COM(78)221 final (Commission of the European Communities, Brussels, 25 May 1978).

11   Commission Decision establishing Community rules for specific aids to the steel industry, *Official Journal*, L29, 6 February 1980.

12   Fourth Council Directive on aid to the shipbuilding industry, 4 April 1978, *Official Journal*, L98, 11 April 1978.

13   *General Objectives for Steel 1980, 1985 and 1990*, SEC(78)3205 (Commission of the European Communities, Brussels, 20 July 1978).

14   'Shipbuilding reorganisation programme', *Bulletin of the European Communities*, Supplement 7/77, Brussels 1977.

15 *Commission Communication to the Council on a Scheme to Promote the Scrapping and Building of Ocean-Going Ships*, COM(79)446 final (Commission of the European Communities, Brussels, 2 October 1979).

16 See, for example, Christopher Layton, *Cross Frontier Mergers in Europe: How Governments Can Help* (Bath University Press, Bath, 1971).

17 Louis Turner, 'The problem of adjustment in the consumer electronics industry', paper to Chatham House Study Group on 'The implications of newly industrialising countries on trade and adjustment policies', mimeographed, April 1980.

18 *Financial Times*, 12 February 1980.

19 Commissioner for Industrial Relations Davignon, in a speech on Europe's new industrial challenge, at the Royal Institute of International Affairs, 22 March 1979.

20 'Proposal for a Council Decision empowering the Commission to issue loans for the purpose of promoting investment in the Community', *Official Journal*, C37, 31 January 1978.

21 See Michael Shanks, 'The European Social Fund', *Common Market Law Review*, vol. 14, 1977.

22 'A new regional policy', *Bulletin of the European Communities*, Supplement 2/77, Brussels, 1977.

23 Council Decision 78/870, 16 October 1978.

24 'Proposal for a Council Regulation on Community aid for industrial restructuring and conversion operation', *Official Journal*, C272/3, 1978.

25 See 'Labour policy and the micro-electronics industry', *Europe Documents*, 1088, 29 February 1980.

26 These unemployment rates refer to regions, for example Wales in the UK. Local unemployment rates will be much higher in some cases.

27 On this and other issues discussed on this page, see the relevant chapters on the Budget and enlargement.

28 'Social aspects of the steel policy', *Official Journal*, C142, 7 June 1979.

29 *First Half-Yearly Report on the State of the Shipbuilding Industry in the Community*, COM(79)469 final (Commission of the European Communities, Brussels, 1979).

30 Various suggestions have been made for a form of 'early warning system' which would also help promote outward-looking adjustment to changes in the international division of labour. See Paul Marc Henry, *The European Community and the International Division of Labour* (Commission of the European Communities, Brussels, 1979).

31 Stephen Woolcock, 'Industrial policy in the European Community', M.Phil. dissertation, University of Edinburgh, 1979.

32 See Maldague Report, op. cit.

5

How to Prevent the EC Budget Reinforcing Divergence: A British View

Geoffrey Denton

The General Budget of the EC has a truly unique significance in the study of the political consequences of economic divergence. This Budget is only a tiny percentage of the GNPs of the member states, and is dwarfed by the size of their own national budgets.[1] But its political significance is out of all proportion to its size, on account of both the key role which any budget must play in the convergence or divergence of a group of regional or national economies, and the peculiar characteristics of this particular budget. National budgets (including in that term the federal government's budget in federal states) have come to fill a vital role in preventing economic divergence and promoting economic convergence. They therefore have an important political role in maintaining unity and coherence among the constituent regions or states. By analogy, the General Budget of the EC could be expected to assume a similar role in the Community, offsetting some of the causes of economic divergence, and positively promoting the convergence of the disparate national economies.

However, any such expectation about the effects of the EC Budget would appear highly academic given the experience so far and political attitudes in some of the member states. The existing Budget has been constructed not as the Budget of an 'ideal' federal Western Europe, but as an instrument for financing a number of policies that the member states have been able to agree: primarily the customs union and common commercial policy, the Common Agricultural Policy, regional, social and overseas aid policies, and a number of minor industrial and research projects. Some of these policies, especially the regional and social policies, tend to promote convergence since they channel expenditure towards member states and regions with high unemployment and low growth rates. But the overwhelmingly important agricultural policy, taking around 70 per cent of the whole Budget, has no such effect. On the contrary, leaving aside the special case of Ireland, almost certainly the CAP redistributes income towards member states with higher levels of income per head, and also has regressive effects within countries. This situation creates difficulties especially for the United Kingdom, and to a lesser extent for Italy, which have two of the poorest economies in the EC. While for a variety of reasons the issue has not assumed great political significance in Italy, it lies at the heart of the political difficulties surrounding UK membership.

The purpose of this chapter is therefore to examine the development of the UK's gross and net contribution[2] to the Budget, to compare it with the budgetary position of other member states, and to assess the way in which the Budget could be restructured in order to make it a promoter of economic convergence, and therefore an instrument for political cohesion, rather than a disruptive element within the Community. The emphasis throughout is on the relevance for the UK, both because Britain came in 1980 to make by far the largest net contribution to the EC Budget, and because the problems of the UK economy show in sharp relief the parameters of the problem of economic divergence for EC policies.

The Gross Contribution

Between 1973 and 1977 the gross contribution of the UK to the EC Budget was determined by direct contributions of percentages of the total Budget, laid down in the Treaty of Accession. For 1978 and 1979 the contributions were due in accordance with the 'own resources' Decision of April 1970, but were restricted, again under the provisions of the Treaty of Accession (Article 131) by a limit on the rate of increase over the preceding year (see Table 5.1). But in and after 1980 the UK contribution is on the full 'own resources' basis, automatically determined by the payment of duties under the common external tariff, levies under the Common Agricultural Policy and VAT revenues calculated by applying the Community 'tranche' to the harmonised basis of assessment agreed in the 6th VAT Directive. The latest available estimate from the Commission in March 1980 is shown in Tables 5.2(*a*) and 5.2(*b*) as 2,908m. EUA, or about £1,775m. (at £1 = 1·64 EUA). This was 21·09 per cent of the estimated total Budget, compared with a share in Community GNP of around 17 per cent.

That the UK gross contribution could be very large was anticipated at the time when the terms of membership were under examination in 1971 and 1972, so the present position is not surprising. The prospective gross contribution, after the end of the transitional

Table 5.1 The trend in the volume of the General Budget of the European Communities, 1973–5

| Year | Unit *1* | General Budget of the European Communities | | | | | General Budget (%) | |
		Total *2*	EAGGF Guarantee *3*	EAGGF Guarantee as % of total *4*	National budgets *5*	GDP (EEC) *6*	National budgets 2:5 *7*	GDP 2:6 *8*
1973	m.u.a.	4,641	3,594	77·4	227,700	867,600	2·0	0·53
1974	m.u.a.	5,037	3,390	67·3	268,300	983,500	1·9	0·54
1975	m.u.a.	6,214	4,327	69·6	337,500	1,110,600	1·8	0·55
1976	m.u.a.	7,993	5,710	71·4	387,900	1,281,600	2·1	0·62
1977	m.u.a.	9,584	7,133	74·4	442,600	1,515,500	2·2	0·63
1977	m.EUA[1]	9,600			405,000	1,388,100	2·4	0·69
1978	m.EUA[1]	12,363	8,677	70·2	473,500	1,535,200	2·6	0·81
1979	m.EUA[1]	13,700[2]	(a) 9,582[3] (b) 9,232[4]	69·9 67·4	518,100	1,696,700	2·6	0·81

Notes:
1 At 1 February rates used for the establishment of the General Budget.
2 Including the preliminary draft for the First Supplementary and Amending Budget; figure rounded off.
3 Including refunds for food aid.
4 Excluding refunds for food aid.

Source: EC Commission, 'Global appraisal of the budgetary problems of the Community', 5528/79, March 1979, Table 1.

arrangements, was also debated at length during the 'renegotiation' of the terms of UK membership in 1974–5, which resulted in the establishment of the Financial Mechanism, providing for partial refunds of excessive gross contributions.

The facts that the budgetary position was not unforeseen, and that the solution of the difficulties was already envisaged as being met by the new Mechanism agreed in 1975, tended to undermine the efforts by the UK since that time to raise the problem again. There are nevertheless four reasons why the question had to be revived. First, with the ending of the transitional arrangements in 1980 the UK felt the full force of the inequity of the original terms, which the Financial Mechanism can only slightly offset. Secondly, the growth of the open-ended CAP expenditures has now pushed up the UK's contribution to levels well in excess of those anticipated in 1975. Thirdly, the weakness of the UK economy has persisted throughout the years since accession, making the EC budgetary burden progressively more serious. Fourthly, the Commission now anticipates that the Budget must be increased in size after 1980 to meet the expenditure needs of a further enlargement of the Community, of the new European Monetary System and of other developments of Community policy. If there is to be a new agreement to increase the 'own resources' of the Community, it is essential that a more equitable system of contributions and benefits should be devised. There is no indication at present that increasing the size of the Budget will have this effect unless consideration is specifically directed at the question of equity in determining how future expenditure should be financed.

The disproportion between the UK's share in gross contributions to the EC Budget and its share in the total GNP of the Community derives from the interaction of the structure of the EC's Budget with the structure of the UK economy. A relatively high dependence on dutiable imports from outside the Community results in the share of duties under the common external tariff being disproportionately high. Imports of a large proportion of food supplies from outside the Community results in a similarly high relative burden of levies on these imports under the Common Agricultural Policy. Finally, even the VAT contributions operate to the disadvantage of the UK, since VAT is effectively a tax on final consumer expenditure. The UK has a higher proportion of consumer expenditure to GNP than other member states, because a lower proportion of GNP is invested, and imports tend to exceed exports (VAT being levied on imports but relieved from exports).

To some extent, therefore, the relatively high gross contribution may be regarded as 'accidental', or even the UK's own responsibility. If the weakness of the economy were corrected the position would improve. However, while this analysis may be appropriate for the

VAT contributions, which are not far from being a neutral tax and broadly related to ability to pay, it is certainly inappropriate for the duty and levy contributions. For example, Britain's budgetary balance with the EC could be radically improved by switching from third country to EC suppliers for more of its agricultural imports. However, the relief from a reduction in levies paid into the Community Budget would be matched by the higher prices it would have to pay for more imports from high-cost producers in other member states. There would therefore be no net *economic*, as opposed to budgetary, improvement in the UK's position to be gained from such a diversion of trade.

The Net Contribution

The *net* contribution of the UK to the EC Budget is also disproportionately high. Table 5.2(*b*) shows receipts in the UK of only 1,095m. EUA (7·9 per cent of the Budget), leaving a negative balance of 1,813m. EUA (£1,100m.). The high net contribution is caused partly by the structure of contributions already referred to, but more by the structure of expenditure. The Community has failed to develop sufficiently the regional, social and industrial spending that might have offset the effects on the UK net position of the concentration of expenditure from the European Agricultural Guarantee and Guidance Fund (EAGGF) in the agricultural producing and exporting countries. The UK was allocated in 1975–8 a national quota of 28 per cent of the European Regional Fund (ERDF) (reduced for 1978–80 to 27·03 per cent), giving a significant net benefit after allowing for its share in budgetary contributions. But the ERDF is small in relation to the EAGGF (in 1978, for example, ERDF payments amounted to only 525m. EUA, against 8,677m. EUA for EAGGF). Since there are no fixed national quotas for the Social Fund, the UK share has varied from year to year. In some years it has exceeded 30 per cent, but in 1978 the UK received only 135m. EUA, about 20 per cent of the total.

Comparisons with Other Member States

There has been considerable reluctance within the Commission and in certain member states to make comparisons of the gross, and especially of the net, contributions to the Budget. Such comparisons are regarded as non-*communautaire*, contrary to the 'own resources' doctrine, and liable through the wrangling they are likely to incite to reduce the commitment to develop Community policies. Thus there has been a strong pressure against even discussing equity in the Budget, despite the obvious link with the question of convergence of the economies. However, following the British demand to revise the

Table 5.2(*a*)   *Expenditures, receipts and balances by member states in 1980; MCAs re-imputed to importing member states*[1]

	Expenditure	Receipts	Balance
a. *In MCAs*			
Belgium	1,320[2]	851	+ 469
Denmark	715	327	+ 388
France	2,655	2,614	+ 41
FRG	2,994	4,110	− 1,116
Ireland	626	124	+ 502
Italy	2,395	1,641	+ 754
Luxembourg	303[3]	16·5	+ 287
Netherlands	1,555	1,197	+ 358
UK	1,225	2,908	− 1,683
Total	13,788	13,788	0
b. *In %*			
Belgium	9·6	6·17	+ 3·4
Denmark	5·2	2·37	+ 2·8
France	19·2	18·96	+ 0·3
FRG	21·7	29·81	− 8·1
Ireland	4·5	0·90	+ 3·6
Italy	17·4	11·90	+ 5·5
Luxembourg	2·2	0·12	+ 2·1
Netherlands	11·3	8·68	+ 2·6
UK	8·9	21·09	− 12·2
Total	100·0	100·00	0

Notes: 1   See this page for an explanation of the differences between Tables 5.2(*a*) and 5.2(*b*).
2   Of which 552m. EUA are administrative expenditures of the EC.
3   Of which 281m. EUA are administrative expenditures of the EC.
Source: EC Commission, COM(80) 147, 20 March 1980.

terms of membership, the Commission produced in 1974 a document which compared the gross contributions with the GNPs of the various member states.[2] Following the Bremen Summit of July 1978 the Commission was instructed by the heads of state to carry out 'concurrent studies' in connection with the proposed EMS, and in turn asked the Economic Policy Committee to carry out these studies. The Committee's (unpublished) report to the Commission in November 1978 contained hypothetical calculations of the possible net contributions in 1980, irrespective of the possible operation of the Financial Mechanism.[3] Then the British demands for a revision of their budgetary position in 1979 and 1980 resulted in the publication of further estimates by the Commission, shown in Tables 5.2(*a*) and 5.2(*b*).

Table 5.2(*b*)   *Expenditures, receipts and balances by member states in 1980; MCAs without re-imputation*

	Expenditure	Receipts	Balance
a. *In MCAs*			
Belgium	1,330[1]	851	+ 479
Denmark	755	327	+ 428
France	2,714	2,614	+ 100
FRG	3,037	4,110	− 1,073
Ireland	664	124	+ 540
Italy	2,299	1,641	+ 658
Luxembourg	303[2]	16·5	+ 287
Netherlands	1,591	1,197	+ 394
UK	1,095	2,908	− 1,813
Total	13,788	13,788	0
b. *In %*			
Belgium	9·7	6·17	+ 3·5
Denmark	5·5	2·37	+ 3·2
France	19·7	18·96	+ 0·7
FRG	22·0	29·81	− 7·8
Ireland	4·8	0·90	+ 3·9
Italy	16·7	11·90	+ 4·8
Luxembourg	2·2	0·12	+ 2·1
Netherlands	11·5	8·68	+ 2·8
UK	7·9	21·09	− 13·2
Total	100·0	100·00	0

Notes: 1   Of which 552m. EUA are administrative expenditures of the EC.
            2   Of which 281m. EUA are administrative expenditures of the EC.
Source: EC Commission, COM(80) 147, 20 March 1980.

A number of problems arise in interpreting and drawing policy conclusions from statistics of gross and net budgetary contributions, and from the comparisons with other member states. The UK suffers 'food costs' over and above the import levies which figure in the gross contribution. Until recently there has been the awkward question of how monetary compensatory amounts (MCAs) should be ascribed. The 'own resources' doctrine makes for difficulties in assessing the economic effects of duty and levy contributions. The use of market exchange rates is held by some to distort the comparisons of GNPs and GNPs per capita, against which the fairness of the gross budgetary contributions has been questioned by the British government.

Food Costs
A reduction in British agricultural levies, by importing more from

other member states and less from third countries, would save contributions to the Budget only at the cost of higher food prices. Levies are based on the differences between the 'world' price, at which food can be imported from third countries, and the EC's common price at which supplies are available inside the Community. Food which is imported from within the Community usually costs more than it would outside the Community, and this cost is in economic terms difficult to disentangle from that of import levies. Successive annual articles on the costs for Britain of EC membership in the *Cambridge Economic Policy Review* and other studies have therefore included an estimate of the higher cost of food from inside the Community, in addition to the levies paid into the Budget. This is based on estimates of the difference between the actual cost of food imports from within the EC, and the hypothetical cost of importing the same quantity of food from non-EC sources. For 1978, for example, these higher food costs were estimated by the Cambridge group to add a 'net trade contribution' of £317m. to the £806m. total 'net budgetary contribution', making a 'total net cash' payment of £1,123m. Table 5.3 gives these estimates and similar calculations for other member states. There may be room for argument about the detail, but there is no doubt that an estimate of the burden of higher food costs should be added to the net budgetary contribution in order to arrive at a comprehensive assessment of the total direct cost to the UK. This is however only one of a number of adjustments needed in order to convert the net budgetary cost into a significant indicator of the true economic burden.

The Treatment of MCAs

MCAs are the border taxes and subsidies made to compensate for the discrepancies between current market exchange rates and the representative or 'green' rates used for conversion into the national currencies from the common prices fixed in terms of the agricultural unit of account. The major effect of MCAs in the late 1970s has been to operate as subsidies to trade between member states such as Germany and Denmark with higher levels of farm prices, and those such as the UK and Italy with lower levels of farm prices. The subsidies enable trade to take place despite the enormous disparities which have existed between the price levels in different member states.[4] There is in administrative practice a choice as to whether these subsidies should be paid in the exporting or the importing country. Until May 1976, the practice was to pay UK and Italian import subsidy MCAs in the importing country; since that date, as a matter of administrative convenience, they have been paid in the exporting country. There is also controversy as to whether the economic effect of MCAs is to subsidise high-cost exporters, or to subsidise consumers in the importing

Table 5.3   *Net cash receipts and payments between EC members, 1978 (£m.)*

	Net budget receipts	Net trade receipts	Total net cash receipts
UK	− 806	− 317	− 1,123
Germany	− 570	− 101	− 671
Italy	− 114	− 532	− 646
Belgium–Luxembourg	+ 312	− 156	+ 156
Ireland	+ 254	+ 221	+ 475
Holland	+ 190	+ 441	+ 631
Denmark	+ 329	+ 289	+ 618
France	+ 114	+ 620	+ 734

Source: *Cambridge Economic Policy Review*, April 1979.

countries. The Commission has tried to stay outside this dispute, and therefore publishes its tables of net contributions or net benefits in two versions, one attributing MCAs as a receipt in the exporting countries, and the other attributing MCAs as a receipt in the importing countries. Since the MCAs have at times been substantial, they have made a substantial difference to the comparisons of net contributions. In 1977, for example, a recorded (net) transfer of 624m. EUA *by* the UK, assuming MCAs benefited the exporting countries, was converted by an MCA totalling 750m. EUA into a 'corrected net transfer' of 126m. EUA *to* the UK. Fortunately, the changes in parities in 1979–80 have greatly reduced the size of the MCAs. In March 1980 the 'negative' MCA in UK imports disappeared altogether, to be replaced by a small *positive* MCA, implying a tax on UK imports (and subsidy on UK imports).

Own Resources
The 'own resources' doctrine of the Community holds that the revenues derived from the operation of Community policies are to be regarded as the property of the Community, and not as specific contributions from individual member states.[5] Avoidance of intergovernmental arguments about contributions was indeed the reason for the Decision to establish the 'own resources' in place of the previous system of direct national contributions. The principle is interpreted by some member states, and by the Commission, to mean that it is invalid to regard as a burden on a member state the budgetary contributions derived from the duties and levies. The member states, it is argued, are acting solely as agents for the Community in collecting these revenues, their costs of collection being compensated by a 10 per cent refund. It is further claimed that when goods are imported into the EC's free

internal market, shippers have a degree of choice as to which ports they use, and thus it is largely accidental whether duties are paid in one member state or another. Reference is frequently made to the entrepôt trade of Rotterdam and Antwerp in support of this view. If this 'logic' were followed absolutely the British case on the revenue side for consideration of the unfair budgetary burden within the Community would be undermined. The UK succeeded in breaching the principle in 1975, since the Financial Mechanism then agreed was based on comparing gross contributions of member states, including duties and levies, with their GNPs per capita. However, the principle continued to be asserted by restricting refunds to a member state to the total of its VAT contributions, on the argument that in no case could a member state be left making a gross contribution less than the total sum of duties and levies it was collecting on behalf of the Community.[6] In *The Way Ahead* in November 1978 the Commission reiterated this principle. Its suggestion for a new approach to equity in the budgetary contributions applied only to the VAT element.[7]

It is highly unsatisfactory that discussion of the fairness of national contributions to the Budget should be conducted in terms of opposite views on whether substantial revenues from duties and levies should or should not be regarded as a burden on the member states in which they arise. It is also unsatisfactory that the compromises contained in the Financial Mechanism and the Commission suggestions in *The Way Ahead* should be so contradictory. In the measurement of national contributions the Commission includes duties and levies, yet it excludes them from any measures adopted or proposed to correct the position. It must be emphasised that budgetary contributions and receipts have economic effects on member states in addition to their narrower financial impact. British concern about these economic effects has contributed to dissatisfaction about the inequity implicit in the current budgetary arrangements. Studies of the structure of the external and internal trade of the EC enable estimates to be made of the incidence of duties and levies, and the Commission published such estimates in 1979.[8] They showed that the extra-EC import content of UK exports is 151 per 1,000, which suggests that at most only 15 per cent of the burden of duties and levies collected in the UK is passed on to other member states. Thus UK duty and levy contributions could be scaled down by that proportion. However, since other member states' contributions would also have to be adjusted, the final effect would be very small, except in the case of countries with a large re-export trade, mainly the Netherlands and Belgium.

Evaluating National GNPs
Some have argued that the base of comparison for national GNPs should be purchasing power parity rather than market exchange

rates.[9] It is widely accepted that comparisons of national products per head can be misleading in periods when exchange rates have been appreciating or depreciating rapidly. If, for example, the present market rate of sterling overvalues its real purchasing power, there could be a case for adjusting the estimates of GNP per capita in the direction of reducing the UK estimate. In 1976 the position was reversed, and the heavily depreciated pound underestimated UK GNP. PPP exchange rates value currencies in terms of their relative purchasing power over a 'standard basket' of goods. There are great difficulties in calculating them, and the results are always controversial.

The Need to Increase 'Own Resources'

A major issue facing the Community is whether it can or should adopt a different approach to revenue-raising once it reaches the limit of the initial 'own resources'. The Commission's Green Paper, *Financing the Community Budget: The Way Ahead*, of November 1978, was a response to the expectation that these resources would become inadequate to finance expected expenditure needs in or after 1981. The possible growth of expenditure needs was also charted in the later Commission paper, *Global Appraisal of the Budgetary Problems of the Community*, March 1979. In Table 5.4, on both the hypotheses chosen for examination, the estimates show that expenditure needs could not be met within the constraint of existing own resources. Two solutions to the problem of raising more revenue were envisaged: either the VAT rate would have to be raised above the limit of 1 per cent set in the April 1970 Decision, or new revenue sources would have to be developed. Each solution would require both governmental agreement and parliamentary ratification of a new Financial Regulation.

The Way Ahead reviewed a number of proposals for new revenue sources, including attributing to the Community part or all of the revenues from excise duties on cigarettes, alcohol duties, corporation taxes and personal income taxes. It also examined briefly the merits of new Community taxes applied to energy consumption in general, or to petrol. Many difficulties were revealed, concerning especially the equity of the incidence of the various taxes in different member states, and the lack of harmonised structures of the existing taxes to which a Community rate could be applied. The Commission therefore concluded that in the immediate future the most practicable source of additional revenue would be an increase in the rate of VAT.

A major review of own resources would offer the EC the opportunity to come to grips with the problem of equity on the revenue side of the Budget. Even in the current system with a larger

VAT element, the principle of equity could be entrenched in the EC Budget. A reduction in agricultural spending would begin to erode the element of the Budget that has strongly regressive effects. Increased spending on regional, social and industrial policies could enable the EC to develop on a larger scale policies with the explicit object of progressive redistribution of resources. A progressive key for the VAT contributions, suggested in *The Way Ahead*, could be used as an alternative or supplementary means of adjusting the balance on the revenue side of the Budget. Lastly, a different version of the 1975 Financial Mechanism could make it a more effective means of adjusting the final outcome of the Budget in relation to the relative economic positions of individual member states.

Reductions in Agricultural Expenditure
The need to hold down agricultural spending has been a constant theme in the British approach to the budgetary problem in recent years. The strategy largely pursued has rested primarily on demands for a freeze on the prices of all products which are in surplus. It is not possible in this chapter to examine agricultural policy in detail, but some of its broad effects must be taken into account in discussing the Budget. The issue of agricultural price levels has been complicated by the effects of setting prices in terms of a common unit of account: until 1979 the agricultural unit of account (AUA), based on the average value of the snake currencies and their conversion into domestic prices at the representative green rates. The use of an AUA based on the stronger currencies which were members of the snake gave an upward bias to the average agricultural price level. This meant that a small increase in the level of intervention prices, decided on at the annual price determinations, was effectively made higher by the tendency for the average value of the snake currencies, centred on the German Mark, to appreciate relative to the average value of all Community currencies. Thus even a nominal price freeze could mean in practice continuing small price increases. The green rates, which are only adjusted to the movements of market rates of exchange by political decisions of the Council at irregular intervals, allow member governments to retain a degree of control over their own agricultural price levels. Thus the need of UK farmers for some increase in their prices, to cover increased costs of labour and farm inputs, could to some extent be met by a devaluation of the green pound, while German farmers could also benefit from a revaluation of the green DM. Meanwhile, a freeze on the overall level of common prices would meet UK interests by holding down both the budgetary cost of agricultural levies, and the price of food imported from other member states, an option that creates problems for all other member states. Thus the manipulation of the MCA system has given some protection

Table 5.4 General trend in expenditure and revenue, 1979–82, in m. EUA (1982 figures rounded off)

Heading	Total appropriations for commitments			Total appropriations for payments		
	1979¹	1982 Hyp. 1	1982 Hyp. 2	1979¹	1982 Hyp. 1	1982 Hyp. 2
a. EXPENDITURE						
1 Agricultural sector of which:	9,875	15,000	12,100	9,713	15,000	12,100
EAGGF Guarantee Section	9,232	14,000	11,100	9,232	14,000	11,100
EAGGF Guidance Section	564	875	875	426	880	880
Fisheries	71	125	125	47	110	110
2 Social sector	842	1,700		582	1,600	
3 Regional sector	945	1,600		499	1,300	
4 ENS subsidies	200	200		200	200	
5 Energy, research, industry and transport sectors	276	800		296	800	
6 Development co-operation sector	997	2,300		849	1,600	
7 Overall operational reserve	100	100		30	100	
8 Administration (Commission and other institutions)	842	1,100		842	1,100	
9 Reimbursements to the member states	737	785		737	785	
10 Enlargement (Greece)	—	150		—	150	
11 GRAND TOTAL	14,814	23,700	20,800	13,728	22,600	19,700
b. REVENUE						
1 Miscellaneous revenue				154	200	200
2 Customs duties				4,746	5,500	5,500
3 Agricultural and sugar levies				2,173	1,900	1,900
4 Expenditure to be covered by VAT				6,655	15,000	12,100
5 TOTAL (– line 11)				13,728	22,600	19,700
6 1% of the VAT assessment base				9,047	11,800	11,800
7 Revenue including 1% of VAT (1 + 2 + 3 + 6)				16,120	19,400	19,400
8 Difference (b.7) – (a.11)				+ 2,392	− 3,200	− 300
9 VAT rate is % (b.4):(b.6)				0.74	(1·27)	(1·08)

Note: 1 Including preliminary draft of the First Supplementary and Amending Budget.
Source: EC Commission, Global appraisal of the budgetary problems of the Community, March 1979, Table 2.

to a relatively poor member state such as the UK, but perversely has also allowed the richest member of the EC to charge the EC Budget for maintaining its farmers' incomes. The British strategy of holding down the budgetary and other costs of membership has been affected by two policy developments. The AUA was replaced in April 1979 by the more representative EUA 'basket' unit of account, in the context of the European Monetary System. The conversion was finally carried out at a ratio of $1 \cdot 21$ ECU:$1 \cdot 00$ AUA which left the price unchanged. However, the change means that for the future the CAP prices will be based on the average value of all, and not only of an unrepresentative sample, of the member states' currencies. Secondly, the strength of the pound gradually eliminated negative MCAs by March 1980, and in April 1980 positive MCAs were introduced, implying a tax on UK imports (and subsidy on UK exports). But this was welcomed by the UK government, as a continuation of the previous strategy of giving UK farmers price increases through manipulating the MCA system, while continuing to oppose increases in the support prices themselves.

The immediate interests of the majority of EC members and the political pressures on them make any reduction in the share of agricultural spending in the EC Budget dependent on the outcome of hard-fought compromises on the determination of common prices, the definition of the unit of account in which they are expressed, and the manipulation of the MCAs. Only the British government has an immediate interest in a severe reduction in CAP expenditure, though increasingly criticisms of the imbalance of an EC Budget so heavily skewed to agriculture are being voiced elsewhere in the EC. However, even with determined efforts from the UK and some support from other governments it will take some years for the balance of the Budget to be substantially altered.

Increased Spending on Regional, Social and Industrial Policies
Increased expenditure on other policies is another route towards a better balanced budget in which criteria of equity could play a central role. The creation of a European Regional Development Fund was, for example, expected to offset to some degree the high UK net contribution and to offer disproportionate and positive benefits to Italy and Ireland. This Fund has indeed brought gains to all three 'less prosperous' countries. In the UK case its share in expenditure has been greater than Britain's share in gross contributions to the Budget as a whole. However, the role of the Regional Fund has so far been quantitatively insignificant. The increase in the size of the Fund for 1979, which was forced on a reluctant Council by the European Parliament, brought a further increase in British, Irish and Italian receipts. It helps to make Ireland the largest recipient per head from

the EC Budget and to make Italy a sizeable net beneficiary. But it only marginally offset Britain's net contribution.

There are, however, substantial obstacles to further increases in the Regional Fund to correct the overall budgetary balance and its effect on the UK. First, there is great opposition to increasing the size of the Fund in those member states that are net contributors to it. Secondly, the European Parliament may not act indefinitely in support of a larger Regional Fund. The resolution of the impasse over the size of the Fund for 1979 also included provisions to ensure that in future the loophole exploited by the Parliament on that occasion is not left open.[10] Thirdly, the enlargement of the Community by the accession of Greece, and later of Portugal and Spain, though it would increase the number of member states wanting a larger Regional Fund, would also bring into the Community three member states which would compete for shares in that Fund. The outcome for the UK, though probably not for Ireland or Italy, could be to reduce substantially, or even eliminate, the net benefit from the Fund.

Neither the Social Fund nor the limited programme of industrial projects has national quotas. Expenditure is allocated primarily by policy criteria, though the resources of the ESF have latterly in practice gone in larger proportions to poorer rather than richer countries. The UK has benefited in most years from receiving a higher share of Social Fund expenditure than its share in gross contributions to the Budget. However, similar reservations to those advanced in connection with the Regional Fund also apply to any expectations that increases in the Social Fund could significantly reduce the UK net budgetary contribution. A major Community effort to finance industrial projects could be geared to the problems of weaker economies in the EC. A policy of aid to older industrial areas in need of restructuring could for instance bring significant net benefits to the UK, though it is worth noting that for an EC industrial policy to be sensitively applied to the different needs of particular national economies would require fine and selective judgements about priorities at the EC level.

This suggests that the UK should press constructively for an expansion of regional, social and industrial policies. The problem is to devise policies that make sense in themselves and that would have the effect of reducing the British net budgetary burden. However, if such policies develop, the distribution of their expenditures could shift, particularly after further enlargement, leaving the UK as the richest of the less prosperous members a net contributor rather than a net beneficiary. Moreover, restructuring of the EC Budget in this direction presupposes a 'larger Budget' strategy which may not be acceptable to many member states, and perhaps not even to the UK. Only Italy and Ireland were prepared at the time of writing to commit themselves to a bigger EC Budget.

The Financial Mechanism

The scope of the Financial Mechanism as agreed in 1975 was severely restricted. Nevertheless, this method of producing a more equitable Budget by using refunds has much to commend it. First, it already exists, which is always an advantage, since it avoids the need to create entirely new structures. Secondly, it leaves largely unaffected the existing size and structure of the Budget, and thus avoids the weaknesses inherent in methods that depend on policy changes. If a well-constructed financial mechanism created the necessary fiscal transfers, individual member states would reach a position commensurate with their economic position automatically, as they do more or less by the practice of fiscal equalisation within Federal Germany. Refunds of this sort are entrenched in the fiscal relations between central and local government in most developed countries, and in relations between federal and state governments in the United States and elsewhere.[11] Given that the structure of budgetary revenues and expenditures has to serve many social and economic objectives besides that of equity, it is probably inevitable that a redistributive mechanism of this kind should figure in all states and communities where public finance is organised on more than one level. The UK would not then need to fight the arduous and unpopular battle to hold down agricultural prices, nor to press for more Community spending against the convictions of many both in Britain and in other member states. Thirdly, a refund system can be adjusted over time in the light of changing circumstances and needs, again without affecting the basic structure of the Budget.

A number of fundamental changes would have to be made in the existing Financial Mechanism before it could play an adequate role in the EC. The 1975 Mechanism already goes further than the suggested 'progressive key' in that it includes the duty and levy contributions in the basis of calculation of the need for a refund. But complex rules limited the actual amount of the refund to the VAT contributions. As in the case of the 'progressive key', it would therefore be necessary to insist on a formula for including the duties and levies in a realistic way in the contributions which could be refunded. It would also be necessary to remove a number of other restrictions on the sums that are allowed to be refunded. The limit of refunds to 3 per cent of the total Budget is illogical; if a member state is making a disproportionate contribution this should be corrected whatever proportion of the Budget is represented by the amounts that have to be refunded. The restriction of refunds if the balance of payments of a member state has remained in surplus, on the basis of a three-year moving average, should also be reconsidered. There is no obvious case for restricting refunds to countries that have payments deficits, though the restriction to member states where the excess budgetary contributions represent a net foreign exchange burden is more justifiable. It allows refunds to be withheld from a member state such as the Netherlands, whose gross contribution to the Budget could be high enough relative to its GNP to qualify for refunds, but which benefits so much from the CAP that it is also a large net recipient from the Budget. However, if another method were devised of estimating the true burden of the duties and levies (which produce the high gross contribution of the Netherlands owing to its large re-export trade), this complication could be resolved more effectively.

At the Dublin Summit in November 1979 the other member states offered to abandon the balance-of-payments condition, the 'tranche' system, and the limit on the total repayment. These changes would have resulted in a refund of 520m. EUA (£350m.) in 1980, and a guarantee that, if the other conditions were fulfilled, similar refunds would be available in future. However, the offer included no action on the larger problem of the shortfall of receipts, and was refused.

Since the UK's budgetary problem is much more the net contribution than the gross, and since the expenditure solution is so problematical, it appears necessary to extend the refund principle to make it apply to the net and not only to the gross contribution. Further work is needed to analyse in detail the ways in which the Financial Mechanism would need to be extended in order to make it an effective instrument for achieving net budgetary equity. However, it appears to be the most promising method of those reviewed for bringing about greater equity, in the context of a reappraisal of the effects of the Budget that must accompany a new Decision by the Community on the necessary extension of its 'own resources' for the 1980s.

The Temporary Settlement of 1980

In the work leading up to the Dublin Summit of November 1979, the British tended to prefer a solution to the Budget imbalance that would guarantee the UK a defined and equitable share of Community Budget receipts irrespective of the particular policies of the EC. The Commission in October 1979 expressed some resistance to such corrections on the expenditure side of the Budget, in common with other member governments. They considered that such mechanisms would come too close to the concept of *juste retour* that had been resisted over many years. It would raise problems about the definition and attribution of Community expenditure, and involve a more radical departure than corrections on the revenue side. There are indeed many obstacles in the way of finding a solution on the expenditure side.

(1)   Any new expenditures clearly could not be made solely in order

to correct the net position of the UK on the Budget but would have to be justified by other objectives.

(2) There has in recent years been great reluctance on the part of all the member states' governments, including the UK government, to accept Commission proposals for increased expenditure.

(3) This reluctance has been reinforced strongly in the last year or two by the pressures in all member states to hold down public expenditure.

(4) Any new programmes which were justified on their merits would attract claims from other member states for a share in the expenditures.

(5) New spending programmes take time to set up and make effective, and they therefore are not very well adapted to providing a quick remedy for a temporary problem. All these considerations throw doubt on the chances of a successful conclusion being found in this direction.

The conclusion of the Commission was that:

A significant movement in the direction of more balanced Community expenditure can only take place if there is a decision to increase the resources available for financing the budget.[12]

But by the time of *the* Solution Paper in November 1979 there appears to have been a change of mind in the Commission:

It would be possible to envisage special, temporary and *ad hoc* measures which would ensure a greater participation by the United Kingdom in a number of policies and which would increase the present low level of Community expenditure in the United Kingdom.[13]

Items mentioned were: exploitation of coal resources, transport infrastructure, agricultural improvement schemes, and (if the UK joined the EMS) interest rebates in respect of Community loans. Such special expenditures should be limited to a period of three or four years, after which the Commission hoped that a better balance within a larger Budget would have been achieved.

At the Luxembourg Summit in April 1980 the other member states offered to support this critical approach to the 'expenditure' solution by cutting through many of the problems mentioned above and looking for ways of reducing the UK net contribution by some £800m. to £325m., but only for 1980. For 1981 the net contribution would rise to £490m. and there was no offer beyond that year. Since it would be in the interests neither of the UK nor of the Community for the arguments of 1979–80 to continue indefinitely, the UK government was right in refusing again to accept the offer.

In Brussels at the end of May the offer for 1980–1 was improved, and rearranged, to produce a net contribution of £370m. in 1980 and £430m. in 1981. More important, a long-term fundamental review of the structure of the Budget was also promised, with an undertaking to use for 1982 similar methods to those for 1980–1 if the review had not been completed in time. This agreement, together with the new treaty needed to increase the 'own resources' when they expire in 1981, or 1982 at the latest, should ensure that a permanent solution is finally achieved. It follows from what has been said above that this solution should be based on a revised and extended financial mechanism.

Conclusion

This chapter has dealt in some detail with the problem of the UK contribution to the EC Budget. It has not discussed the concept of convergence as such. Nevertheless, the issues of divergence or convergence, both economic and political, are implicit throughout. The UK Budget problem arises because the structure of the UK economy is different from that of most other member states: in the smallness of the agricultural sector, the larger dependence on imports of both agricultural and industrial products from outside the Community, even the higher rate of consumers' expenditure as a proportion of GNP. The problem has been exacerbated by the divergence of the economic performance of the UK: the slow rate of economic growth, the increasing gap between productivity levels in the UK and those in other member states, even, ironically, the *higher* levels of labour productivity in UK agriculture than in other member states. The Community Budget, which reflects the structure of the EC itself, is clearly not directed at the problem of divergence, despite the fine words of the Treaty and the minor cosmetics of the Regional and Social Funds. In practice, its major effect is to promote divergence in the British case, by saddling a country which on most indicators is less prosperous than all except two other member states with a large net burden, while subsidising countries with much higher incomes per head. While the Budget, and the agricultural policy it mainly reflects, happily promote convergence in the poorest country, Ireland, and to a lesser extent in Italy (see Table 5.2), these results also are in the most accurate sense accidental, since there is no general commitment of principle and policy to this objective. The Community, by the essentially random nature of its economic effects, which are reflected only in part in the Budget, also promotes political divergence, at least in the British case. Awareness that the economic structure of the Community would not suit Britain's economic structure was one reason why the UK failed to join in 1958; continuing fears on this score, and their recognition in other member states, delayed British entry until the Heath government was prepared to take the gamble; and now the actualisation of what had been feared all along has created a tense situation between the British and the other governments, and a climate of public opinion in the UK and other member states which is, to say the least, unenthusiastic about continued British membership. All this has come about because the governments have failed to take seriously the problem of divergence of economic structures and peformance, and have persisted in assuming that a collection of 'managed free trade' policies can automatically respond to the interests of all member states. While it is correct to assume that the elimination of barriers to trade, both in the industrial and the agricultural sectors, can produce net benefits for all, the distribution of the gains and the associated costs of adjustment need to be considered and where necessary corrected, in order to promote convergence, and to assure all member states that the benefits are fairly distributed.

Notes: Chapter 5

1 Table 5.1 shows the trend in the Budget since UK accession to the Community. The EC Budget has grown from 2·0 per cent of the total of national budgets of the member states in 1973, to 2·6 per cent in 1979. As a proportion of the gross national product of the member states it has grown from 0·53 per cent to 0·81 per cent over the same period. The Budget is therefore relatively small, reflecting the narrow basis of the common policies it has to finance. Of the total, between 67 and 77 per cent each year between 1973 and 1978 has been spent on the guarantee section of the European Agricultural and Guidance Fund.

2 *Inventory of the Community's Economic and Financial Situation since Enlargement and Survey of Future Developments* (Commission of the European Communities, Brussels, October 1974).

3 See *The Economist*, 18 November 1978.

4 At one time these exceeded 40 per cent, but they have fluctuated widely as relative exchange rates have altered, and the representative ('green') rates of exchange used for converting prices set in terms of the agricultural unit of account into national currencies have been revalued or devalued.

5 See the Council Decision of 21 April 1970 on the replacement of financial contributions from member states by the Community's 'own resources'.

6 See Geoffrey Denton *et al., The Economics of Renegotiation* (Federal Trust, London, 1975), for a discussion of the Financial Mechanism.

7 *Financing the Community Budget: The Way Ahead* (Commission of the European Communities, Brussels, November 1978).

8 *Document de référence sur les questions budgétaires*, COM(79) 462 final (Commission of the European Communities, Brussels, September 1979).

9 In its document setting out the proposed Financial Mechanism in 1975, the Commission concluded that market rates should be used 'pending the introduction of a theoretically more satisfactory system of assessing rates of exchange in terms of purchasing power'. See EC Commission, *The Unacceptable Situation and the Correcting Mechanism* (Brussels, January 1975).

10   See House of Lords Select Committee on the European Communities, Session 1979–80, 2nd Report, *EEC Budget*, for an account of the problems that arose in the adoption of the 1979 Budget and the solution that was agreed in March 1979.
11   On this point see especially the MacDougall Report: EC Commission, *Report of the Study Group on the Role of Public Finance in European Integration* (Brussels, April 1977).
12   EC Commission, *Convergence and Budgetary Questions*, COM(79) 620, 31 October 1979, para. 48.
13   EC Commission, *Convergence and Budgetary Questions*, COM(79) 680, 21 November 1979, para. 15.

6

EMS: Cul-de-Sac or Signpost on the Road to EMU?

Jocelyn Statler

> The new European Monetary System (EMS) must not be confused with the projected economic and monetary union, let alone with a common currency. Its immediate limited objective is to create a zone of monetary stability in Europe by closer monetary policy cooperation. (*European Economic and Monetary Union*, Commission of the European Communities, Periodical 3/79, p. 29)

The Resolution of the European Council of 5 December 1978 on the establishment of the EMS and related matters makes it clear that the EMS was not intended to be consolidated into a final system, which would include a European Monetary Fund and full utilisation of the ECU as a reserve asset and means of settlement, until two years after the inception of the scheme. The resolution also makes it clear that, while convergence of economic policies towards greater stability must be the most important concern of all participants in the EMS, measures to strengthen the economic potential of the less prosperous countries of the Community were to be primarily the responsibility of the member states concerned. Community measures are seen as playing a supporting role. Even so, the Commission's injunction 'not to confuse' will not disperse the troublesome horde of questions which still remain to be answered on the wider and long-term function of the EMS within the European Community (EC), and on some of the more immediate aims of those whose views did not prevail when the resolution was drawn up – members of the Community who regarded economic convergence as a necessary basis for greater monetary stability. The aims and motives of those who have been instrumental in the evolution of the EMS are still obscure. The system cannot be understood in isolation and this chapter will look at the background from which it has developed, the form in which it has evolved, and its possibility for future development, in order to try to elucidate its relationship to the trends towards convergence or divergence in the Community.

Bretton Woods Breakdown

Full realisation of the aims of the Common Market requires the establishment of an Economic and Monetary Union (EMU), though this concept is nowhere mentioned in the Treaty of Rome. A common market aimed at the free movement of goods and services, labour and capital, comparable to that existing in a national market, can only be fully realised in an Economic and Monetary Union which involves fixed exchange rates between national currencies and, at a later stage, their replacement by a common currency managed by a single Community central bank. In spite of this, the members of the EC have not committed themselves to EMU. In the early years of the Community's existence no need was felt for an exclusively Community arrangement in this area and, more recently, because of a reluctance to forfeit national autonomy, no commitment has been made.

Article 3 of the Treaty of Rome says that the activities of the Community shall include the application of procedures by which the economic policies of member states can be co-ordinated and disequilibria in their balance of payments remedied. Chapter 2 of the Treaty, on Balance of Payments, sets out guidelines to be followed in this respect and on the setting-up of a Monetary Committee with advisory status to keep under review the monetary and financial conditions of members and to report to the Council and the Commission.

The lack of precision in the terms of the Treaty in this respect was due to the apparent stability of the international arrangements then in operation. Members' trade and payments were carried on within the framework of the Bretton Woods system of fixed but adjustable exchange rates, which seemed to answer the requirements of the time and only a few, notably the American economist Robert Triffin, questioned the durability of the system.[1] The United States exercised responsible hegemony at the time, supplying the Western world's requirements for liquidity through its balance-of-payments deficit. In the absence of a common currency of their own, the members of the EC relied on the dollar 'to achieve a kind of informal monetary integration'.[2]

In the second half of the 1960s there were several major currency crises. In November 1967 the pound was devalued; there was a dollar crisis in March 1968 and a crisis involving the French franc and the German Mark in November 1968, as funds were moved from any currency which showed signs of weakness. The Bretton Woods system hinged on the key role of the dollar, which was the standard for fixing all other currencies' exchange rates, and was convertible into gold at $35 an ounce.[3] Towards the end of the 1960s, the dollar became overvalued due to the inflationary consequences of the American government's high spending at home and abroad. From 1965 the US current account started to move into increasingly large deficit.

The international monetary system had become highly integrated. It was possible for large sums of capital to flow through the system and this began to occur increasingly as confidence in the dollar waned. The United States wanted to retain the pivotal role of the dollar and rather than accept a devaluation itself put pressure on other countries to revalue their currencies. This caused ill-feeling and a breakdown of co-operation. From 1968 America was following a policy of 'benign neglect', or withdrawal from responsible leadership. It disregarded the international consequences of its policies and allowed huge dollar outflows to continue. By 1971 there was a decline in the American gold stock to $10 billion, while outstanding foreign dollar holdings were estimated at about $80 billion. The United States had to renounce officially its commitment to convert the dollar into gold at $35 an ounce. Robert Triffin's forecast had been realised and the foundations of the fixed rate system, as it had developed, were crumbling. A brief period of generalised floating followed until, in the Smithsonian Agreement of December 1971, the overdue devaluation of the dollar finally took place. This was accompanied by the realignment of European currencies and an attempt to get back to the security of fixed rates of exchange, albeit with a wider band of 4·50 per cent allowed for exchange rate movements.

Confidence in fixed rates had been shaken and more changes were anticipated. Large movements of capital continued, with outflows from weak currencies and mounting pressure against strong currencies, so that the attempt to maintain a system of fixed rates could not hold in such conditions. A return to floating began with sterling's abandonment of fixed rates in 1972. By March 1973 the system of fixed rates that had survived since the end of the war had given way to one in which the eighteen countries that accounted for 70 per cent of the trade of members of the International Monetary Fund (IMF) were floating, either independently or in a joint float.

Reassessing the Route

It was against this background and particularly as a result of the currency crises of 1968 and 1969, when the French and Germans suffered from speculative pressures against the franc and in favour of the Mark, and exchange rate instability began to threaten the policies of the European Community, that members of the Community were forced to reconsider the implications of their Treaty with regard to Economic and Monetary Union. The shortcomings of the international system as it was being managed by the United States, and the difficulties in these conditions of maintaining the fixed rate system, which was assumed as a basis for the policies of the Community, prompted the members to consider the advantages of closer co-operation among themselves in the monetary sphere. In spite of the apparent shortcomings of a fixed rate system in coping with the conditions prevailing at the time, a core group of European countries was not willing to accept a general move to a system of floating rates.

The two leading members of the European Community had a variety of motives for giving attention to a Community-based monetary plan, although both the Germans and the French had previously shown a lack of enthusiasm for the idea. General de Gaulle did not favour any scheme which would encroach on French sovereignty and the Germans preferred to approach monetary problems in the framework of the IMF. Nevertheless, the French had a long commitment to fixed rates, partly as a result of national pride and a desire to maintain their standing in the international system. They were also particularly concerned over the threat to the Common Agricultural Policy (CAP) from floating rates. The CAP depended on stable rates for its successful working and France's support for the establishment of the Community had been closely linked with the benefits it expected to reap from the CAP, in return for which France had agreed to open up its industrial markets to German competition. The growing power of the German nation was also alarming to the French. Following the French currency crisis of May 1968 the Germans refused to revalue the Mark in spite of considerable pressure from other countries. The French took this as a warning. A Community Economic and Monetary Union could serve to bind the Germans more securely to their allies in the West and curb their growing strength.

The Germans themselves were beginning to feel that the progress the Community had made up to that time would be threatened in the unstable conditions prevailing unless there were some impetus towards new goals. They were anxious to maintain the stability of the Community at a time when they were embarking on their new venture in Ostpolitik and needed a secure base from which to conduct their negotiations. They were also having doubts about the future strength of American support in political and defence matters.

For all the members of the Community, the question of enlargement was coming to the fore, presenting a possible threat to the character of the Community from the new membership. If the Community achieved Economic and Monetary Union, the new members would have to commit themselves to its constraints and their influence on the EC's policies would be lessened. This influenced the French attitude to Britain's case for membership. If the British were willing to accept the implications of a European monetary union for the role of sterling, this would be a good test for the strength of the UK's commitment to a fully integrated Europe.[4]

President Georges Pompidou, who led the French delegation to the Hague Summit of EC members in December 1969, was more favourably disposed to closer European integration than his predecessor, Charles de Gaulle, and made a speech advocating the 'completion, deepening and enlargement' of the Community. The category of 'deepening' had no very precise content, but was soon utilised to accommodate the creation of a European monetary union, which the leader of the German delegation, Chancellor Brandt, proposed in his speech. The French response was favourable, for the reasons set out above, and in addition President Pompidou made the point that 'the Europe of the Six and even more an enlarged Europe will exercise all its weight in international discussions' through such a union.[5]

The French and Germans had their individual economic and political motives for favouring closer integration at this point and the manner in which they sought to arrive at this closer union was also very different. The German Chancellor regarded the co-ordination of economic policies as a prerequisite for any progress towards EMU; the French President placed more emphasis on immediate measures in the monetary field and on setting up the foundations for the creation of a regional monetary bloc. The communiqué issued at the end of the summit seemed to indicate that the German view had prevailed. The Council was asked to draw up a plan leading by stages to an EMU in which the development of monetary co-operation was to be based on the harmonisation of economic policies. The culmination of the process would be the establishment of a European Reserve Fund.

An Early Model

A group was set up under the chairmanship of Pierre Werner in March 1970 to follow up the decisions of the Hague Summit. The Werner group brought out two reports, the second of which was not accepted until February 1971 − the exchange rate crises which occurred in the interim delaying the process and making it doubtful at times whether the Community would ever embark on its plan. The first Werner Report drew on two earlier plans which had been produced in response to the worsening conditions in the international sphere. These plans are of interest, not just as the basis of the Werner Report, but because they contained the elements of the opposing points of view on the best way to arrive at EMU which have characterised the debate from the time the French and German leaders took their positions at the Hague Summit. The adherents of the two approaches became known as the 'economists' and the 'monetarists'.

The Schiller Plan, supported by the Germans and the Dutch (the 'economists'), had as its principle objective the co-ordination of economic policies to be phased over ten years in four stages, and contained provisions for the liberalisation of intra-European capital flows. The second Barre Plan, which reflected the views of the French, Belgians and the EC Commission (the 'monetarists'), gave priority to the establishment of fixed exchange rates. Once rates were fixed, member countries would be forced to take steps required to co-ordinate their economic policies to ensure maintenance of those rates. The plan called for immediate reduction of margins of fluctuation around existing parity rates.

The first Werner Report was keenly debated. The advocates of the Barre Plan stressed the importance of the creation of a Community personality in the international monetary sphere and proposed the immediate establishment of a European Stabilisation Fund. Those who supported the Schiller Plan felt that the creation of a reserve fund during the first stage was premature. Once harmonisation of economic policies had been achieved, exchange rate stability would follow. Fixing exchange rates at levels then current would be inappropriate as there was no guarantee that these were the rates which would emerge as the ultimate equilibrium rates of exchange. Following this line of reasoning, a reserve fund to support currencies should await the achievement of the goal of policy harmonisation.

Only a general commitment to EMU and an agreement that existing intra-European parity margins would not be widened, even if wider bands were accepted by the IMF, resulted from the first Werner Report. The committee went back to work, but the second report, issued on 8 October 1970, was not very different from the first and the resolution finally adopted by the Council on 22 March 1971, was the result of considerable compromise between the 'monetarists' and the 'economists'.

The Werner Reports had advocated a step-by-step approach to EMU, the final stage to be achieved by 1980. In the compromise, no binding commitment to the 1980 deadline was made and only the details of the monetary measures for the first stage of the plan were agreed. Since the French would not commit themselves to the plan in its entirety, the Germans inserted a safeguard clause which guaranteed the reversibility of the monetary measures of the first stage by limiting their application to five years if the transition to the second stage and the desired parallelism between progress in the economic and monetary fields had not been ensured. During the first stage of the plan, there was to be a gradual narrowing of the margins within which the exchange rates of members' currencies would be permitted to fluctuate *vis-à-vis* each other; a \$2 billion reserve fund would be created to provide medium-term assistance to members to supplement the short-term arrangements already in existence; and a report was to be prepared on the feasibility of establishing a European Fund for Monetary Co-operation. In the meantime, central banks would be urged to increase their co-operation and to co-ordinate their policies.

The increasing turbulence in world currency markets immediately following the acceptance of these arrangements made it look doubtful whether even these limited measures could be implemented. The EC Commission called meetings to try to co-ordinate response to the crisis but no agreement could be reached and it was necessary to postpone the planned narrowing of exchange rate margins. No common approach could be arrived at when the convertibility of the dollar was suspended in August 1971. Germany proposed a joint float of EC currencies against the dollar but this was rejected by France which maintained its existing parity while the other EC currencies floated. Confusion continued until a temporary calm was achieved with the signing of the Smithsonian Agreement in December.

A Trial Run

The EC members took advantage of this pause to implement in March 1972 the first stage of their planned progress towards monetary union. The original plan for narrowing exchange rate margins had to be revised in the light of the Smithsonian arrangements and the wider band this allowed against the dollar. Each European currency could deviate as much as 2¼ per cent on either side of the dollar central rate, which would have allowed them to deviate by 4½ per cent on either side of their bilateral parity rates against each other. This was considered to be too lax to help the Community and the EC members agreed to restrict themselves to 2¼ per cent on either side of existing intra-EC parity rates. This narrow EC band within the wider dollar band became known as the 'snake in the tunnel' arrangement, and was launched on 24 April 1972. Agreement was reached on intervention procedures to support this arrangement which can be compared with the later arrangements in the EMS. Central banks whose currencies reached the limit of the community band were to intervene using EC currencies only. If the limits of the dollar band were reached, intervention in dollars could occur. This was designed to avoid conflict in the intervention policies of the member states.

When the snake went into operation, the membership included the UK, Ireland, Denmark, Sweden and Norway as well as the six original members of the EC. The pound sterling soon came under speculative pressure and had to withdraw after seven weeks, closely followed by the Irish punt and the Danish krone. Italy only remained a member with the help of special concessions. France left the snake for the first time in January 1974, rejoining in July 1975. After the French franc's second and final exit in 1976, the snake was reduced to a group of small countries with very close trading ties with Germany, that is, to a Deutsche Mark zone. The currencies outside the Deutsche Mark zone embarked on a period of managed floating in the hope that this would prove a more favourable method of coping with their difficulties.

The snake had not held firm against the destabilising forces of the 1973/4 oil price crisis and the widening of inflation and growth rate differentials among EC member states, but valuable experience had been gained of the difficulties with which any successful system had to cope. Adjustment of central rates among the remaining member states did occur with sufficient frequency for its supporters to argue that one of the faults in the Bretton Woods system had been overcome in the snake. Proposals continued to be put forward for means by which the Community could maintain its progress towards monetary union and build on its past experience. These proposals were not taken up straight away, but in several cases contained elements which were included in the EMS, or which influenced its form when it was put into practice.

In April 1974 the Commission submitted a proposal on the pooling of reserves within the Community. In May 1975 French Finance Minister Fourcade submitted a plan which called for the use of the European Unit of Account in intra-European exchange rate relationships, in order to assign the burden of adjustment to the currency which was moving out of line with the Community average. This would mean that when a strong currency moved up, it would not be a weak currency which would have to take measures to adjust. The plan emphasised the need for a joint policy towards the dollar. In February 1976 the Netherlands Finance Minister Duisenberg submitted a plan which had as its objective the establishment of a device to trigger consultation among member states in order to co-ordinate members' policies. Target zones were to be established for containing effective trade-weighted exchange rates, although members were to have only a negative obligation not to follow policies which would push their rates out of these zones. The movement of exchange rates outside the zone would be the indicator which would trigger discussions on policy co-ordination.

The report submitted by Mr Tindemans and the European Commission contained support for the idea of a two-tier Community and for the use of the snake as a motor for further monetary and economic integration. The obligations emanating from membership of the snake were not to be limited to external monetary policy, but were to extend to internal monetary and budgetary policy and all key aspects of economic policy. The European Commission's report on European Union of June 1975 took up the idea of creating a common currency as a preferred method to the Werner Plan's approach of gradual narrowing of exchange rate margins, which had not succeeded. The 'Europa' was to be used first as a reserve currency by central banks. This was in contrast to the strategy recommended in the report of the All Saints' Day group, published in November 1975, by nine independent economists, which advocated the use of the Europa as a private asset which would have the advantage of having stability of purchasing power.

Werner Fails the Test

The debate continued, but actual progress in the Community towards EMU had not been encouraging. The Marjolin Committee, set up to assess the situation, reported in March 1975 that national economic and monetary policies were more discordant than at any time since the EC was set up. The report saw no point, in the circumstances of the time, in an attempt to try to proceed to the second stage of EMU as outlined in the Werner Plan. The report attributed the failure of the Werner Plan to 'unfavourable events, a lack of political will and insufficient understanding',[6] all relevant points to be borne in mind when future attempts were being considered. The Marjolin Committee's report made proposals which showed how experience was pushing the Community towards acceptance of more far-reaching measures which would make it possible for the weaker members to stay within a Community monetary system. It stressed the need for the issue of Community loans and the setting up of an Exchange Stabilisation Fund of $10 billion to support intervention in the exchange markets. It suggested that the new European Unit of Account (EUA) should be used as a reserve asset and a means of financial settlement in the operation of the European Monetary Co-operation Fund. It also referred to the possibility of using EUAs in denominating Community loans.

These suggestions were not taken up at the time they were made. The political will to utilise them was lacking. Even so, they provided a source of ideas which could be drawn on when interest revived. Roy Jenkins's speech, attempting to relaunch the idea of EMU in October 1977, appeared to be one more in the list of attempts which fell on stony ground. Looking back from the events of 1978, it was possible to recognise it as the oratory of a John the Baptist.

Schmidt takes the Wheel

Chancellor Schmidt's proposal in the spring of 1978 for a fresh attempt at a Community system of fixed but adjustable exhange rates took most observers by surprise. There were many factors which made it seem unlikely that such an attempt would be made. The IMF meeting in Jamaica, in January 1976, had marked the acceptance by that institution of the reality of the floating rate system, and the general mood seemed to be one of willingness to go along with floating rates as the only way to cope with the volatile conditions in the international monetary system. The dollar overhang and the size of the Euromarkets was still growing, so that destabilising capital flows were as disruptive as ever, inflation rates were still high, though stabilising somewhat at their higher level, and exchange rate movements in the currencies outside the snake had been too large to make an attempt to keep them within narrow margins appear at all feasible, the experience of sterling in 1976/7 being a dramatic example here. Balance-of-payments positions were among the few indicators which showed any signs of improvement.

In spite of these apparently unfavourable circumstances, the EMS bandwagon started to roll. The most potent force behind it was the provision of strong political support – most important by the West German Chancellor – one of the necessary ingredients lacking at the time of the Werner Plan, as Marjolin had recognised. The explanation for this revival of 'political will' is still a matter for speculation, as the aims and motives of those involved were complex and never clearly stated. However, an attempt to clarify them helps to explain why the EMS emerged in the form it finally took. The idea of an EMU was out of keeping with the mood of the times – no one was ready to face the implications this held for national sovereignty – and the hard realists, that is, Chancellor Schmidt and President Giscard d'Estaing, insisted that the aims of the EMS were more limited for the immediate future. Willy-nilly, the system they produced may have implications for convergence within the Community going beyond their primary aims.

In spite of the acceptance by the IMF of floating rates, and the United States' continued adherence to the system, it is possible, especially with hindsight, to detect a growing disenchantment among some of the European countries with more open economies with the results of the floating rate system at the time the EMS idea was put forward. Although floating rates had allowed Western economies to survive the effects of the flight from the dollar and the balance-of-payments disturbances following on the oil price rises of 1973/4, there was dissatisfaction on several counts. There were the problems caused by excessive fluctuations in exchange rates – the phenomenon of 'overshooting'. Capital flows resulting from lack of confidence in the dollar could cause the rate of a European currency such as the Deutsche Mark to rise, pushing up the value of the currency beyond what would be justified by any objective measure such as purchasing power parity. Market forces could be slow in restoring equilibrium. This concerned weak currency countries also. They complained that their currencies dropped below a level justified by objective criteria during bouts of panic selling due to the psychological influence of loss of confidence. Again, a lot of damage could be done before market forces restored a more acceptable rate for the currency concerned, as they were supposed to do in theory. There were also increasing doubts as to whether the benefits of currency depreciations in helping a country improve its competitiveness in trade were large enough or permanent enough to outweigh the costs in terms of inflation.[7] The 'vicious circle' argument, which describes the self-reinforcing character of the relationship between declining exchange rates and rising prices for weak currency countries, was used to substantiate these doubts.

The position with regard to inflation rates, growth rates and unemployment was found equally unsatisfactory during the period of generalised floating. Various strategies to promote non-inflationary growth had been tried with the backing of such international organisations as the OECD and the IMF. The locomotive theory, according to which the strong economies would expand and drag forward the weaker ones, had been replaced by the convoy theory, promoted by the British Prime Minister, James Callaghan. Mr Callaghan put forward a five-point plan in March 1978 to promote an integrated programme in which all the major economies would combine their efforts to increase growth, conserve energy and establish currency stability within the framework of the IMF.

The extent to which these policies' lack of immediate success was related to the effects of floating rates is much debated. The arguments in favour of floating and the beneficial effects of depreciation for weak currency countries were not without their supporters. However, the West German Chancellor was not satisfied with the results which were being achieved. It is true that until 1978 the German government had shown no sign of moving from its position, which was still in line with the arguments of the 'economists' put forward early in the 1970s, that, in the absence of substantial progress towards greater economic convergence, the Germans would have no interest in locking their economy into a fixed exchange rate system with the high inflation rate countries of Western Europe outside the snake. The Germans were running a tight and successful monetarist policy and maintaining a low inflation rate. They seemed to have little to gain by widening the snake. Yet Herr Schmidt changed his stance and this must be explained in terms of his assessment of the political situation at the time, combined with broad economic considerations.

Among the economic considerations which influenced Herr Schmidt was the belief that exchange rate instability and rising inflation had undermined business confidence in the Community, harming trade and investment and thus stunting growth and leading to unemployment. The success of Germany's own policies and the apparently salutary effect that membership of the snake had had on the economies of those countries which had remained in it suggested that there was a case for holding that other European countries could benefit by subjecting themselves to similar disciplines. Herr Schmidt had the problems of his own business community in mind, as well as the problems that he saw around him in the rest of Europe as he sought a solution. The Chancellor was not perhaps so obsessed with the fear of even slight rises in the inflation rate which made the Bundesbank view plans for widening the snake with disfavour. In addition, he was interested in the possibility that membership of the wider EMS might help control the appreciation of the Deutsche Mark.

The political arguments centred on the German Chancellor's dissatisfaction with American leadership and policy. Germany suffered from America's policy of benign neglect as the Deutsche Mark was the most favoured alternative to the declining dollar as a reserve asset, and Germany was reluctant to see the Deutsch Mark become a reserve currency. There seemed to be no evidence that the Americans could be relied upon to adhere consistently to policies which would stem the decline of the dollar and reverse the inflationary trends in the American economy. The decline of the dollar's value also helped to make American goods more competitive in world markets, often at the expense of German products. There were other areas where American interests seemed to diverge from those of Europe, in defence and energy for instance, and where the quality of leadership coming from the United States seemed to indicate that Europe would do well to look to its own institutions to develop a more independent and internationally influential presence of its own.

The French, who at the time of the Werner Plan had been the leaders in the 'monetarist' camp, once again had reasons for favouring membership of a fixed exchange rate system. Under the leadership of President Giscard d'Estaing and Prime Minister Raymond Barre, the French were engaged in a programme to restructure the French economy so that it could compete with the most advanced industrialised countries' products. A period of relative exchange rate stability would help to build the confidence of the French industrial sector to undertake the long-term investment which would be necessary if the plan were to succeed. If a return to a fixed rate system could be arranged in such a way as not to stir memories of France's two earlier exits from the snake, then the French would enjoy once again the prestige of keeping up with the strongest economies in the Community, which would help to allay the ever-present fear, as in the earlier years, of Germany's still increasing strength.

A close association had grown up between the President of France and the German Chancellor, and it was following weekend discussions between the two leaders that Chancellor Schmidt took the opportunity of the meeting of the European Council in Copenhagen on 7 April 1978 to launch what President Giscard described to the press afterwards as 'a zone of monetary stability'. In supporting the idea of a scheme based on the close linkage of exchange rates, the West German Chancellor was moving into the camp of the 'monetarists', leaving the British (not among the members of the Community at the time the Werner Plan was launched) to argue for the 'economist' approach, and lead the other less prosperous members of the Community in the struggle to gain concessions to offset the consequences of renouncing exchange rate flexibility and tying their exchange rates to those of the stronger, less inflation-prone EC countries.

At this stage, concern for convergence, as such, was not apparently at the forefront of the minds of those involved in the negotiations to establish an EMS. Their economic aims were connected with finding a solution to the immediate problems of inflation and low growth; in so far as there was concern to forge a closer bond between Community members it was the result of a desire to establish a political presence as a counterweight to American influence in the world. Even so, the steps proposed on the economic side might, if successful, be accompanied by closer convergence of members' economic policies and performance which could pave the way towards a full monetary union.

Bremen: An Uneasy Compromise

The attempt to accomodate the interests of the two groups within the Community was evident in the first publicly announced outline of the plans which were afoot — the Annex to the communiqué issued after the Bremen meeting of EC leaders in July 1978. It reported that the Council had discussed a scheme for closer monetary co-operation leading to a zone of monetary stability in Europe. Community bodies were to draw up by the end of that October the necessary provisions for the scheme. The basic elements of the system as it was to emerge in its final form were all in the Bremen outline: arrangements for linking of exchange rates, provisions for a newly named European Currency Unit to be at the centre of the system, and provisions for improved credit mechanisms, these arrangements to be consolidated with the creation of a single European Monetary Fund two years from the start of the scheme.

The position of the less prosperous countries is reflected in the clause which reads:

There will be concurrent studies of the action needed to be taken to strengthen the economies of the less prosperous member countries in the context of such a scheme; such measures will be essential if the zone of monetary stability is to succeed.

The uneasy compromise achieved between the members at this stage is evident in the last clause:

A system of closer monetary co-operation will only be successful if participating countries pursue policies conducive to greater stability at home and abroad; this applies to deficit and surplus countries alike.

The system was to be founded on 'monetarist' principles, but there was no illusion that the fixing of exchange rates alone could be successful unless the necessary domestic economic policies were followed. However, the weaker economies were making it clear that they did not intend to be landed with the entire burden of adjustment this time round. The issue of concurrent studies and the desired outcome in parallel measures was formally on the agenda.

In order to win the allegiance of the strong currency members of the EC, the new system had to be 'at least as strict as the "Snake"', as the Bremen Annex described it. As in the snake, changes in central rates 'subject to mutual consent' would be allowed. In making this concession, and in agreeing to accept the dangers of increased inflation, so much feared by the Bundesbank, the Germans felt that they had sacrificed as much as could be asked by the weak currency countries. They could not reasonably be expected to 'pay twice' in the form of further concessions such as resource transfers. However, Britain and the other weaker countries were by no means satisfied by this. Whether the further concessions they wanted would actually lead to closer convergence of the EC economies' performance, or whether such concessions would only encourage them to continue in the error of their ways was one of the points at issue.

The position of the weaker member countries was set out in the Green Paper on the European Monetary System,[8] issued by the British government. The Green Paper pointed out that the Bremen statement had recognised the importance of economic convergence as a necessary basis for greater monetary stability and stressed that the British government's position had always been that the system 'would not be durable and effective unless it were soundly based in appropriate economic policies'. The Green Paper laid out eight points which should characterise the system if it were to meet the British requirements. These specified that the system should be durable and effective. It should be capable of containing all members of the Community and should provide a basis for improved economic growth and higher employment in the Community, rather than impose further constraints on growth and employment. The fourth point then specified that:

> For this reason, the system should impose obligations on its stronger members symmetrical with those falling on its weaker members.

And section 8 read:

> The system should be accompanied by clear progress in making the operation of Community policies as a whole assist in promoting convergence of economic performance of member states. In particular, there should be net transfers of resources on the right scale to the less prosperous members.

Here lay the nub of the difference between the weak and strong members of the Community. Both sides could agree on the aims set out in the first three provisions of the Green Paper, and the following requirements, 5, 6 and 7 (that there should be adequate funds for intervention, that provision should be made for realignments of exchange rates, that the system should reinforce efforts to improve currency stability worldwide and should not be detrimental to other currencies, including the dollar, or to the standing and effectiveness of the IMF), were all accepted in the final form of the EMS. It was section 4 and section 8 which indicated the difficulty of accommodating the full requirements of the two parties within one system which would be acceptable to both.

Grid versus Basket: More than a Mechanical Problem

The struggle over these two central points became focused, as far as section 4 was concerned, on the bargaining over the type of exchange rate mechanism to be used in the EMS, the 'grid versus basket' controversy, as it became known in the press. This had the appearance of a highly technical, and almost irrelevant squabble, but actually was the manifestation of the basic difference of attitude on the way the system should work. The requirement specified in section 8 was fought over in the debates on concurrent studies and parallel measures to lead to actions to strengthen the economies of the less prosperous member states, such action to entail net transfers of resources, 'in conformity with the Community's objective of bringing about convergence in the economic performance of member states'.[9] The weaker states were in effect throwing down the gauntlet before the stronger members. They were challenging them to make clear whether they were concerned with the long-term and often proclaimed aims of the Community to bring about a closer convergence in the economic performance of its members, whether they were prepared to accept the full consequences of the system on which they were hoping to embark, or whether they were determined to ignore the implications of their actions and hope that a system with the limited aims of combating excessive fluctuations in exchange rates and hence reducing a factor of uncertainty in trade and payments between member states, could succeed. As the Green Paper put it,

> Some may regard the EMS as little more than an exchange rate mechanism, supported by central bank swap arrangements. The Government see it as much more than that. They believe it was conceived as more than that at Bremen and that it needs to be more than that if it is to contribute to greater stability in the international monetary system.

The controversy over the alternative exchange rate mechanisms which could be used in the EMS to govern central bank intervention and maintain parity levels centred on the question of whether the mechanism used in the old snake system of bilateral cross rates between each pair of currencies involved should pass over unchanged to the new system.[10] The important difference from the point of view of those who were advocating greater symmetry of obligations in the new system was that the basket arrangement would mean that when disequilibrium was caused by a strong currency getting out of line with the average of the other members' currencies, as calculated in the ECU, the obligation to undertake corrective measures would fall on that strong currency country without necessarily involving a weak currency. Under the parity grid system of bilateral rates, two currencies would always be involved, and the weak currency countries argued that the measures they would have to take were more punishing than those open to the strong currency countries (see explanation earlier in the chapter).

The British argued strongly for the basket mechanism and at first had considerable support, including that of the French. When it began to look as though the Germans were so opposed to making concessions on this point that they might withdraw support from the whole scheme, the French gave way. Jacques van Ypersele, of Belgium, proposed as a compromise that while the basis of the new system would be a parity grid, it should also include the basket mechanism as a divergence indicator to give a preliminary warning when a currency was starting to diverge against the Community average. After further bargaining it was agreed that when a currency crossed its threshold of divergence as indicated by the basket mechanism, this would trigger, not a rigid obligation for corrective action, but a 'presumption' that action would be taken. If actions were not taken, then the country involved, in the terms of the carefully worded clause, 'shall' give its reasons to the other authorities. The action which was to follow a crossing of the threshold could take the form of diversified intervention – that is, intervention in various currencies rather than just the currency which was furthest away from the currency of the intervening country, a method aimed at spreading the burden of intervention among currencies of the EMS – measures of domestic monetary policy, changes in central rates, or other measures of economic policy.

The Divergence Indicator: Optional Extra or Essential Feature?

When the compromise was first reached, there was perhaps a feeling that very little had been gained by the less prosperous countries. A sceptic has referred to the divergence indicator as 'a bureaucratic nicety offering jobs for computers and statisticians'.[11] More recently, some very positive assessments have been given. Professor Thygesen has said that 'it represents for the first time in Community and world monetary history an agreement on the use of an objective indicator as a trigger for policy co-ordination' without which policy co-ordination in the past has tended to degenerate into a mere exchange of information.[12] It was the intention of van Ypersele in proposing the divergence indicator that it should function not only as a trigger for intervention but for policy co-ordination. It is early yet to give a balanced assessment of the success of this mechanism but in so far as it establishes a presumption that there will be discussion and co-ordination of the range of policies outlined above, it marks an advance on previous attempts at co-ordination. The discussions held so far on exchange rate adjustments have been heated and in some cases not without rancour, but at least members have established the habit of thrashing out these difficult questions amongst themselves and have a forum in which they can voice their views.

Where the decision is taken to intervene, the credit available to members is now of substantial proportions to give credibility to any stand which is taken. The credit mechanisms have been extended to an amount of 25 billion ECUs which is about 2½ times the amount previously available. With this backing, the EMS incorporates and expands the three previously existing credit mechanisms.[13] Large amounts are therefore available to counter speculative movements. Van Ypersele has argued that the system, which has taken the form of an adjustable peg, does not encourage speculation against member currencies by offering a one-way option for adjustment. 'To the extent that changes in central rates are smaller than twice the width of the margin of fluctuation, it is not at all sure that speculation will gain.'[14] Lessons had been learned from the inflexibility which developed in the Bretton Woods system, as mentioned earlier, and led to countries defending unrealistic rates. The freedom to adjust was used in the previous snake arrangement, and it remains to be seen whether the option available in the EMS will strengthen the system, or as its detractors might suggest, make it a weaker instrument of convergence by allowing its members to avoid the corrective measures in domestic economic policy which a fixed rate system would have forced upon them.

The British government made it clear in its Green Paper that it considered the concurrent studies (on the action to be taken to strengthen the economies of the less prosperous member countries in the context of the EMS) of critical importance. The task of producing a report on this was given to the Community's Economic Policy Committee. The British government felt that participation in the exchange rate regime might be difficult to reconcile with its goals for growth and employment if it were forced to follow deflationary policies in an effort to defend the exchange rate level. The position was well described by Sir Donald MacDougall, author of the Commission study on the role of public finance in European economic integration,[15] when he said that, whereas in a full monetary union a large budget and considerable transfer of resources would be needed, this was not a necessary requirement to support an adjustable peg arrangement.

> EMS is quite different from a full monetary union; and the argument is the quite understandable one about how far countries that may be less keen than others to join an adjustable peg system on a European basis can bargain to get a better deal for themselves regarding contributions, the CAP, help from the Regional Fund, and so on. I certainly would not want to argue that a large transfer of resources or a much larger Community budget is necessary to support an adjustable peg system in Europe if countries want one.

The Economic Policy Committee was able to agree on the basic requirements for the smooth functioning of the system,[16] as was acknowledged in the Green Paper: 'Our partners agree unanimously that one necessary condition for the system to be effective and durable, is that inflation rates should converge at as low a level as possible, without this having a deflationary effect.'[17] It was to offset this deflationary effect that the less prosperous countries were, as Sir Donald phrased it, 'bargaining to get a better deal for themselves', and it was the question of the role which resource transfers should play in this context which brought disagreement in the Economic Policy Committee.

It will be recalled that the second Barre plan (see page 106) referred to earlier had set out the position that in a fixed rate system members would be forced to co-ordinate their economic policies to ensure maintenance of those rates. Once again in 1978 the 'monetarists', this time with Germany at their head, were arguing that monetary discipline would force 'sensible' economic policies on the less prosperous countries, which would lead to an improvement in their economic performance. The less prosperous countries were worried about the consequences of those 'sensible' policies for their growth and employment rates and were trying to ensure that suitable parallel measures would recompense them for the problems they would have to face.

There was further disagreement on the assessment of net receipts and contributions to the Community Budget which the British wanted to include as an 'essential instrument' to achieve the objective of narrowing the gap between the more and less prosperous countries in the Community. The arguments here have been dealt with in Geoffrey Denton's chapter on the Budget. No country wished to see itself in the role of philanthropist, especially when many members of the more prosperous countries regarded the misfortunes of the less prosperous as largely of their own making. At this distance from the heat of the debate, the British blanket demand for 'net transfers of resources' strikes the observer as, at the very least, a bold position, even acknowledging that the prosperous countries expected to reap their own rewards from membership of the EMS. The rather meagre concessions made in the final agreement come, therefore, as no very great surprise.

A separate section of the Resolution of the European Council of 5 December 1978 on the establishment of the European Monetary System is devoted to 'Measures designed to strengthen the economies of the less prosperous Member States of the European Monetary System' (Section B). For those looking for hard cash, Section B starts promisingly. 'We stress that, within the context of a broadly-based strategy aimed at improving the prospects of economic development and based on symmetrical rights and obligations of all participants, the most important concern should be to enhance the convergence of economic policies towards greater stability.' When it comes to the actual measures to be taken, however, improved co-ordination was all that was to be offered. 'We request the Council [Economic and Finance Ministers] to strengthen its procedures for co-ordination in order to improve that convergence.' The second clause makes it quite clear where the real burden of economic adjustment was to lie. 'We are aware that the convergence of economic policies and of economic performance will not be easy to achieve. Therefore, steps must be taken to strengthen the economic potential of the less prosperous countries of the Community. This is primarily the responsibility of the Member States concerned. Community measures can and should serve a supporting role.'

The real meat of the concessions is found in section 3.

3.1   The European Council requests the Community Institutions by the utilisation of the new financial instrument and the European Investment Bank to make available for a period of five years loans of up to 1,000 million EUA per year to these countries on special conditions.

3.2   The European Council requests the Commission to submit a proposal to provide interest rate subsidies of 3 per cent for these loans, with the following elements: the total cost of this measure, divided into annual tranches of 200 million EUA each over a period of five years, shall not exceed 1,000 million EUA.

'Le NIC': A Second-hand Facility?

The 'new financial instrument' mentioned in section 3.1 was first heard of in June 1977 when M. Ortoli, the Commissioner for Economic Affairs, announced a Commission proposal to take advantage of the Community's 'triple A' credit rating to raise money on the international money markets which could then be re-lent at preferential rates for Community projects in energy, industrial restructuring and regional development. This was to supplement the funds available from the EIB and ECSC, and to make up an anticipated shortfall in Community funds that would be available to finance a policy which it was intended should provide selective stimulus to investment without fuelling inflation. With the Council's usual caution in extending the executive power of the Commission, it was not until 16 October 1978 that the Commission was empowered to contract loans for this purpose. Even then the power to administer the loans was divided between the Council, the Commission and the EIB and the arrangements were 'tentative', to be reviewed in two years.[18] The instrument is variously referred to by the press and the Commission as the Ortoli facility, the New Community Facility or Instrument (NCF or NCI), or by the French, 'Nouvel Instrument Communautaire' (*le NIC*). Under the name of the 'new financial instrument' it was adopted by the Community to provide the means of channelling funds to the less prosperous members of the Community in the final arrangements for the EMS. The 'new financial instrument', although unused up to that time, was not in fact 'new' − all that was new was the special provisions for interest rate subsidies of 3 per cent to be available only to those countries 'effectively and fully participating in the Exchange Rate and

Intervention Mechanism'. This explains why, when the first loans were announced on 17 September 1979, Ireland, Italy and the UK were to benefit, though the UK would not receive any interest rate subsidies. Britain was to receive £66·3m. for electricity and water supply projects, Ireland £58m. for electricity, water, road-building and telecommunications projects, and Italy L45b. for water supply projects.

The operation of the facility has been criticised in the Ruffolo Report on the EMS prepared for the European Parliament.[19] According to this report, progress towards economic convergence had been negligible, partly because of the ambiguity of the real meaning of the 'parallel measures'. The report suggests that the more prosperous countries understood convergence to mean the imposition of stabilising restraints, that is, anti-inflationary measures, while the less prosperous countries took it to mean co-ordination of growth objectives to eliminate the possible deflationary effects of participation in the exchange agreements, and the full use of supranational policies and instruments in order to redistribute resources. The report does not regard the New Community Instrument as carrying out this aim and, therefore, considers that at this level, the parallel measures have become meaningless. It must be said that anyone reading the December Resolution in the cold light of morning could hardly say there was any ambiguity about the promises made therein. However, the less prosperous countries might well have been justified in some disappointment that so little was finally conceded. Even the outcome of the dispute over the amount to be allocated to the Regional Fund was only a small rise over that originally proposed for 1979, when it was finally agreed in March 1979.

Ireland decided to join the EMS and the 2¼ per cent margin arrangements for exchange rates after it had secured promises of bilateral loans to help it maintain its rapid economic development, and Italy, in the hope that the EMS would help it achieve its domestic stabilisation plans, joined, taking advantage of the 6 per cent intervention margin and some bilateral loan agreements.[20] Britain alone was not satisfied with the final arrangements, which left the UK Budget problem unsettled.

The EMS as finally agreed in the December 1978 Resolution of the European Council is described in the British government White Paper (Cmnd 7419). Its main features were the exchange rate system (an adjustable peg with substantial credit facilities to support intervention); the creation of a new European unit of account, the European Currency Unit (ECU) (with the potential to become a European currency); and the first steps towards the establishment of a European Monetary Fund.

Purpose-built Exercise: the ECU and the EMF

The December Resolution of the Council took up the commitment made in the Bremen Annex that the ECU would be at the centre of the EMS. It was to be used as the denominator or numeraire for the exchange rate mechanism, as the basis for a divergence indicator, as the denominator for operations in the intervention and credit mechanisms and as a means of settlement between monetary authorities. The ECU is a basket of the nine member states' currencies, with the amount of each currency in the basket corresponding to the economic importance of the country in question. The weight of each currency influences the value of the ECU basket, which is calculated each day by the Commission. It was intended as the new European unit of account which could be used increasingly as a means of payment, initially between member states' central banks and later perhaps in connection with international capital movements. The possibility is there for the ECU to be a key factor in the linking of Community monetary mechanisms and consequently policies. It can be the medium for the establishment of a parallel currency (see John Pinder's chapter). The December Resolution pledged the Community to full utilisation of the ECU at the end of two years as a reserve asset and means of settlement. The options were left open and much would depend on whether and how it would be utilised.

The less prosperous countries had called for an expansion of the credit facilities which had been set up in connection with the snake. The EMS incorporates and expands the three existing credit mechanisms, the very short-term financing, the short-term monetary support (STMS) and the medium-term financial assistance (MTFA). The amount of these credit mechanisms was extended to 25 billion ECUs and the periods within which settlements had to be made were extended. These were to be forty-five days after the end of the month of intervention for the very short-term facility, with a possible three months' extension; the STMS was to be for three months with the possibility of two extensions of three months each; the MTFA was to be repayable within a period of two to five years.[21]

A European Monetary Fund (EMF) was to be set up two years after the system came into effect. For the time being, members deposit with the existing European Monetary Co-operation Fund (EMCF) 20 per cent of their gold and dollar reserves and receive in return a corresponding amount of ECUs, which can be used to settle balances connected with intervention and short-term monetary support. This is intended to make it easier to repay currency credits since members can use them in certain proportions[22] to help settle their debts. For the initial period the reserves remain the property of member states and are lodged with the Fund on a swap basis for use as reserve assets and as means of settlement. The implication is that once part of the currency reserves is managed jointly, the Community will also have to pursue a common foreign exchange policy towards non-member countries' currencies, in particular the dollar.

Annual Check-up

Although the EMS has been in operation for a little over a year, it is still rather early to assess the effects it may have had on the convergence of members' policies. To the surprise of many who predicted almost instant disaster for the scheme, as had been predicted for the snake, it survived its first year with its membership of eight countries (Great Britain having remained outside the exchange rate mechanism, though participating in the arrangements for the pooling of reserves) intact. On two occasions it was necessary to realign central rates. On 24 September 1979, after a fifteen-hour meeting in Brussels of the finance ministers, the Deutsche Mark was revalued by 2 per cent against the other currencies in the system and the Danish krone was devalued by 3 per cent. On 29 November the Danish krone was devalued by 5 per cent *vis-à-vis* the other EMS currencies.

The stability of the early months was partly due to the fact that there had been a realignment of currencies in October 1978, in anticipation of possible tensions between the Deutsche Mark and other currencies, and partly to the fact that following the package of measures introduced by the American government in November 1978, the dollar entered a period of relative stability. In addition, the fear that the strength of the Deutsche Mark would strain the system was mitigated by the reversal in balance-of-payments positions of the member countries. Germany moved into current account deficit after a decade of surplus and this helped to hold the Deutsche Mark down. France and Italy had strong surpluses and this helped to give unusual strength to the franc and the lira. Stability was not achieved without regular heavy intervention, however. This caused considerable concern in Germany where the Bundesbank had been intervening in support of both the dollar and the Danish krone and Belgian franc. The Germans argued that this swelled the domestic money supply and therefore added to inflation.

Members' inflation rates have not shown the improvement that might have been hoped for during this period. It was never claimed that membership of the EMS would produce a quick cure for inflation but rather that by imposing discipline, particularly on monetary expansion, the EMS would help to curb inflation. The situation is described in the Commission's monthly report for March 1980 and illustrated by the figures in Table 6.1.

The Commission considers the rise of the Community's average

Table 6.1   *Cost and price indicators*

	Consumer price deflator			Wholesale prices	
	1973–8 average	*1979*	*1980*	*1973–8 average*	*1979*
a. In national currencies					
Denmark	10·2	9·5	12·5	10·4	9·0
FRG	5·3	4·1	5·0	5·1	6·9
France	9·6	10·5	12·1	9·6	11·7
Ireland	14·8	13·2	15·5	16·7	(12½)
Italy	15·4	15·0	17·1	18·7	15·4
Netherlands	8·1	4·7	6·8	6·2	(3)
Belgium	8·3	4·5	6·9	6·1	6·3
Luxembourg	7·5	4·5	6·5		
UK	14·6	13·2	18·9	16·6	12·1
EC	9·9	9·0	11·3	10·9	(10½)
USA	7·0	9·0	9·5	9·9	12·2
Japan	10·2	4·0	5·5	8·5	7·3
b. In ECUs					
Denmark	12·2	6·7		12·4	6·3
FRG	11·4	6·2		11·1	9·0
France	9·3	9·0		9·4	10·2
Ireland	7·6	12·4		9·3	(11·7)
Italy	6·1	9·2		9·2	9·6
Netherlands	13·1	5·0		11·1	(3·3)
Belgium	12·2	4·4		9·9	6·2
Luxembourg	11·4	4·4			
UK	7·4	16·1		9·3	15·0
EC	9·9	9·0		10·9	(10½)
USA	4·8	1·4		9·9	4·3
Japan	14·7	−7·4		8·5	−4·5

Source: Eurostat and Commission staff.

inflation rate since 1978 as 'very serious'. The acceleration of inflation during 1978–9 was common to all members but was accompanied by renewed divergence. Among the more prosperous countries of the Community, the rise of the rate of inflation (measured as the annual average forecast for the private consumption deflator in 1980 over the annual averages recorded in 1978) was within the range of +2·4 to +3·3 per cent. Among the less prosperous countries the acceleration was much more marked with the rates reaching +4·4 per cent for Italy, +6·6 per cent for Ireland and +10·5 per cent for the UK. Undoubtedly, the UK, outside the EMS, has fared worst, but its rate of inflation would have been higher if the sterling exchange rate had not been allowed to strengthen during 1979. Had Britain been a member of the exchange rate mechanism, it would have had to intervene to sell sterling. This would have increased the money supply, which might have had severe inflationary consequences, and would certainly have led the government to adopt an economic policy that implied greater divergence. The less prosperous countries are getting no more and no less than was promised in the December Resolution. The main burden of achieving economic convergence is primarily their own responsibility and the results of their policy decisions are reflected in their performances. Even accepting that the results have not been good in this area, there are those who feel that the differing rates of inflation within the Community need not necessarily prove an insuperable difficulty for the EMS. There was quite a wide divergence of inflation rates among the members of the snake from its early days, but they managed to cope by means of fairly frequent realignments, and the same could happen in the EMS.

Missing Parts

The two largest gaps in the EMS's procedures so far have been the lack of a policy towards the dollar and of a formally co-ordinated monetary policy. Hans-Eckart Scharrer, writing on the need for joint monetary management in the EMS, has commented that 'the European Council's complete neglect of the problem of policy co-ordination [in this area] is quite incomprehensible. This is all the more so since not only the EC Commission but also Prime Minister Tindemans in his report on European Union delivered to the Council have stressed this basic issue of monetary integration.' He adds that 'efforts to harmonise national money supply policies are of paramount importance if exchange rates are effectively to be stabilised in the new system'.[23] There has not been a lack of suggestions as to how this could be achieved. The German Council of Economic Experts in their Annual Report for 1976/7 presented a set of proposals for coherent monetary policies with fixed or adjustable exchange rates. Armin Gutowski, a member of the group, has explained that this would involve making 'multilateral assistance from other member states conditional on all member states' forsaking some of their independence in national monetary policy and adhering to jointly agreed upon monetary policy targets'.[24] The need that would arise to forsake some independence gives a clue as to why no such policy has so far been agreed. There has been an increasing degree of consensus in member states' attitudes to monetary policy. The four major countries of the Community have recently aimed at the control of money or credit aggregates, with some secondary convergence for

1979 in the technical design of targets.[25] But no coherent policy for the Community as a whole has been attempted.

The EMS cannot be a fortress of stability independent of the dollar. World financial markets are highly integrated and the fate of the EMS is inextricably linked with that of the dollar. The Europeans felt a need for a Community-based monetary system in the early 1970s as a result of America's dollar policy and the resulting instability in the international monetary system. The decline in the dollar during the years 1977 and 1978 again prompted a further attempt to seek stability within the Community. EMS is partly a reaction to dollar instability yet it cannot prosper unless in partnership with a stable dollar. The system could contribute to dollar stability with a co-ordinated support policy towards the dollar and with the development of the ECU as an alternative reserve asset, gradually sharing some of the burden of this role with the dollar, as is discussed in a later section of this chapter. The lack of a co-ordinated policy is partly the result of caution lest the scheme should appear as antagonistic to the dollar in any way, and partly the result of Germany's reluctance to share its role as policy-maker in this vital area.

The stability of the dollar–Deutsche Mark relationship is a key factor in the solution of this problem, yet the relationship has been most precarious. The erratic behaviour of the US monetary authorities, who switched from periods of tight monetary control to periods of expansionary monetary policy, has provoked a not always helpful response from the Germans. Even the measures of November 1978, which ushered in a period of six months during which the Federal Reserve lowered the growth rate of the monetary base by 50 per cent relative to the previous six months, were followed by a period of six months from early April when the Federal Reserve reversed its policy and doubled the growth rate of the monetary base. The United States seems to have reverted to the paths of monetarist virtue since Federal Reserve Chairman Volcker abruptly returned to Washington from the IMF meeting in the autumn of 1979 to set things on the right course again. Some commentators remain sceptical as to whether this is a lasting policy. Karl Brunner believes that 'There is little evidence from past behavior assuring any reliable prospects of responsible international (or domestic) monetary policymaking in the USA'.[26] At times the Germans have intervened heavily in support of the dollar and helped stabilise the relationship but they have been anxious to recoup any losses incurred in recent years (having experience of losses sustained in the past) and their subsequent selling of dollars may have contributed to renewed weakness in that currency.

All the official statements have expressed awareness of the need for such a policy from the time of the Bremen Annex, where it was stipulated that

Participating countries will co-ordinate their exchange rate policies *vis-à-vis* third countries. To this end they will intensify the consultations in the appropriate bodies and between central banks participating in the scheme. Ways to co-ordinate dollar interventions should be sought which avoid simultaneous reverse interventions.

The commitment to co-ordination *vis-à-vis* third countries was repeated in the December Resolution. In spite of these good resolutions, the recent Ruffolo Report has pointed out that 'The most important source of external strains is the almost total absence of a joint policy towards the dollar'.

The absence of a dollar policy was one of the main points which the British took up in their criticism of the proposed EMS. Mr Callaghan, drawing on Britain's past experience of the problems of a reserve currency, was very much aware of the difficulties involved in this role for the dollar. The British pushed strongly for progress on a dollar policy at the time of the negotiations, but the Germans were unwilling to discuss it. Christopher McMahon, of the Bank of England, in his evidence to the House of Lords Select Committee on the European Communities inquiry into progress in the EMS (July 1979), reported that 'When Sir Kenneth [Couzens] and I took part in the autumn negotiations, we and others attempted to persuade the Germans that we needed a coherent dollar policy'. The Germans had borne the brunt of the cost of intervention for some time and as a result may have felt that they had a right to determine the policy. However, what they did out of concern for their own inflation rate was of considerable concern to their European partners, whether in intervention, or interest rate policy, an aspect of their conduct which has provoked much criticism.

In spite of the lack of progress so far, this does seem to be an area where the prospects for the future allow some optimism, on the assumption that the system remains in operation. American dollar policy since the autumn of 1979, with the US authorities taking a more responsible attitude, in the sense of being willing to intervene themselves in support of the dollar and following monetarist policies at home, has left the Germans with less ground for criticism − even though they may not be entirely happy with the results of their own prescription now that the Deutsche Mark itself is not so strong. In addition, the increased amount of intervention in support of the dollar undertaken by others, such as the Bank of England, has given them a less exclusive right to determine policy.

With the American authorities following a more predictable policy of intervention to support the dollar there is opportunity for co-ordination and co-operation. In Community committees and meetings of central bank and monetary authorities there is now more overt and explicit discussion between the Germans and their EMS partners on dollar policy, including such questions as whether or not German intervention should take place. As Sir Kenneth Couzens said in his evidence to the House of Lords Committee, there has been some success in the difficult area of arrangements 'which spread the responsibility and the power of making decisions'. Continued stability for the dollar is not assured, is even unlikely, but there is a better ground from which to build a co-ordinated and co-operative response, and this seems to be one area where there is a possibility of convergence in Community policy and where the rewards would seem to make the derogation of national independence well worthwhile.

Election Ahead: Proceed with Caution

The communiqué issued at the Dublin summit in November 1979 confirmed the Community's commitment to move to the second stage of the EMS in March 1981. This would involve the setting-up of the European Monetary Fund and the acceptance of the ECU in its full role of reserve asset and settlement currency. However, reports in February 1980 said this was to be delayed. The French and German heads of state met on 3 February and though no announcement was made, government sources said that it had been decided to postpone any positive action until after the German and French elections in the following autumn and the spring of 1981. With elections on hand, neither leader wanted to tackle the difficult questions of national control over monetary policy that would arise in connection with the establishment of the EMF.

Even though the political will to move forward was in abeyance, the theoretical and technical side of the work on the future development of the EMS had not come to a standstill. The review which had been planned to take place at the end of the first six months had been brushed over in only a few minutes at a meeting on 17 September 1979. There was said to be no need for technical modification at that stage, though the exchange rate realignments which took place a few days later suggested that there was a desire not to unsettle the markets by stimulating speculation about possible changes.

The Commission prepared reports on alternative ways forward for the EMS during its first year and technical studies continued in the EC's Monetary Committee. The standing of this committee was strengthened by a change of membership in January 1980, to include more senior men from treasuries and finance ministries of member countries. While the decision-making capacity of the committee was improved, thus removing some of the burden of co-ordinating monetary policy from the level of the finance ministers, the new members were on the whole men less known for their favourable attitude to the development of the EMS. Jacques van Ypersele, a strong supporter of progress towards monetary union, retired and the chairmanship was taken by M. Jean-Yves Haberer, director of France's Treasury. Also appointed were Herr Manfred Lahnstein, state secretary in the German Finance Ministry and Sir Kenneth Couzens, second permanent secretary in the UK Treasury. The character of the new membership seemed to indicate a desire to have the system working efficiently in its present form rather than any preparation for renewed progress towards monetary union.

Movement to the second stage of the EMS's development would provide a clear test of the commitment of the EMS members to greater convergence of monetary policies. At this stage, the EMCF (the functions of which are carried out at present by the Bank for International Settlements – BIS) would become a European Monetary Fund (EMF). Community documents available so far do not specify clearly what this would involve. It could be very little more than a change of name, or it could mean a fully independent central bank, which would become the owner of the 20 per cent of gold and foreign currency reserves now lent to the EMCF on a revolving swap basis, to help members deal with pressures on their exchange rates and balance-of-payments problems. Since the time the system was set up these have increased in value from 25 billion ECUs to about 40 billion ECUs, due to the rise in the price of gold. The ECU could become a genuine reserve currency issued to members against the gold and currency in the Fund, instead of the accounting device it is at present. It could be used for settling international debts[27] and members could borrow ECUs from the Fund on the condition they adopted the economic policies it recommended. If the Fund had the ability to create ECUs against credits it would give it the means to impose tighter monetary discipline within the Community, or, as some observers fear, the power to follow more relaxed policies than individual members might choose for themselves. Such developments would raise technical problems. Member states would have to enact legislation to abolish the limits on the acceptability of ECUs to central banks, and the terms of the ECU's convertibility and yield would have to be settled to make it sufficiently attractive to compete with other reserve assets.

The Commission has produced an internal report on the possible options for development of the EMS which suggests that the EC's agreement in July 1978 to aim for the full utilisation of the ECU as a reserve asset and means of settlement implies the creation of a fund with extensive responsibilities for monetary matters, now divided between central banks and ministries of finance. Whether member countries would accept this is at the moment hard to predict. There would have to be strong arguments to convince central banks to give up their powers, especially the Bundesbank with its considerable independence at the moment, and there would be opposition on political grounds to loss of national independence.[28] There would be the difficult question of who would control the new EMF, whether central bankers, the European Monetary Committee, or a newly created group of EC officials, independent of their national governments.

The incentives to accept such a development may look rather thin at this moment, but there are pressures resulting from developments in the international system which could possibly help to over-ride domestic objections. At the international level the problems of recycling oil money and providing a stable reserve asset to offset the volatility of the dollar have been occupying policy-makers. Much work had gone into the development of the IMF's substitution account as a possible answer to some of the difficulties and it was hoped that it would be endorsed at the IMF's Interim Committee meeting in April 1980. In this plan, dollar reserves could be swapped for the SDR, thus enhancing the role of this artificial reserve asset and adding a stabilising element to the international monetary system. However, with the increased stabilisation of the dollar in 1980 and the growing current account deficits of Germany and Japan, support for the plan vanished in April and suggestions were made that the development of the ECU might fill the gap left in its absence. The IMF would not want the ECU to rival the SDR, but might accept it as playing a complementary role in a multiple reserve asset system. Interest has been expressed in several quarters, including the Arab countries, in wider use of the ECU. They might well, for a combination of technical reasons – the tradability of ECU currencies – and reasons of political preference or financial prudence, prefer to make use of the ECU basket.[29]

Intervention policy is another area where EMS activity is developing on independent lines. In the old snake arrangement, it was intended that intervention to support a currency should be carried out using European currencies, as noted earlier. This occurred occasionally but the bulk of intervention was in dollars. In the EMS members are now gaining increasing experience in using national currencies of member states for intervention. Dollars are still used for bilateral currency-to-currency intervention, but members' currencies are used for intervention against the ECU. In addition, national currencies of the relevant EC creditor states in the EMS are given priority in settlements which have to be made within forty-five days after the end of each month, between central banks for bilateral currency-to-currency intervention. Thereafter, ECUs (up to a maximum of 50 per cent of the remaining debts), gold and other currencies may be used for settlement purposes. Peter Coffey has commented on this, 'Thus, in a somewhat complex manner, experience is finally being gained in the use of the national currencies of the Member States of the Common Market'.[30]

Postcard Dated 1980

Renewed suggestions from Germany in the spring of 1980 that Britain might consider membership of the EMS as part of a package deal to settle the Budget dispute pointed once again to one of the most obvious shortcomings of the EMS. It had not proved to be a system that could accommodate all the requirements of the entire membership of the European Community. Its future development has been delayed until after the French and German elections, though the French are said to be working on a plan for the reform of the international monetary system which would seek to tie the EMS, the dollar and the yen together more closely, thus going some way to remedying the lack of a dollar policy in the EMS. This was due to be presented to the international summit of Western leaders in June 1980. Whether Britain would then reconsider joining will depend on the developments in the UK economy in the meantime, but its inflation rate trend makes this look unlikely for 1980.

An assessment at this stage in the progress of the system must reveal rather limited achievements, but the potentials of the scheme are waiting to be exploited. There are positive elements which can be built on and which show an advance over previous efforts, and the structure of the scheme is more comprehensive than anything attempted in the past. There has been development, not only of the habit, but the mechanisms for consultation and co-operation. The experience of the debates prompted by the workings of the divergence indicator has established for all members a precedent for the expectation that the Community will come together for frank discussions of policy options. The discussions between central banks and the work of the Monetary Committee could doubtless have developed without the EMS, but its existence heightens the need and the constraint to make greater use of these channels. The presumption that countries have the right to act in isolation is gradually being undermined. The system is better able to support its aims with increased credit and availability of loans.

External pressures are also helping to push the EMS along the road to closer convergence. There is a growing interest in the ECU's possible role in the future after the failure in April 1980 of the IMF plan for a substitution account to gain acceptance. This development illustrates the strength of the EMS as a regional arrangement where progress and development, though difficult, are often easier and speedier than that which can be achieved in an international body like the IMF. The reorientation of power between Europe and America, with the continuation of strain in US-German relations in 1980, could mean that Germany will once again look to development of Europe as a power base. This may not meet opposition from other power blocs, including the Americans, who would often prefer, for the sake of simplicity, to deal with a single European unit.

A further internal factor which may promote the role of the EMS in convergence is the interest of the directly elected Parliament in the system. The European Parliament has not been satisfied with past monitoring of economic policies, and as Niels Thygesen has commented, 'the ambitions of the directly elected European Parliament to engage itself in the supervision of decision-making on money and exchange rates are likely to be considerable'.[31] The work of the European Parliament Committee under Mr Ruffolo which sees the way forward for the EMS as requiring 'a more solidly-based ECU, a reorganisation of the Community institutions and greater consistency between European monetary policies', illustrates the direction such involvement is likely to take.[32]

Many problems remain for the economists and the politicians. It is by no means clear yet that a system such as the EMS which links the exchange rates of member states with widely differing economic performances can survive in its present form. If its more prosperous members value the continued existence of the scheme they may have to face the cost of a closer union within which net transfers of resources would be feasible. The delay in progress to the next stage of the EMS means that the system will have to survive a difficult period when the problem of inflation will test the strength of the scheme and when discontent among member states may grow.[33] In similar troubled circumstances, the first stage of the Werner Plan based on limited monetary measures never moved on to the wider scope of its second stage. Difficult political decisions would have had to be faced then as now. The EMS is not as well able to cope with the problems of the times as a full Economic and Monetary Union, yet the desire to progress to EMU is not present. The lines between the EMS and EMU have remained clearly drawn – there has been no confusion on that score – but as the extracts from the Ruffolo Report have shown, there are those who would like to see the EMS developed further in the future, those who have never been satisfied with the 'compromise' agreement of December 1978 which favoured the 'monetarist' approach and skimped on the parallel measures.

The EMS has made some contributions towards convergence of policy-making in the Community. Convergence of economic performance has been slower to emerge. The leading member states of the Community prefer for the present to try to get through the difficult economic circumstances facing them as members of an association with limited aims. They prefer to make slow but steady progress in improved co-ordination and co-operation rather than to make a dash for full monetary union. Nevertheless, the potential for development is there and valuable experience has been gained. In this context, the EMS should not be seen as a cul-de-sac, but as a signpost on a road with many turnings.

Notes: Chapter 6

1 In his testimony before the Joint Economic Committee of Congress, 28 October 1959, Robert Triffin pointed out that the form of the world monetary system was not viable. In what came to be known as the Triffin Dilemma, he forecast (*a*) if the United States corrected its persistent deficits, the growth of world reserves could not be fed adequately by gold production at $35 an ounce; (*b*) if US deficits continued their trend, America's foreign liabilities would far exceed its ability to convert them into gold upon demand, which would bring about a gold and dollar crisis.

2 Benjamin Cohen, 'Europe's money, America's problem', *Foreign Policy*, Summer 1979.

3 The Bretton Woods system of fixed but adjustable rates officially allowed a movement of only 1 per cent on each side of a currency's central rate. While freedom to adjust central rates after consultation was allowed within the system, one of the weaknesses which developed in it was that this adjustment concession was not used. Countries were reluctant to accept the consequences of revaluation or devaluation and pressures grew up within the system which were not corrected.

   The system was criticised for its asymmetry − a situation which the British, as will be seen later, did not want to see repeated in the EMS. The pressure to adjust fell on the countries with weak currencies which had the limited options of drawing on their reserves or adopting deflationary domestic policies, if they did not want to adjust their central rates. The strong countries, it was argued, could tolerate the consequences of an undervalued currency (expanding reserves, overshooting on monetary targets) with more equanimity.

4 See Loukas Tsoukalis, *The Politics and Economics of European Monetary Integration* (Allen & Unwin, London, 1977), for a detailed study of this subject, and particularly p. 84 with reference to this point.

5 *The Times*, 3 December 1969.

6 *Report of the Study Group 'Economic and Monetary Union 1980'*, Vol. I (Commission of the European Communities, Brussels, 1975), p. 3.

7 A study by Ball, Burns and Laury of the London Business School, 'The role of exchange rate changes in balance of payments adjustment', *Economic Journal*, March 1977, notes that 'the output effect of the single exchange rate change is effectively transitory since the competitive advantage is subsequently wiped out by the adjustment of incomes to import prices restoring domestic costs to previous levels'.

8 Green Paper on the European Monetary System, Cmnd 7405 (HMSO, London, November 1978).

9 ibid., section 28.

10 The mechanics of the two arrangements have been described in Cohen's article, op. cit., and in the Green Paper, op. cit. The 'grid versus basket' controversy is described in my article 'EMS: from conception to birth', *International Affairs*, April 1979.

11 Karl Brunner, 'Reflections on the state of international monetary policy', Banca Nazionale del Lavoro, *Quarterly Review*, December 1979, pp. 361–75.

12 N. Thygesen, 'The emerging European Monetary System: precursors, first steps and policy options', in J. Williamson *et al.*, *Bulletin of the National Bank of Belgium*, LIVth year, vol. I, no. 4, April 1979.

13 *European Economy*, July 1979, p. 76.

14 Jacques van Ypersele de Strihou, 'Operating principles and procedures of the European Monetary System', in Philip H. Trezise (ed.), *The EMS: Its Promise and Prospects* (Brookings Institution, Washington DC, 1979).

15 Address to the Royal Institute of International Affairs, London, 16 January 1979.

16 Alessandro Leipold, 'The EMS: technical features and initial experience of its operations', paper prepared for conference on the European Monetary System held at Reading University, 11–13 July 1979.

17 Green Paper, op. cit., section 25.

18 *Bulletin of the European Communities*, 10/78.

19 *The EMS as an Aspect of the International Monetary System*, Report of the Economic and Monetary Affairs Committee of the European Parliament (Ruffolo Report), Working Document No. 1/63/80, 1980.

20 Ireland was reported to have arranged £255m. in bilateral loans. The Italian arrangements were less specific and Sig. Andreotti spoke in terms of an 'act of faith' when describing Italy's decision to join; *Financial Times*, 13 December 1978.

21 *European Economy*, July 1979, p. 77.

22 Members can use their ECU credits to repay 50 per cent of their debts while the remainder must be covered from national reserves.

23 Hans-Eckart Scharrer, 'Problems of monetary integration in Europe', *Intereconomics*, no. 11/12, 1978.

24 Samuel J. Katz (ed.), *US–European Monetary Relations* (American Enterprise Institute for Public Policy Research, Washington, DC, 1979), p. 73.

25 See Michael Emerson, 'The EMS in the broader setting of the Community's economic and political development', in Philip H. Trezise, op. cit., p. 37.

26 Brunner, op. cit., p. 365.

27 The Commission has suggested this would allow the EMS to 'establish its "monetary identity at the international level"'; *Financial Times*, 28 March 1980.

28 See *New York Times*, 19 February 1980, 'Delay seen in European monetary plans'. In France, the left-wing opposition parties joined forces with the right-wing neo-Gaullist followers of Mayor Jacques Chirac of Paris, who is expected to challenge President Giscard in next year's elections, in attacking plans to hand over the country's gold to a faceless, new international bureaucracy.

29 *Financial Weekly*, 21 December 1979, 'Moves to invigorate the ECU'.

30 Peter Coffey, 'The European Monetary System – six months later', *Three Banks Review*, no. 124, December 1979.

31 Niels Thygesen, 'Community decision-making on exchange rates and money', *Journal of Common Market Studies*, vol. XVII, no. 4, June 1979.

32 Ruffolo Report, op. cit., p. 17.

33 Signor Guido Carli, a former manager of the Bank of Italy, is reported in *The Times*, 7 May 1980, as saying that though the Italian economy is increasingly dependent on international markets its room for manoeuvre has been narrowed by membership of the EMS. 'Doubts are beginning to arise on the wisdom of accepting the links imposed by EMS membership.'

7

Regional Divergence and Policy in the Community, with Special Reference to Enlargement

Geoffrey Denton

Geographical disparities and divergence among regions are now accepted as a concern by most governments throughout the world. Certainly in Western European countries policies to promote convergence of the economic and cultural development of the various regions are highly developed. For the European Community regional disparities are a problem both because they affect the willingness of industry and workers in the member states to accept the impact of free competition within the wider Community market, and because integration of the national economies does not affect all regions uniformly. Some regions may be better placed than others to exploit the gains from specialisation – economies of scale and faster economic growth within the unified market – with the consequence that at best the gains from integration may be unevenly distributed, and at worst the economic welfare of some regions may even be damaged. The variations in the incidence of regional problems in the different member states can also affect the distribution of gains from integration measured at the national level, and could in principle cause some member states not to benefit from membership of the Community. But even if a member state benefits as a whole, if some regions within it suffer from the intensification of competition, the economic and political consequences may be unacceptable.

An account of regional problems and policies is therefore central to a discussion of economic convergence or divergence within the EC, not only in the narrow context of the operations of the Regional Development Fund, but also including the regional impact of other policies, and the control of regional aids under the competition policy. The third part briefly examines the implications for the regions of progress towards monetary union. The discussion is related throughout to the original Community of the Six, to the nine members of the existing Community, and to the problems, so far as they can be foreseen, which will be created by the further enlargement of the EC to take in Greece, Spain and Portugal in the early 1980s.

The Problem of Defining Regions in the EC

Before one can discuss the issues it is essential to clarify some conceptual and statistical difficulties. There is no satisfactory definition of a region. Economists have usually defined a region, putting it very simply, as an area within which capital and labour are mobile, but across the borders of which they are relatively immobile.[1] There are, of course, many difficulties with this approach, including the definition and measurement of mobility, differences between the behaviour of capital and of labour, and the direction in which they may be mobile across the borders. Many other indicators besides mobility of factors may be used, but the more indicators there are the more difficult it becomes to obtain an unambiguous definition. It is no use trying to avoid the problem of definition by a 'practical man's' approach of defining problem regions as those in which governments have intervened. Not only is this question-begging, but in practice governments have intervened in a bewildering variety of regions.

Another approach is to define regions in terms of the criteria which may be agreed to define the existence of a regional problem, though this is also question-begging, and the criteria are numerous and frequently contra-indicative. Some of the most often cited are: unemployment rates, activity rates, incomes per head, rates of emigration, rates of economic growth, age and class structure of the population, industrial structure, degree of spatial congestion and environmental conditions. Each of these criteria raises complex issues of comparability (for example, the statistical coverage of unemployment is notoriously variable between one country and another, and even within one country over time). Even if comparable statistics could be obtained, the relative incidence of regional problems would still be difficult to measure since social preference patterns vary from one country to another, and what is perceived as a problem in one country or region may not be so regarded in another. There is therefore no single 'regional problem' to be defined by some combination of these indicators; there are rather a number of different regional problems defined in terms of different selections from the list. It follows that problem regions may have little in common, and need different solutions.

These problems of definition are sufficiently severe at the national level (for example, the very different nature of the regional problem as between the industrial north-west of England and the agricultural Scottish Highlands); at the Community level they are magnified. It is not easy to find a common basis for discussion as between the United Kingdom, where regional disparities have been high in unemployment but small in incomes per head, and the Italian Mezzogiorno, where not only is unemployment much higher than in the north of Italy, but incomes are extremely low and outward migration is heavy. In the Community of Twelve, after the second enlargement, it will be even more difficult to discuss on a common basis the regional problems of Portugal, where even the wealthiest region, Lisbon, has a per capita gross domestic product only slightly more than half, and the poorest regions less than one-fifth, of the average for the Community of Nine.[2]

There is a particularly awkward problem in defining regions for the purpose of discussing the impact of the EC on the regions and for developing the Community's own regional policy. Apart from the difficulties caused by the immense variety of the problems facing different kinds of areas, there is a total failure even to attempt so far to arrive at any harmony in the matter of defining regions. The regions that are distinguished for the purposes of national statistics and national policies have completely different bases. For example, while the British statistics are provided for eleven economic planning regions, in Germany, with a similar population, there are thirty-four regions. The city Länder of Hamburg and Bremen stand out at the head of the German and EC league table with GDPs per capita (in 1976) of 229·5 and 177·5 per cent of the EC average.[3] But if they were included within their surrounding provinces, with GDPs per capita little above the EC average, their ranking would fall considerably. The large British regions hide so much of the regional discrepancies that they all fall within 60–83 per cent of the EC average. In Spain, with a population much lower than that of Britain or Germany, each of fifty provinces is listed as a region, which tends to magnify the extent of regional discrepancies. These obvious problems of lack of comparability are of course only the first of a series of statistical obstacles to a true understanding of the EC's regional problems. Any attempts at sophisticated analysis of the economic prosperity of the various regions appears misguided while the basic data are so unreliable.

The Nature of Regional Problems in the EC(6), EC(9) and EC(12)

The major regional disparities existing in the original Community of the Six in and after 1958 were those of the large agricultural regions of the Mezzogiorno of Italy and the south and west of France, which did not share in the rapid industrialisation which took place in those two countries from the mid-1950s onwards. They therefore suffered from low levels of income per head relative to the more prosperous regions, high levels of unemployment, high outward migration rates, and indeed a progressive depopulation. There were other regional problems within the Six in the 1960s (for example, the high unemployment in the declining industrial area of southern Belgium), but such problems of industrial regions were far outweighed by those of the major rural areas.

The first enlargement of the Community brought new dimensions to the regional problems contained within its member states. Denmark added a small country that constituted in itself a very high income region relative to the rest of the Community's regions. Ireland was a member state which constituted a single largely agricultural region with a level of income per head less than half the Community average, and comparable with all but the poorest regions of the Mezzogiorno. The major change concerned the accession of the United Kingdom. With a high level of productivity and income in its small agricultural sector, the regional problems were those of declining industrial areas. And the regional problems of these northern and western regions were characterised not so much by income disparities as by differences in the levels of unemployment. Outward migration, which was an important indicator of the regional problems in the Six, hardly figures in the UK's regional problems.

Accession of the three applicants in the second enlargement will again alter the overall balance of the regional problem within the Community. Here the regional problems are characterised by the concentration of most industrial development in a single region in Portugal and Greece, or a few regions in Spain, to the neglect and depopulation of much of the rest of the national territory. While Spain's regional distribution of income per head is similar to that of Italy, most of the Portuguese regions are much poorer. Thus the second enlargement will increase the maximum disparity between the richest and the poorest regions within the Community. At the same time it will re-emphasise the type of regional problem which was most prominent in the EC(6), rather than that which the UK contributed to the EC(9). However, economic trends in the 1970s have caused other industrial regions within the Community to share the UK problem.

The Effects of Economic Integration on Regional Problems

Economic integration may have two kinds of effects on regional disparities. First, there is a purely statistical effect mentioned above, that the pattern of regional differences under the various indicators will be different for a larger group of countries than within the individual member states, or within the smaller Community before enlargement. Though purely statistical, such an effect may have political consequences, since attention is drawn to the wider disparities, and there may be demands for the Community to take action to reduce them.

The second effect, that the integration of the national economies and the harmonisation of policies may itself create or exacerbate regional problems, is more important. In the EC(6) three main reasons were adduced why integration might worsen the regional problems of the member states.[4] Intensification of competition after the removal of tariffs and other barriers to trade would, deliberately, drive out of business inefficient and high-cost firms. If within the same region other firms expanded and new firms were established to create as much or more new employment and income, there could be a positive, or at least not a negative, overall effect. But some problem regions, which already suffered a relatively high-cost, uncompetitive economic structure, might be badly placed to create new employment in a more competitive environment. A second effect would be that the common market would create a tendency towards an equalisation of the earnings of labour and capital throughout the Community, as a result of the growth of trade, and of mobility of labour and capital. Although this might increase the incomes per head of those in work in the less prosperous regions, it would also tend to increase their unemployment rates, and slow down their economic development. Thirdly, it was feared that these effects of integration would harm especially those regions most remote from the market centres of the Community. There was much evidence to suggest that remote location was a major cause of regional problems, and unification of the markets throughout the EC would make some regions more remote than they had been in their national economies. For example, while the Saar and Lorraine became more central within the EC, the Mezzogiorno and south-west France became more peripheral. Although these arguments for the effects of integration on regions are not easily tested, they are certainly plausible. Their significance is also increased by Myrdal's concept of 'cumulative causation', whereby an initial loss of competitive strength, possibly deriving from effects of integration, may bring about a progressive decline in the prosperity of a region.

So far as the applicant countries are concerned, there is every indication that membership of the Community, whatever other advantages it may bring, will intensify regional imbalances. The three countries have in the past decade been undergoing a process of rapid industrialisation. They have therefore also experienced a similar rural exodus to that experienced some decades earlier in other parts of the EC, and much earlier in the case of the United Kingdom. The population of the urban and industrial centres has swollen as people have left the countryside. Although the benefits of industrialisation are appreciated, there has been a desire to moderate this movement in order to avoid the depopulation of vast areas of the country. A major aim of regional policy has therefore been to foster the development of smaller urban centres, outside the major industrial growth areas, so as to spread economic development more widely through the national territory. Regional policy has been little developed in Greece and Portugal, but in the context of the Spanish development plans attempts have been made to develop suitable industries in smaller centres, such as Burgos, Valladolid and Zaragoza, to avoid the congestion of industrial and population growth in Madrid, Barcelona and the northern coast. At the same time a feature of Spanish industrial growth has been that production is protected by tariffs, and carried on at relatively high costs to meet demand in the domestic market. Many products are therefore uncompetitive in terms of quality, marketability, and so on, in other EC countries. Following entry into the Community and the removal of the tariffs during the transitional period, it will be necessary to meet the keener competition both in the domestic market and in the wider Community market. It will therefore be necessary to shift the strategy of industrial development away from the elements of import substitution which characterise the present position, towards an export-oriented growth. If this transition is to be made successfully, it will be necessary to concentrate efforts on achieving internal and external economies of scale in the most favoured industrial centres. This may mean emphasising the development of Athens, Lisbon, Madrid, Barcelona, Guipuzcoa and Vizcaya, to the detriment of smaller industrial centres. This in turn could intensify the process of 'desertification' of rural areas, which will be deprived of the closer contact with urban centres that national regional policies have aimed to provide. If these broad generalisations are near to describing what is, of course, a more complicated picture, membership of the EC poses a serious dilemma for regional policy in the applicant countries. It raises the strong possibility that membership of the Community will not only bring about a statistical increase in the indicators of regional disparities, but also a real divergence, an increase in the gap between the richest and the poorest regions of the EC(12).

The Regional Policy of the European Community

Despite the difficulty of measuring the regional effects of the EC on its member states, the arguments about the possible effects of integration were broadly accepted. It was therefore thought to be socially and politically essential to redistribute some of the gains from integration to those regions that were supposed to have suffered, at least relatively, from the process of integration. This meant, in the main, assistance to the major problem region of the Six, the

Mezzogiorno, and took the form of the use of the Social Fund, and the channelling of a large proportion of the loans from the European Investment Bank in that direction. The sums involved were small relative to the size of the problem, and relative to the size of the regional efforts being made by the Italian government. The impetus to create a more effective regional policy came with British accession in 1973. Since the British were sensitive to the fact that the balance of existing Community policies meant that they would have to make large contributions of duties, levies and value-added tax to the Community Budget after the end of the transitional arrangements in 1980, they pressed for a shift in the balance which would have the effect of increasing their receipts.[5] A new Community regional fund appeared a satisfactory way to achieve this shift, without endangering the *acquis communautaire* of the Common Agricultural Policy.

However, in creating a new European Regional Development Fund (ERDF), it was hardly possible to direct all the EC subsidies to the UK's industrial problem regions, while ignoring the rural areas that had so far been assisted in other ways within the Six. The new Fund therefore had to develop complicated criteria for both kinds of regions. Given the greater poverty of the Italian regions, Italy was allocated the largest share, 40 per cent, for the first three years 1975–7. The UK was allocated a quota of 28 per cent, slightly altered for the following three years, 1978–80. But the detail of the operation of the ERDF will not be discussed in this chapter. The important feature of this Fund in relation to the present discussion is that it is very small. For the three years 1978–80 the total commitment agreed by the Council of Ministers is 1,850m. EUA (about £1,230m.). This compares with a total Community Budget for the single year 1979 of 13,700m. EUA. This total Budget is in turn only some 2½ per cent of the total of all national budgets of the member states, or 0·8 per cent of their total GDP. In discussing the Regional Fund of the EC, it is therefore important to remember that at least until 1980 it was merely a token contribution to the solution of regional problems. To say this is not to criticise the efforts made by the Regional Policy Directorate-General of the EC Commission to make a real contribution in addition to the much larger regional policies operated by the member states. The reason for the smallness of the ERDF is the refusal of the governments of the member states to agree in the Council to increase its size. Even when, in the autumn of 1978, the self-interest of Italy and the United Kingdom led them to refrain from voting in the Council of Finance Ministers to reject the proposal of the European Parliament for a substantial increase in the Fund for 1979, British reluctance to allow a development that might seem to increase the powers of the Parliament, and therefore to undermine UK sovereignty, led the UK to refuse to vote for the increase in the total size of the Budget that was needed to give effect to the increase in the ERDF.[6]

In considering the relevance of the ERDF to the regional problems of the applicants it is essential to bear in mind both the smallness of the present Fund and the obstacles in the way of substantially increasing it. It is true that the regional policies of the three applicant countries are so little developed that even a share in the small ERDF would make a proportionally more significant contribution to regional policy in those countries than it does in the existing member states. Yet the total aid seems likely to be small relative to the GDPs of those countries. It is impossible to forecast how much they might receive after accession, but a Commission simulation, based on 1978 data for Spain and Portugal, suggested that they might receive respectively 190m. EUA and 125m. EUA from the ERDF.[7] Naturally, following the accession of three countries with such severe regional problems there will be a strong pressure for an increase in the size of the Regional Fund. But there will also be powerful resistances to its increase, and it would be wrong to be too hopeful that it could bring massive help to the new members. Resistance on the part of the wealthier member states must be expected to continue, for reasons of *parsimony* (the financial burden would fall mostly on them) and of *economic ideology* (opposition, especially in Germany, to too much state intervention). Enlargement might also turn the UK from a supporter of a larger regional fund into an opponent, because in the revision of national quotas that would ensue, the British proportion might be reduced to a point close to its share in total contributions to the Budget, thus removing the net transfer that has so far been received from the Regional Fund.

The small payments out of the ERDF are made in supplementation of national regional aids, and there are detailed rules for the acceptability of projects for this additional aid which cannot be examined here. But there is an important issue concerning the relationship between Community and national aids which must be discussed. The Community in developing its regional policy has attempted to avoid raising the issue of income transfers among the member states. This is consistent with its general approach to the discussion of contributions to and receipts from the Budget, and more generally to the question of the costs and benefits of integration. The Commission has attempted (for good motives of attempting to increase political solidarity in the Community, and avoiding arguments among the member states about who is benefiting the most) to discourage member states from thinking in terms of *juste retour*, and to develop the concept of the *ressources propres* which the Community will dispense in accordance with common needs. The regional aspect of this general approach is the concept of 'additionality': that ERDF grants are made in addition to whatever the member states may be doing to help their regions, and that what the member states do should not be reduced on account of their receipts from the ERDF. As the Thomson Report stated back in 1973: 'it should be emphasised that the Community is here concerned with problems linked to certain limited geographical areas. For it is not the role of Community regional policy to act as an overall corrective to all economic problems affecting the growth rate of a member state'.[8] This principle entailed that the Fund should be 'used in a manner quite independent of any criterion of *juste retour*, to tackle regional problems according to their size and urgency'.

However, the economic growth of a national 'region' cannot in practice be dissociated from the progress of its component subregions. And if Community funds are directed towards the more urgent and significant regional problems, as judged by Community-wide criteria, the possibility of transfers among the member states must be a real one, whatever attempts are made to hide what is happening. It is thus superfluous to argue whether or not Community funds should give regional aid to member states. If regions are to be given effective aids not based on *juste retour*, member states will *ipso facto* have to receive transfers. This effect is quite transparent in the general acceptance that the Fund, while it may directly finance its own programmes in 'non-quota' areas of special common interest, such as cross-border regions, normally works indirectly by financing national programmes of aid to regions. Since regional aids continue to be financed largely from national funds, the possibility is left open for national governments to diminish national financing in line with the growth of Community financing. No doubt this is contary to Community policy, but unless done blatantly it is impossible to police. Community regional aids are thus in practice indistinguishable from Community subventions to member states. But even if earmarking were carried out so successfully that Community aids did represent a net addition to total aids to a region, economic interdependence of the regions with their national economies could result in the leakage of much of the aid. Community checks on the type of activity eligible for Community-financed assistance could be nullified by the switch of nationally financed programmes towards projects with high spillovers outside the regions.

A Broader View of Community Regional Policy

Community policies other than the Regional Fund have an impact on the national economies and on their regions. This was recognised in a decision in 1977 to include 'regional impact' assessment in the assessment of all policy proposals. But to do this in respect of the detail of new policy proposals may not be sufficient. It is also necessary to assess the regional impact of existing Community policies, since the overall regional effects of the EC are determined by these, as well as by the ERDF. Two major areas need examination. The first is the regional impact of the Common Agricultural Policy. The second is the action of the Community to prevent distortion of trade.

A comprehensive assessment of the regional impact of the Agricultural Policy would be beyond the scope of this chapter. It would require an economic analysis of the effects not only of the distribution of EAGGF spending, but also of the burden of the duties and levies that finance the Budget, and of the true incidence of the monetary compensatory amounts which are associated with the maintenance of the special 'green' exchange rates for the operation of the policy. It is generally accepted that the EAGGF expenditures are concentrated on some of the wealthier member states (Denmark, Netherlands, France, Germany) as well as on one of the poorer member states (Ireland). The MCAs appeared in the late 1970s to assist especially the high-cost but wealthy German farmers to compete with lower-cost French, Italian and British farmers.[9] However, they also benefit consumers in those countries by keeping down the prices of foodstuffs. Duties and levies fall heavily on one relatively poor member state, the UK, whose imports from third countries are relatively high. The EAGGF certainly benefits northern agricultural producers, for whose products high prices are maintained by mostly open-ended support regimes, rather than Mediterranean producers, for whom generous regimes have not yet been adopted. Within each member state the EAGGF appears to operate regressively, because the method of supporting incomes of farmers via the prices of farm products concentrates assistance on the large (and efficient) producers in the more favoured regions.

These questions concerning the regional impact of the EAGGF are highly relevant to the question of enlargement. The Commission points out, for example, that Spanish price support and other assistance for the production of beef and maize in the north-western regions, with a productivity less than 50 per cent of the Spanish national average, have been higher in recent years than those available under the Common Agricultural Policy.[10] Adoption of the CAP could therefore in this instance undermine the economy of an already poor region. Even more serious could be the effect of the overall structure of the CAP on the Portuguese economy. Because Portugal imports a high proportion of its foodstuffs, there would be a heavy burden of levies or of higher-cost imports if they were diverted to come from the EC instead of from third countries. Export restitutions affecting existing imports from the Community would also be lost. Unless the policy were considerably adapted to meet the needs of Portugal, it could therefore operate in a regressive way. Thus while most farmers in all three countries might expect to gain from EAGGF expenditures, some farmers would probably lose, and the overall effect of the policy could even be negative for the nation as a whole.

The applicant countries would benefit from the Guidance section of the EAGGF, and this would in fact bring financial assistance to agriculture of a similar order of magnitude to the receipts from the ERDF. The Commission estimated that Spain would have received 200–250m. EUA and Portugal 50–100m. EUA if they had been members in 1978 and existing policies had been applied in those countries.[11] But the Guidance section is only a tiny proportion of the EAGGF, and the Guarantee section expenditures are made largely without reference to regional needs. Indeed, as noted above, they are at present concentrated in the northern areas of the existing Community.

As in the case of the Regional Fund, there would be pressure after enlargement for a revision of the Common Agricultural Policy to direct more of the EAGGF expenditures towards the poorer southern European farmers, though this would meet with strong resistance in the existing member states. They have already resisted British attempts to alter the balance of the Policy to make it more helpful to poorer consumers. And while Italy and France are to some extent allies in attempting to shift the balance more towards Mediterranean producers, the British would be on the other side in this matter, since they would see it as an attempt to ensure that British consumers pay high prices not only for northern but also for southern agricultural products.

Regional Aids and Competition Policy

In discussing regional policy it is often forgotten that the Community has a separate strand of regional policy, which consists in the attempts to control distortions of competition in the free internal market. The necessity of subsidies provided under national programmes of regional aid is accepted, and indeed the Commission attempts to promote effective programmes through its own research, advice and conferences, in addition to the use of its own Regional Fund to provide additional financial assistance. But this 'positive' policy is not at all inconsistent with a 'negative' policy which should at the same time control and harmonise regional aids in order to create and maintain fair conditions for trade within the Community. While there have been a few instances of national regional policies being abandoned or adapted in the light of objections raised by the Commission under Articles 92 and 93 of the Rome Treaty (for example the UK Selective Employment Tax and its associated Regional Employment Premium), this aspect of regional policy appears to have had only slight effect. However, it could become more serious as a constraint on national policies if the Community should succeed in developing a common industrial policy. At present unharmonised national regional policies are merely one aspect of competitive industrial promotion which prevents the creation of viable European industrial structures.

The impact of this aspect of EC policy on regional balance in the applicant countries after membership can only be assessed in broad outline. They would benefit from any increase in the effectiveness of Community attempts to control the proliferation of regional aids in the central areas of the Community. However, the past few years of rising unemployment throughout the EC have seen a great extension of industrial aids, and also restrictive policies, some organised at Community level, as in the case of steel and textiles, which if continued would assist sensitive industries to compete in some of the industries that are of most interest to the applicant countries. Accommodation of these industries in the new members within existing EC policies is already being developed, but the outcome may not be to give them the freedom to compete which might be considered a natural benefit to be expected from membership. The question of a more far-reaching industrial strategy for the Community appears so unrealistic as to be hardly worth discussing. It may however be noted that if any such strategy were devised, and if the new members were given a fair participation in the 'allocation' of industrial production that would be envisaged, it would be unlikely that this would be such as to assist them in spreading industrial development more evenly through their territories. The natural result of such a policy would be to strengthen the concentration on their already highly developed regions.

Another aspect of the operation of a free internal market that should be mentioned here is free movement of labour. In the past years of rapid movement of labour out of the agricultural sector in the three applicant countries an important social and economic safety valve, given the inability of the cities and industry to absorb all the manpower involved, has been emigration to the industrial areas of the EC. Although the Rome Treaty provisions for free movement do not apply to workers from the applicant countries so far, the major flows of labour have been, with the exception of Italy, from the applicant countries (and Yugoslavia and Turkey). One advantage of membership should be that the right of free movement will have to be granted to the applicants, so ensuring this important element in their economic development. However, the situation has changed radically in recent years, and it now appears likely that free movement will be modified by restrictions during a long transitional period (seven years in the Greek case) and that in any case it will not be as important an assistance to their industrialisation as had appeared. The chief determinant of emigration appears to be the demand for workers in the labour importing countries. With higher levels of unemployment in the 1970s this demand has fallen away, and the prospects for its revival in the 1980s appear to be poor. Thus another negative item needs to be noted by the applicants in respect of the economic, and especially regional, implications of membership.

EMS, Monetary Union and Regional Disparities[12]

The regional impact of monetary union has so far been a problem primarily for Italy and the United Kingdom within the existing Community. Though both countries joined in the initial attempt to move towards monetary union, the 'snake' arrangement for limiting the margins of short-term fluctuation of the exchange rates in 1972, both were forced to withdraw after a short while. Since the experience of operating a floating currency has in both cases, however, not been at all successful, they have both participated in the development of the new European Monetary System (EMS) in 1978–9. Italy has joined the system formally, though with a wider margin of 6½ per cent. Britain, for both economic and political reasons, remains only associated with the EMS for the moment. Although the EMS is only a small step towards monetary union, and one whose success must remain doubtful until there is more experience of its operation, its existence poses the question of the exchange rate policy of the three applicant countries, as well as the more general question of the macroeconomic effects of membership. Will they remain outside this system, and other moves which may be made towards monetary union, for a decade or more? What would be the consequences of this policy for their economies and for their position in the Community? Or will they seek to join at an early date, and what would be the consequences of keeping their exchange rates more closely in line, and eventually fixed, with those of the stronger economies in the EC?

The natural method by which weak countries and regions within a monetary union are assisted to stay within it, and by which its consequences for them are made acceptable, is that financial transfers are made from the wealthier towards the poorer regions. Within an EC monetary union, the solution appears to be the same. However, there is by no means unanimous agreement that this should happen, and indeed there is strong pressure to retain the existing EC budgetary situation, in which the overall position of regressivity which arises from the predominance of the EAGGF and the structure of the Agricultural Policy is only slightly offset by the small Regional Fund and other structural funds such as the Guidance section of the EAGGF and the Social Fund.

Transfers of funds could take place in two ways: by means of transfers within the Community Budget, or by way of loans which could be channelled through the Budget or could be derived from the European Investment Bank, or even through bilateral inter-state loans. Examples exist of all three methods of making loans, though the totals so far have not been very great. It is also possible to link loans and outright grants, by giving subsidies to the interest payable on the loans. This method has been developed by the EC in connection specifically with the EMS; loans to Italy and to Ireland to assist them to stay within the system will be supported by interest rate subsidies of 3 per cent through the Budget. But the sums involved are again small, and indeed much smaller than those countries had requested. The loans, and interest subsidies, that would have to be given to the three applicants if they joined the EMS might be larger. Moreover, since the EMS leaves the power to change the central rate in the hands of the national governments (though after consultation), it presents a much smaller problem of transfers than would a full monetary union. If the EMS is to develop into a monetary union, the size of the transfers would thus have to be much greater.

More fundamentally, one may question whether the approach via loans is realistic. To support the new members in this way even if they remained outside the EMS, and certainly if they were to participate in a monetary union, would be to push them into long-term indebtedness. For the issue is not merely one of short-term needs for balance-of-payments' support, but one of long-term structural imbalance, which must be expected to persist for many years. The regional problems of the individual member states of the EC have proved remarkably difficult to solve, despite years of active and generous regional policies. It is unlikely that the regional problems of the Community as a whole will be solved in a shorter period. Moreover, the weaker regions within the member states are supported not only by regional policy as such but by the whole transfer system of the unitary state. Unemployment benefits, relief of income and corporation tax, and other income transfers, many of which go unrecorded because they are so automatic, maintain the economies of the weaker regions. Within the European Community not only will such transfers (which are effectively grants, not loans) not take place, but if recent trends persist there may actually continue to be regressive income transfers from the weaker to the stronger economies.

Concluding Comments

The conclusion of this analysis is that there will need to be a radical reappraisal of the structure of the EC's policies and of its Budget if enlargement is to promote the convergence of the new members and especially of their weaker regions. Reliance on the supposed dynamic gains from trade, and on an expected expansion of regional policy at the Community level, would be hazardous, as the British experience has shown. The Community need not bring benefits to the economies of the new members as a whole; it will probably operate to worsen rather than to improve their regional problems; and the likelihood of adequate compensation through development of the existing Regional Fund of the Community, and generally through the Budget, is small. Joining the EMS, and eventual monetary union, would exacerbate the problems of membership for the weaker economies and regions. Development of income transfers to help the weaker member states and regions could redress the position. But of this there is no sign; on the contrary, the stronger member states show every sign of continuing to hold on to the advantages they derive from the customs union itself, from the Agricultural Policy, from the EMS, and to make only token gestures towards the type of progressive inter-regional income transfers that are an integral part of existing economic unions.

It may well be that the three applicants, like those of the first round of enlargement of the EC, can see no alternative to membership, both politically and economically. However, they should at least be clear about the difficulties, and understand that they face a hard struggle, during their entry negotiations and later, to ensure that the Community operates to the advantage and not to the detriment of their economies as a whole and of their weaker regions in particular. For a Community of Six, regional policy was a problem of limited dimensions, which agricultural transfers in some ways assisted. For a Community of Nine, regional divergence has proved a far more complex problem, which has met with only a token response. For a Community of Twelve it will present a much larger challenge, which the member states have so far shown themselves reluctant in the extreme to meet.

Notes: Chapter 7

1 This simplification is based on Robert Mundell, 'The theory of optimum currency areas', *American Economic Review*, 1961.
2 These data are derived from D. Biehl, 'The impact of enlargement on the regional development and regional policy in the European Community', in W. Wallace and I. Herreman (eds.), *A Community of Twelve?: The Impact of Further Enlargement on the European Communies* (De Tempel, Bruges, 1978).
3 Biehl, op. cit.
4 This account is based on that contained in G. McCrone, 'Regional policy in the European Communities', in G. R. Denton (ed.), *Economic Integration in Europe* (Weidenfeld & Nicolson, London, 1969).

5 See Chapter 5 on the Budget problem.
6 House of Lords, Select Committee on the European Communities, Session 1979–1980, 2nd Report, *EEC Budget* (HMSO, London, June 1979).
7 'Enlargement of the Community: economic and sectoral aspects', *Bulletin of the European Communities*, Supplement 3/78, Brussels, 1978.
8 *Report on the Regional Problems in the Enlarged Community* (Thomson Report), COM(73)550 (Commission of the European Communities, Brussels, 1973).
9 Y. S. Hu, 'German agricultural power: the impact on France and Britain', *The World Today*, November 1979.
10 'Opinion on Spain's application for membership', *Bulletin of the European Communities*, Supplement 9/78, Brussels, 1978.
11 ibid.
12 See Chapter 6 on the European Monetary System.

8

Economic Divergence and Enlargement

Loukas Tsoukalis

While people are extremely worried about the continuing divergence in economic performance and its adverse effects on the cohesion of the Community of Nine, the second round of enlargement with the accession of Greece, Portugal and Spain can only worsen the present situation. The entry of the three southern European countries, which are usually classified in the group of 'newly industrialising countries' (NICs), will add considerably to the economic divergence within the Community, manifested in terms of rates of inflation and unemployment, or in levels of industrialisation and income. During the 1960s discussions about convergence were usually centred on the need to co-ordinate short-term economic policies. This remained true of the early approaches towards economic and monetary union (EMU). It was therefore inevitable that people would tend to concentrate on short-term trends of which inflation rates constituted the main focus of attention. After the entry of Britain, Ireland and Denmark, which also coincided with the first major economic crisis since the end of the Second World War, the emphasis has gradually switched towards structural differences. Although the recent creation of the European Monetary System (EMS) brought the continuing divergence in inflation rates into the limelight again, nobody still seriously believes that an effective co-ordination of short-term economic policies can be a necessary and sufficient prerequisite for the creation of a complete EMU. Persisting structural differences and the experience of the early 1970s made political leaders in member countries more cautious about their long-term objectives.

With respect to the Mediterranean enlargement of the Community, it can be argued that the motivations have been predominantly political on both sides of the negotiating table. The pro-marketeers in the three applicant countries saw membership of the Community as a means of consolidating parliamentary democracy and obtaining international recognition after long years of isolation. The governments of the Nine saw enlargement as contributing to political stability in the region. Moreover, no one seemed prepared to veto an application coming from a democratic European country which declared itself prepared to accept the *acquis communautaire*. But although both sides have tended to concentrate on the political aspects of enlargement, the success of the whole operation will be decided mainly in the economic area. This success will depend on the ability of the three economies to withstand the shock of Community membership and the ability of both sides to adjust. Ideally, policies should be designed to promote the process of adjustment.

Given the limited space available here, it is virtually impossible to tackle the subject of economic divergence and enlargement in a satisfactory way. Of necessity I shall have to concentrate on the analysis of some macro variables, while what we surely need, if we want to have a better understanding of the recent economic development of the three Mediterranean countries and also make some projections into the future, is more disaggregated data and a sector-by-sector analysis. Moreover, we also need to look into socioeconomic variables and, therefore, avoid the trap of a simple, economistic approach to the subject.

The above is a list of good intentions and objectives which can be fulfilled only partly in the space of this chapter. What follows is some preliminary ideas about the implications of enlargement for economic divergence in the European Community. I start with some general indicators of recent economic performance in the Nine and the Three and then proceed to discuss the likely effects of accession of Greece, Spain and Portugal on both sides. I end with three different scenarios for the development of the Community of Twelve, and it seems only fair that the reader should be warned of the strong voluntaristic approach adopted there.

Some General Comparisons

All three applicant countries have relatively low GDPs per capita. The difference from the Community average varies considerably depending on whether GDP is measured at current prices and exchange rates or on the basis of some form of purchasing power parity. In 1977 GDP per capita in Spain, at current prices and exchange rates, was 51·6 per cent of the Community average. The corresponding figures were 46·4 per cent for Greece and 27·4 per cent for Portugal.[1] According to calculations made by the Commission for 1976, using purchasing power parities, the figures obtained were considerably more favourable for the three countries, namely, 65·3 per cent for Greece, 64·5 per cent for Spain and 41·9 per cent for

Portugal.[2] Greece and Spain are therefore at about the same level as Ireland and only a small distance behind Italy, while the third applicant country lags far behind. National income statistics, however, give only a very broad indication of the level of welfare in different countries. Leaving aside the problem of exchange rate variability, we are still faced with another variable factor, the so-called 'hidden economy', which seems to have acquired an increasing importance during the recent economic recession.

Regional inequalities will be much worse. According to estimates in the MacDougall Report, the ratio between the richest and the poorest region in the Community of Nine was 4·4:1 in 1970.[3] This estimate was based on GDP figures at purchasing power parity exchange rates. On the basis of available data for the fifty provinces in Spain, this ratio would slightly worsen when Spain becomes a member of the Community. The ten poorest provinces situated around Madrid and along the frontier with Portugal have a per capita GDP which in 1975 was between 32 and 37 per cent of the Community average.[4] Regional data for Greece and Portugal are not available and we can only guess that the minimum/maximum ratio of regional disparities in the Community of Twelve will be worse than 1:10, given the level of per capita income in Portugal.[5]

During the period 1960–73 all three countries enjoyed higher rates of growth than the Community of Six or Nine (Table 8.1) or even any individual member country. The figures in this table also suggest that fast growth was mainly industry-induced (at least as far as the manufacturing sector is concerned). But the relatively low rates of growth for agriculture should not also be taken to imply slow growth in productivity rates. As data in Table 8.2 show, there has been a radical transformation in the distribution of the labour force, particularly in Greece and Spain which both lost more than half of their farming population in the course of seventeen years. In the case of Portugal, the sudden reversal of the downward trend which appears in 1977 can be attributed to the 1974 revolution and the subsequent land reform, the massive inflow of 'retornados' and the dramatic fall in manufacturing output. Nevertheless, the three countries still have a much higher percentage of their labour force engaged in agriculture than is true of the Community as a whole and than any individual member country with the exception of Ireland. Going back to Table 8.1, the experience of the years 1973–7 suggests that although the economies of the three countries used to grow at a faster rate than those of the existing members of the Community, they were, however, seriously affected by the international recession and the political transition at home.

During the 1960s, Greece achieved a remarkable combination of fast rates of growth and price stability (Table 8.3). Since 1970 Greece

Table 8.1　*Growth rates*

	1960–5	1965–70	1970–3	1973–7
Greece				
GDP per capita (volume)	7·3	6·7	7·2	2·0
GDP (volume)	7·9	7·3	7·8	2·9
Manufacturing	9·1	10·0	12·1	4·1[2]
Agriculture	6·4	2·4	1·9	2·9[2]
Portugal				
GDP per capita (volume)	5·7	6·6	8·9	0·0
GDP (volume)	6·3	6·2	8·6	2·1
Manufacturing	9·1	8·3	11·5	−3·3[3]
Agriculture	2·2	1·3	0·0	−2·0[3]
Spain				
GDP per capita (volume)	7·5	5·3	6·0	1·4
GDP (volume)	8·6	6·4	7·2	2·6
Manufacturing	12·1	7·8	11·0	3·1[3]
Agriculture	2·9	3·5	3·8	1·7[3]
EC[1]				
GDP per capita (volume)	3·8	4·0	3·8	1·6
GDP volume	4·8	4·7	4·5	1·8

Notes:　1　Data for the EC until 1973 cover only the six original members. This will also apply subsequently, unless otherwise mentioned.
　　　　　2　1973–6.
　　　　　3　1973–5.
Sources:　OECD, *National Accounts*, various issues, and OECD, *Main Economic Indicators*, various issues.

has climbed up many steps of the inflation ladder and has now caught up with the fastest inflating countries of the Community, namely, the UK, Ireland and Italy. On the other hand, Spain has been consistently running at faster rates of inflation than those experienced by Community countries. The same applies to post-1974 Portugal, where the various governments formed after the revolution proved unable to regain control over prices. But one should also bear in mind that after 1974 the three countries experienced a wage explosion which followed the fall of dictatorships and a long period of political oppression which had, among other things, kept wages down.

　　In all three countries the state has played a decisive role in economic development. In Spain its area of activities has been the most extensive, with the state engaged in indicative planning and also acting as an important entrepreneur. In Greece its main power lay in its control over the financial system. As far as Portugal is concerned, the

Table 8.2 *Distribution of the labour force*

	1960	1965	1970	1973	1977
Greece					
Agriculture	57·0	52·4	47·2	35·1	28·4
Industry	17·8	19·7	22·4	28·0	30·3
Other activities	25·2	27·9	30·5	36·9	41·3
Portugal					
Agriculture	42·8	37·1	33·0	27·0	32·5
Industry	29·5	33·4	35·7	34·4	33·1
Other activities	27·7	29·5	31·2	38·5	34·4
Spain					
Agriculture	42·3	33·6	29·6	24·3	20·7
Industry	32·5	35·9	37·4	36·7	37·6
Other activities	25·7	30·6	33·0	39·0	41·7
EC					
Agriculture	21·0	16·4	10·6	9·3	8·2
Industry	42·2	44·2	43·1	42·0	39·8
Other activities	36·8	39·4	46·3	48·7	51·9

Source: OECD, *Labour Force Statistics*, various issues.

Salazar−Caetano regime almost identified the 'national interest' with the interests of an economic oligarchy. After the revolution the public sector was considerably increased and now the state has direct control over the financial sector and a major part of the manufacturing sector. In both Spain and Greece the state has also played an important supporting role by providing the economic infrastructure and also offering a series of different incentives and subsidies with the aim of encouraging domestic and foreign investment. On the other hand, we could debate for a long time as to whether the low level of research and development (with the consequent high dependence on foreign technology), the regional disequilibria and the inequality of income distribution, to mention but a few of the problems associated with economic development in the three countries, were inevitable in view of the development model adopted or were mainly a function of the kind of political regimes they had. One obvious failure in all three countries has been the low labour absorption of the industrialisation process. In this respect, and apart from the human cost involved, labour migration may have played a very negative role by providing the safety valve for the governments concerned.

Fast rates of growth have also coincided with the gradual opening of the three economies to international economic exchange. The timing was very close and certainly not coincidental. Governments

Table 8.3   *Consumer prices (averages of annual rates)*

	1961–70	1971–9
Belgium	3·0	7·5
Denmark	5·9	9·5
France	4·0	9·2
Germany	2·7	5·1
Ireland	4·8	13·2
Italy[1]	3·9	13·0
Luxembourg	2·6	6·7
Netherlands	4·1	7·4
UK	4·1	13·2
EC-9[2]	3·7	9·0
Greece	2·1	13·2
Portugal[1, 3]	3·9	18·8
Spain[1]	6·0	15·3

Notes: 1   Break in series: 1977.
2   Calculated as weighted averages of percentage changes, using private consumption weights and exchange rates.
3   Excluding rent.
Source: OECD, *Economic Surveys*.

were influenced by the advice offered by international organisations, the process of economic liberalisation which was taking place in the Western system, and European economic integration. The opening of the three economies was greatly facilitated by the economic boom of the 1960s and early 1970s. Their integration into the Western economic system played a determining role in the rapid industrialisation of Greece, Portugal and Spain. It provided them with markets for their exports, which in many cases was of fundamental importance given the small size of domestic markets. Invisible earnings and capital inflows provided the foreign exchange which was necessary for the balancing of trade deficits. Investment by transnational enterprises added to domestic savings, while it also provided access to technology and oligopolistic markets. Export of capital to the three countries was matched, so to speak, by an export of labour to the north which played an important political and economic role.

There is certainly an alternative way of presenting the effects of 'outward-looking' policies in the three countries. If we approach the problem from a more critical angle, we can talk of an industrialisation process which has led to an increasing dependence on foreign trade and technology, which has created a dualistic economy, serious regional and structural disequilibria and a highly unequal distribution of income. It has also brought about the adoption of foreign consumption habits which do not correspond to the standard of living already achieved in those countries. Last but not least, this rapid process of industrialisation did not solve the problem of unemployment and this forced hundreds of thousands of workers to leave their country in search of jobs abroad.

The two pictures presented above do not actually contradict each other. The development of the three Mediterranean countries has not been an autonomous development – whatever this word actually means in the post-war economic system. The development model adopted did not lead to the creation of an integrated industrial structure and it often implied a high price in social terms. Having said that, we can go on to question, together with Munoz, Roldan and Serrano,[6] the feasibility of 'autonomous miracles' in our time. On the other hand, we can add some qualifications to the conclusions reached by centre-periphery theorists. On the export side, the three countries are still below the world average in terms of their dependence on exports (their share of world exports of manufactures being lower than their share of world industrial production).[7] As regards their dependence on foreign capital, this is certainly not higher than what we find in small member countries of the Community, such as Belgium. We also have to bear in mind that the bargaining power of relatively small countries in their early stages of industrialisation, with shortages of capital and technology, cannot be very strong. However, this will not necessarily change in a period of prolonged international recession, when unemployment is rising and local entrepreneurs are not ready to undertake new investment.

Together with all existing members of the Community, the three applicant countries have been hit hard by the world recession and the energy crisis. On the one hand they are all heavily dependent on imported energy resources, while on the other they cannot balance the negative effect in their terms of trade by passing on the price increases to foreign consumers of their own products. Foreign demand for their exports of traditional consumer goods is more price-elastic than the demand for capital and high-technology goods which are more characteristic of the exports of advanced industrialised countries. The economic crisis led to a worsening of their balance of payments. It was most strongly felt in Portugal which in the end was forced to accept the full rigour of the IMF therapy in order to obtain much-needed international credit. For the other two countries, and especially Greece, the balance of payments could very quickly become a serious constraint on economic growth.

With the collapse of the Bretton Woods system and faced with a worsening situation in their balance of payments, the three southern European countries floated their currencies downwards. According to the effective exchange rate index constructed by the IMF for each individual currency,[8] the depreciation between 1970 and 1978 was 43·71 per cent for the escudo, 36·29 per cent for the drachma and 23·60 per cent for the peseta. For the sake of comparison, the corresponding figures for the same period were 42·45 per cent for the lira and 30·63 per cent for the pound sterling. The realisation that devaluations in open economies can have only a limited effect on the balance of payments while at the same time contributing to the creation of an inflationary spiral in the country partly accounts for the renewed interest in stable exchange rates and the EMS.[9]

Although institutional relations with the European Community have differed from one country to the other, the degree of dependence reached in trade with the Nine is very similar. In 1977 exports to the Community as a percentage of total exports of goods ranged from 46·3 to 51·7 per cent, with an average of intra-Community trade for existing members of 50·7 per cent. Their import dependence was considerably lower; it ranged from 33·8 to 43·6 per cent compared with an average of 49·4 per cent for intra-Community trade.[10] This difference can be explained in terms of the much higher rates of protection in the three countries. Greece's Association Agreement with the Community played an important role in the growth of its dynamic industries. Almost the same seems to apply to the Portuguese experience with EFTA. Spanish industrialisation has depended less on access to foreign markets. The size of the domestic market made a policy of import substitution no longer viable in Spain.

Implications for the Enlarged Community

Economic divergence in its different forms may be important in the European Community in so far as it has negative effects on the co-ordination of economic policies and the adoption of new common policies. Alternatively, it may have wider political repercussions in a Community which purports to have long-term political goals, notably to the extent that large income disparities persist despite, or because of, the opening of national frontiers. In a Community with members as different from each other as the Federal Republic of Germany and Portugal, the reconciliation of different economic interests may prove virtually impossible and may prejudice the emergence of a federation. In a political culture where equity ranks very high indeed on the ladder of social and political priorities, the creation of a political Community may not be feasible because of the internal tensions provoked by such wide income disparities. One remedy would be to reduce those disparities by transferring resources from rich to poor areas. But the scale of transfers needed would be huge, so the argument goes, and therefore politically unrealistic.

This argument has been voiced more frequently with the prospect of a Community of Twelve with wide economic divergences and income disparities. It is, however, open to question whether a Community of Nine makes much better sense. If the object is an economically cohesive group, or an 'optimum currency area' as some call it, then this would be viable only with those countries which remained in the old snake, namely, Germany, Benelux and Denmark. The Community of Nine has had many problems; the effect of the second round of enlargement may simply be to worsen them.

Economic divergence cannot be discussed in a vacuum. Its importance derives from the constraints that it sets on political and economic integration in the Community. Often the discussion about economic divergence appears to be one way of evading a fundamental and highly controversial question, namely, who gains and who loses from the process of integration. So far economic divergence between the Three and the Nine has been examined in purely static terms. But the marriage itself, which is in fact closer to polygamy, is likely to have important repercussions for both sides. These will depend largely on the kind of policies adopted as well as the type and length of transition periods after accession. Can we safely assume that Community policies and the model of integration it has followed until now will survive intact the entry of three new members? It is interesting to note that the first round of enlargement, when Britain, Ireland and Denmark became members, seems to have had very little effect on the package deal which had characterised until then the integration of the six founding members. This could be explained both in terms of the strong forces of inertia developed in the Community and in terms of the inability or unwillingness of a country like Britain to play an active role. But still, the discussion of the Mediterranean enlargement on the basis of a ceteris paribus assumption appears somewhat dubious if we look at some of the broad effects for both sides.[11]

The first question to ask about the three applicant countries is whether they will continue to grow faster than the existing members of the Community and therefore gradually close the income gap which separates them from most member countries. Trade liberalisation may lead to the extinction of a large number of small and inefficient firms which have survived until now behind protective barriers catering for the domestic market. This would have adverse repercussions on growth. Moreover, if trade liberalisation leads to a worsening of the balance-of-payments deficit which is not compensated for by an adequate transfer of resources from the rest of the Community, then deflationary policies would become necessary with further negative effects on growth. Commission estimates projected on the 1978 Budget for a Community of Twelve suggest that the net transfer through the Budget would amount to about 2·3 per cent of GDP for

Greece, 3·3 per cent for Portugal and 0·4 per cent for Spain.[12] These would be supplemented by loans through the European Investment Bank: the Ortoli facility as well as balance-of-payments aid within the framework of the EMS.

These would be very considerable amounts, especially for the two small countries, but they would only become available very gradually during the transition period. During the first years, which are likely to be the most difficult ones for the new members, transfers through the Community Budget would be very small indeed. Moreover, the figures cited above verge on the optimistic side – particularly for Portugal, which is also likely to end up as a net loser, at least in trade terms, as a result of its participation in the Common Agricultural Policy (CAP). The balance of payments will probably remain an important constraint on growth for the three countries and membership could thus have a very beneficial effect if it contributed to the lessening of this constraint. Portuguese policy-makers are keen on early accession to the Community partly in the hope that membership will bring about a positive transfer of resources and that it will also enable them to raise loans in Community and third markets so as to avoid the full rigours of the IMF therapy which could have disastrous consequences for growth and for political stability in the country.

Commissioner Natali originally spoke of special aid for all Mediterranean regions of the enlarged Community. In its 'fresco' on enlargement, the Commission was much less ambitious in its proposals. It now thought that the ordinary transfers through the Community Budget would be sufficient for both Greece and Spain; but it still believed that special economic aid would be needed for Portugal.[13] The German social democrats have also been talking for some considerable time about a solidarity fund for southern Europe, but nothing concrete has emerged as yet.[14]

The structure of industrial trade between the existing members of the Community and the three applicant countries suggests that there is still a vertical division of labour between the two sides, with the latter specialising in the production of traditional labour-intensive goods. It is not in anybody's interest that this division of labour be frozen after enlargement. First of all, specialisation in labour-intensive goods means that wages will have to be kept down. Apart from personal preferences that one may have about a more equal distribution of income, such a situation would have highly destabilising effects for the political system of these countries. On the other hand, continued specialisation in sectors such as textiles and clothing would strengthen the protectionist tendencies *vis-à-vis* third countries. For the Community, which is heavily dependent on external trade and even more so on imports of energy and other raw materials, protectionism is a very dangerous policy indeed.

The three governments will have to recover their control over domestic prices, which began soaring up in recent years. Given the perverse effects of devaluation on domestic inflation, the need for internal stabilisation policies in Spain, Portugal and Greece becomes very apparent if these countries are to retain their competitiveness in international markets. It is possible that external discipline via the EMS could be seen as another means of strengthening the hand of governments in their fight against inflation.

Dudley Seers has argued that 'inflation in the periphery is due to structural causes; it would be too much of a coincidence to believe that all finance ministers of the periphery were irresponsible, but none of their counterparts of the core'.[15] His definition of the European periphery includes the United Kingdom, Ireland, Italy, Finland and Turkey together with the three applicant countries. Although the experience of Greece in the 1960s does not fit Seers's model, it is true that there is a strong correlation in the 1970s between low inflation rates and high levels of income. Other definitions of what constitutes the 'core' and what the 'periphery' are somewhat dubious and, therefore, I leave them aside here. Growth rates are certainly not one of the defining variables because otherwise the relationship would be inverse. Although a structural analysis of inflation is indispensable, I remain very sceptical about the usefulness of lumping together countries like Britain and Portugal. Moreover, it is probably worth pointing out that all the 'core' countries, with low rates of inflation, have participated, for all or part of the time, in the snake arrangement. Their currencies have appreciated, in contrast with the experience of 'peripheral' countries. Should we entirely dismiss the theory of the virtuous circle, as it applies to the exchange rates and domestic inflation?

Enlargement will add considerably to the Community's regional problem. The industrialisation process of the 1960s in the three Mediterranean countries led to a heavy concentration of economic activity in the region of Attica, around Lisbon/Setubal and Oporto and a few provinces in Spain. Regional policy, in strictly economic terms, is an inefficient way of allocating scarce resources and it seems that rapid industrialisation was seen in the three countries until recently as too high a priority for policy-makers to afford the luxury of paying attention to regional imbalances.

As we should expect from any form of trade liberalisation, it is the dynamic sectors of the economy on both sides which stand to gain while the weak ones – sectors or regions – are likely to lose. Enlargement and the integration of the three economies into the common market do not seem to provide an exception to the rule. Farmers in the French Midi and the Mezzogiorno, with low incomes per capita relative to those enjoyed by other farmers in the

Community, are likely to suffer as a result of competition from the three new members. In the north-west provinces of Spain where the production of beef and maize is characterised by lower productivity relative to that in other parts of the country, farmers may suffer similarly. Enlargement will give more weapons to those who argue against an incomes-oriented agricultural policy based on a system of price intervention. There will also be strong pressure for a new policy directed at the special problems of Mediterranean agricultural regions and for a much larger Guidance section for the EAGGF.

The entry of Greece, Spain and Portugal is also likely to increase the problems of surplus capacity and growing unemployment in textiles, steel and even shipbuilding, sectors often concentrated in the declining areas of the Community. The Commission constantly insists on the need for the three countries to diversify their industrial production and to avoid investing heavily in the so-called 'sensitive' sectors. But as the Commission rightly adds, this can make sense only if the new members receive sufficient financial aid to enable them to bring about the necessary diversification.[16] This also implies a more urgent need for the management of industrial surplus capacity at the Community level and an effective industrial policy. At the same time dynamic firms in sectors with advanced technology and high productivity, like electronics, machinery, telecommunications and chemicals, stand to gain from the opening of three new markets. It may be instructive to compare the defensive attitude of British businessmen in view of enlargement with the more optimistic and aggressive one adopted by their German counterparts.[17]

The negotiations between an applicant country and the Community are only about the type and length of the transitional period which follows accession. The *acquis communautaire* itself does not come into question during those negotiations. The purpose of the transition period is to provide both sides with a breathing space so as to make the necessary adjustments to their economy and institutions. This will certainly be more difficult for the new members. It is therefore in the interest of both sides that some flexibility is shown during the early stages; otherwise, enlargement could have some catastrophic results and could also lead to a situation where emergency measures become the rule rather than the exception. A great deal will depend on government policy in the three countries, political stability and the creation of the climate of confidence necessary to attract investment. On the other hand, adjustment will be much easier for both sides if it coincides with higher rates of growth than those currently experienced by all Western European countries. But most analyses suggest that the second round of enlargement will take place in a very difficult economic environment where people are more likely to concentrate on short-term problems and adopt the attitude of 'sauve qui peut'.

Alternative Scenarios for the Future

One possible scenario for the Community of Twelve would be that, with increasing economic divergence and the need for unanimity in a club with growing membership, decisions will become virtually impossible and the Community will gradually be diluted into a free trade area. Growing income disparities, even in purely monetary terms, will make, for example, the system of common agricultural prices increasingly difficult to sustain. The dilution of the Community would defeat the whole purpose of enlargement since it is not a free trade area that the three applicant countries are so keen to join. Concern to prevent this may not prove compelling enough in practice to prevent such a scenario being realised. European integration has been based on a package deal that goes far beyond a simple free trade area. The crucial issue is whether this package deal will be redefined in the next few years both because of the partly regressive nature of the current Community Budget and because of the new forces unleashed by the second enlargement. But a new package deal would acquire larger financial resources than hitherto and new common instruments.

A free trade area on its own is at odds with the type of welfare state that exists in all Western European countries. Furthermore, it would mark a regression from the long tradition of co-operation in the Community and the degree of economic interdependence already achieved. The clear implication of this argument is that the Community, transformed into a free trade area, would be in danger of breaking down completely because free trade can hardly survive on its own. This is also confirmed by recent trends in international trade and by what politicians and journalists often refer to as a movement towards 'organised trade'. Changes in the external economic environment have direct repercussions on internal Community developments. The need to accommodate external demands and accept changes in the international division of labour may bring about pressures for the adoption of common internal policies. Some recent examples spring to mind such as the ratification of the UNCTAD liner code and international negotiations on textiles and steel. Last but not least, if there is a tendency for international negotiations, which came to supplement the market as a mechanism for the allocation of resources at the world level, to take the form of bloc-to-bloc diplomacy, then the importance of the Community for its members is bound to be strengthened.

The second possible scenario is the creation of a Community *à la carte*. Agreement may be reached on particular common policies but these will not necessarily entail the participation of all member countries. This may be coupled with an increasing number of derogations and exceptions made for the weak members with respect to sacrosanct parts of the *acquis communautaire* such as the customs union. If the countries participating in different policies or institutions cluster into definable groups, we would in effect be moving towards a two-tier or multi-tier Community. This concept was first introduced by Willy Brandt and later taken up by Leo Tindemans in his report on European Union. We can already find a number of instances in which there has been a division between members of the Community in terms of decision-making or policies or both. The best known example was the operation of the snake, participation in which was confined to only five member countries whose finance ministers met separately in an attempt to co-ordinate national economic policies. Another example has been the exclusion of small member countries and representatives of the Community as such from international summits of the Big Four (or Five or Six) in which important decisions were taken also pertaining to supposedly Community matters. Although the institutionalisation of a two- or multi-tier Community is unlikely and would be tantamount to the breaking-up of the Community as we have known it, the creation of common policies in which some member countries find themselves unable to participate is not very unlikely. The EMS could be only one example. On the other hand, there have been various inspired leaks in the French press about the need to form a directorate of big countries in the Community in order to avoid total paralysis after the second enlargement.[18] But the response of other member countries has been very negative and thus nothing has happened on this front.

The third scenario posits the Community as gradually moving away from the old model of economic *laissez-faire* and towards the creation of a minimum welfare state at the Community level which would complement free trade. The main objective could be the reduction of inter-regional as opposed to international disparities. This might help to by-pass the unreal dilemma of intergovernmentalism and supra-nationalism.[19] Considerable inter-regional resource transfers could result from the adoption of structural, cyclical, employment and even agricultural policies. If the emphasis is to be on the redistributive function of the Community Budget, then the increase in expenditure would have to be financed on a progressive basis. The proposals made in the MacDougall Report run along similar lines. The pessimists would argue that the Federal Republic, backed by the other rich members of the club, would never accept a new package deal in which both redistribution and intervention at the Community level would be two important elements. But this responsibility has been accepted by all modern governments within the boundaries of the traditional economic unit, namely, the nation state. The richer members of the Community may have to pay this price for the preservation of free trade on which much of their economic advantage depends. However, it would be unrealistic to keep after enlargement the same targets as to the reduction of regional disparities, which would have been adopted for the Community of Six or even Nine.

The creation of a single market inside the Community would have to be coupled with a common commercial policy, an agricultural policy with a strong social and regional dimension and an industrial policy concentrating on bringing about the necessary adjustment at a socially acceptable cost. The single market would also rely on a Community monetary system where policy-makers would accept the hard fact that independent national monetary policies are almost 'a snare and a delusion' and that floating exchange rates are not a free ticket to paradise.

All the above may not amount to a real federation but would be more than a justification for the existence of a Community with twelve members. It would be an attempt to manage as well as to continue to enjoy the benefits from growing economic inter-dependence. European integration has been a very gradual and slow process and is likely to continue to be so in the future, if no major external shocks from the East or the West or the emergence of a hegemonial power within the Community come to act as the federator. On the basis of those assumptions, a combination of scenarios two and three seems quite probable for the Community of Twelve. It should also be clear by now where the preferences of the author lie.

Notes: Chapter 8

This chapter contains some preliminary ideas arising from research on the second round of enlargement, financed by the SSRC. See Loukas Tsoukalis, *The European Community and its Mediterranean Enlargement* (Allen & Unwin, London, forthcoming).

1 OECD data.
2 'Opinion on Spain's application for membership', *Bulletin of the European Communities*, Supplement 9/78, Brussels, 1978, Table 1, p. 43.
3 *Report of the Study Group on the Role of Public Finance in European Integration* (Commission of the European Communities, Brussels, 1977), Vol. I, Table 1, p. 27.
4 'Opinion on Spain's application', op. cit., p. 33.
5 Dieter Biehl has made estimates of the regional GDP per capita in Greece and Portugal, which is assumed to be a function of distance from the economic core area of the Community (Düsseldorf/Cologne), the density of population and the number of inhabitants. This has produced some rather dubious results which suggest, for example, that the fertile areas of Crete are poorer than some desolate areas of Greece. See Dieter Biehl, 'The impact of enlargement on regional development and regional policy in the European Community', in W. Wallace and I. Herreman (eds.), *A Community of Twelve?: The Impact of Further Enlargement on the European Communities* (De Tempel, Bruges, 1978), pp. 240–6.
6 Juan Munoz, Santiago Roldán and Angel Serrano, 'The growing dependence of Spanish industrialisation on foreign investment', in D. Seers, B. Schaffer and M.

L. Kiljunen (eds.), *Under-Developed Europe: Studies in Core–Periphery Relations* (Harvester, Hassocks, 1979), p. 173.

7   OECD, *The Impact of the Newly Industrialising Countries* (OECD, Paris, 1979), Tables 1 and 2, pp. 18–19.

8   The effective exchange rate index is a composite measure of the external value of each currency in terms of twenty-seven selected currencies and is computed by averaging the export- and import-weighted indices. Data provided by the IMF.

9   See R. J. Ball, T. Burns and J. S. E. Laury, 'The role of exchange rate changes in balance of payments adjustment – the United Kingdom case', *Economic Journal*, March 1977.

10   Calculated on the basis of OECD data.

11   See also Loukas Tsoukalis, 'A Community of Twelve in search of an identity', *International Affairs*, July 1978.

12   'Enlargement of the Community: economic and sectoral aspects', *Bulletin of the European Communities*, Supplement 3/78, Brussels, 1978, pp. 37–9.

13   'Enlargement of the Community: general considerations', *Bulletin of the European Communities*, Supplement 1/78, Brussels, 1978, p. 8.

14   See, for example, Christian Deubner, 'The southern enlargement of the European Community: opportunities and dilemmas from a West German point of view', *Journal of Common Market Studies*, March 1980.

15   Dudley Seers, 'The periphery of Europe' in Seers, Schaffer and Kiljunen, op. cit., p. 25.

16   The link between financial aid and diversification of industrial production in the three applicant countries was made much clearer in the paper submitted by Commissioner Natali (September 1977) than in subsequent reports on enlargement published by the Commission.

17   See Beate Kohler, 'Germany and the further enlargement of the European Community', *The World Economy*, May 1979, pp. 204–5, and the evidence submitted by British industry to the House of Lords Select Committee on the European Communities, Session 1977–78, 17th Report, *Enlargement of the Community*, Vol. II, pp. 329–94.

18   *Le Monde*, 11 February 1976, 7 March 1977, 13–14 September 1978.

19   The role of regions in a new model of European federalism is discussed in B. Burrows, G. Denton and G. Edwards (eds.), *Federal Solutions to European Issues* (Macmillan/Federal Trust, London, 1978), pp. 1–14.

9

Convergence at the Core?
The Franco-German Relationship
and its Implications for
the Community

Jonathan Story

At the European Council in April 1980 the nine heads of government failed to reach agreement on Prime Minister Thatcher's demands for reform of the Community's budgetary arrangments, though they declared partial support of the United States over Iran. Such facility for pious rhetoric on general foreign policy, combined with difficulty in reaching agreement on substantive economic issues, marks a turn-around from the 1960s. Then the Community of Six was able to reach agreement on the formation of the customs union and of the Common Agricultural Policy, but the members disagreed sharply on foreign policy issues.

Two explanations may be advanced for this shift of emphasis from internal European to international affairs as the bond among the member states. First, the relative decline of American power in the world during the 1970s contrasts with President de Gaulle's views in the 1960s of the United States as an expansionary power. Western European countries share a common dependency on imported energy resources and raw materials; all face growing industrial competition, not just from the United States and Japan, but from Eastern Europe and developing countries. Continental states are reluctant to jeopardise relations with the Soviet Union, and are more than ever aware of the complexities of reconciling the need for good relations with the states in the Middle East and the Gulf with the equally pressing matter of relations with the United States. Foreign policy considerations of Europe's place in the world have thus moved to the forefront of European concerns.

Secondly, the member states of the European Community appear less able to achieve progress in common economic policies than was the case in the 1960s. One of the grander assumptions contained in Article 2 of the Rome Treaty was that governments would be willing and able to pursue economic policies leading to ever-closer relations. Through the establishment of a common market and the progressive alignment of economic policies among member states, the aim of the Community was 'to promote the harmonious development of economic activities throughout the Community'. But as tariffs were lowered, national governments sought to counter the redistributive effects of more competitive conditions through policies of institutional reform, economic growth, industrial intervention and social expenditure. Reforms and policies were adapted to particular national conditions, and their distinct methods and objectives submerged in the general prosperity. When world economic conditions deteriorated in the 1970s, differences in national practices and institutions became more visible.[1] As the 'Three Wise Men' lamented in their report to the European Council in 1979 on reform of Community institutions: 'We realise that the deeper causes for the malfunctioning of the Community are not due to mechanisms and procedures. These play only a secondary role in reality. Economic difficulties and divergences of interests and ideas between member states are more serious obstacles.'[2]

It is tempting to ascribe these 'divergences of interests and ideas between member states' to deep-seated cultural differences, as de Gaulle often argued. His foreign policies were influenced none the less by more pragmatic considerations. De Gaulle's proposals for a European Union, in which the six member countries were to co-operate on welfare economics, 'culture' and foreign policy, enabled him to speak as a 'European', while the ensuing debates on a supra-national versus confederal Europe revealed the limits which other states set on abandoning national powers to new authorities.[3] Their failure opened the way for his diplomatic attacks on the 'Anglo-Saxons', his first 'non' to Britain's membership, and the Franco-German Treaty of Co-operation in 1963. The Common Agricultural Policy emerged through the diplomacy surrounding France's attack on the Commission in 1965, resulting in an enlargement of the Commission's functions as supervisor of the farm policy and as Community negotiator in the Kennedy round of trade negotiations in the GATT. But de Gaulle's policy of détente with the Soviet Union between 1964 and 1968, coupled with his withdrawal of France from the integrated command structure of the Atlantic alliance in 1966, smoothed the way for the Federal Republic to develop its own Ostpolitik. This shift in the focus of political initiative from Paris to Bonn coincided with the social and economic upheavals of the late 1960s. The convergence of shared economic and social experiences with a realisation of the risks in pursuing divergent foreign policies in world affairs contributed to considerable changes in governmental and national attitudes towards the Community's development in the subsequent decade.

Shared experiences and converging views on foreign policy were offset by differing vulnerabilities of states to transnational flows and interstate relations. In the late 1960s the future nine member countries of the Community – as well as the Scandinavian and Mediterranean states, and the neutral countries of Finland, Austria and Switzerland – faced different predicaments arising out of four related developments. First, the United States and the Soviet Union moved to talks on arms limitations and balanced force reductions in Europe while American diplomacy laid the basis for President Nixon's visit to Peking in 1972. Secondly, the deterioration in the gold exchange standard enshrined in the Bretton Woods agreements led to the *de facto* non-convertibility of the dollar into gold in 1968, the parity realignments of sterling, franc and Deutsche Mark, and the gradual move to floating exchange rates. Thirdly, member governments of the European Community initiated co-operation between foreign ministries alongside the institutional and economic aspects of the Rome Treaty.[4] Finally, all member governments faced more militant labour forces.

In the late 1960s, too, when German economic performances began to outstrip those of the rest of the Community, France faced major foreign and domestic political problems. By the mid-1970s France had adopted a policy of accommodation with the Federal Republic, with the result that France and Germany together set the tone for the Community's development and jointly evolved policies of 'parallel convergence' towards world affairs.

German Divergence from the European Community

Since the late 1960s individual West European countries have become increasingly sensitive to their shared economic and social predicament and to the risks of divergent positions on foreign policy. National foreign policies began to alter, with the Federal Republic embracing a new Ostpolitik and the modification of French attitudes to the 'Anglo-Saxons' and to the Atlantic alliance. At the Hague Summit of 1969, President Pompidou lifted his predecessor's veto on the enlargement of the Community to include Britain; French relations with the United States were also gradually improved. Substantial changes occurred in the economic sphere, particularly, with the wage explosion of 1968–9 and exchange rate alterations *vis-à-vis* the dollar. The Federal Republic embarked on a policy of upward revaluations of the Deutsche Mark, while the French, along with the British and Italians, preferred periodic devaluations, even at the cost of increased inflation. The incompatibility between the German and French policies became evident in April 1973, when the Germans finally opted for a managed float and domestic price stability.

These different policy approaches were rooted in different national political conditions. Whereas the French electorate after the May 1968 events returned a conservative majority to the National Assembly, the election of the Social Democrat and Liberal government in the Federal Republic allowed for reform in foreign policy and, to a lesser extent, in domestic affairs. In France, Pompidou's conservative coalition flirted with reform, but finally chose to meet higher wage costs and international competition by a policy of accelerated economic growth. By contrast the Federal Republic moved to a slower rate of economic growth combined with industrial restructuring and currency alignments. In the early 1970s the British and Italian governments proved unable to take either path. Finally, differing political conditions in the major West European countries led to different reactions to the transformation of world politics that followed the oil price rise and the demands of developing countries for a new international economic order. The Federal Republic broke free of dollar turbulence in April 1973 by a stabilisation policy, high interest rates and an upward float of the Deutsche Mark. Faced with the dual impact of the German trade surplus and the OPEC price rises, other countries followed foreign policies reflecting their individual domestic situations. A 'European' foreign policy was conspicuous by its absence at the Copenhagen Summit in December 1973 and at the Washington Energy Conference in February 1974.

When Helmut Schmidt succeeded Willy Brandt in May 1974 the tone was set for a more assertive German policy in Europe. France's eight partners were figuratively speaking lined up eight square behind the United States in an 'Atlantic' approach to the foreign policy problems of higher oil prices, financial reform, Community institutional and economic policies and, above all, of relations with the Soviet Union and Eastern Europe.[5] This was made possible by Germany's economic and financial weight in the European Community after the shocks of 1973, reflected especially in its trade surplus and financial reserves. The outcome of its April 1973 measures was that Germany's trade surplus with the rest of the Community expanded from DM0·8 billion in 1972 to DM8·5 billion in 1973 and to DM17·3 billion in 1974. The surplus rose with Austria, Switzerland and Sweden, as well as with the United States and the Soviet bloc.[6] The Federal Republic emerged as the centre of a currency zone, exercising a polar attraction on lesser currencies in Western Europe.[7] France had to detach the franc from the Deutsche Mark early in 1974 and again in 1976, and higher inflation rates in Britain, Italy and Ireland took their currencies out of the snake. Germany's strong external position, based on exports in manufactured goods, machinery and transport equipment, heightened the Federal Republic's visibility as workshop and banker of Western Europe.

The country's new-found prominence raised problems of style, priorities and coherence for West German policies towards the Community. None of these issues could be divorced from the wider context of Germany's position within the existing constellation of international politics. Thus, an American proposal for a relationship of 'bigemony' between the United States and the Federal Republic to promote open world markets and to provide Western leadership was criticised for understating the disparities in terms of defence, raw material dependence and relative openness on world economic conditions.[8] The proposal also ignored West German political interdependence with other West European countries, where governments favourable to the Federal Republic's orientations none the less had to contend with domestic oppositions hostile to Germany. The most tenacious campaign against 'German–American hegemony' was conducted by the French Communist Party during the 1970s. Another view current in American foreign policy circles, which influenced German official attitudes towards the European Community, held that a hierarchy of priorities running from defence, or 'high politics', through to European integration, or 'low politics', should inform German foreign policies.[9] This deceptively neat compartmentalisation of politics into 'high' and 'low' corresponded to the long-standing American view on the appropriate division of labour between a United States as guarantor of Europe's defence, and the European Community as the political expression of the Federal Republic's Western economic orientation. As the first was assumed to provide the international framework for the second, there was some reluctance in Washington and Bonn to recognise that West Germany's economic integration into Western Europe, and its dependence on stable world economic conditions, could lead to conflict with the United States over a widening range of issues. Thus the European region had become the single most important area for German trade: by 1978, the United States accounted for only 7 per cent of West German imports and exports, as against 12 per cent in 1970, and over 20 per cent in the 1950s. American policies that had the effect of damaging other European countries' policies could not leave the Federal Republic untouched.

A middle way between 'bigemony' and regionalism was for the Federal Republic to act as honest broker between the United States and other countries, supplementing American policies in some circumstances, while agreeing to differ in others. The Federal Republic's trade surplus with OPEC countries from 1976 narrowed America's capacity to correct the trade deficit on oil but could be seen as helping to bind the Middle East and Gulf countries into relations of interdependence with Western countries. The Federal Republic, with a moral debt to Israel, could strike a balance that would meet OPEC demands for economic development and counter French inclinations to push the European Community towards a North–South dialogue not wholly compatible with American interests in the Middle East, Africa and Israel. Similarly, the Federal Republic could reinforce American policy in Greece and Turkey, and help to repair the damage to Washington's relations with Athens and Ankara that had resulted from the fall of the Greek dictatorship, the Turkish invasion of Cyprus and the United States Congress embargo on arms to Turkey.

Such a prescription for German foreign policy barely concealed the assertion of a more distinct German national interest within the Atlantic alliance and the European Community.[10] The Americans were surprised by the German–Brazilian agreement on the supply of nuclear plant in 1975 and Germany's more flexible attitude towards Eurocommunism in the following two years. There were differences of policy towards Spain, with the Americans emphasising the risks of the transition from Franco to Juan Carlos, while the Germans, prompted by the anti-fascist convictions of their political parties and trade unions, pushed for peaceful evolution to a democratic system and, indirectly, for the legalisation of the Communist Party.[11]

Ideological competition between the Federal Republic and the German Democratic Republic[12] stimulated rivalry between socialist and communist parties throughout southern Europe: inner-German relations thus were reflected in Mediterranean countries' domestic political wrangles. In France, the formation of the Union of the Left between the Socialist and Communist parties in 1972 stimulated the perennial debate in French politics over the role of the French state in the economy. The debate evolved along four different lines, reflecting the policies of the four major political groupings which contended in the general elections of March 1978. The governmental position (presented by Premier Barre in late 1977 as the Programme de Blois and providing the platform of the conservative–centrist grouping – the Union pour la Démocratie Française) identified the 'Modell Deutschland' of the Federal Republic as worthy of emulation. Government intervention had to be reduced, price controls lifted, profits reconstituted and financial mechanisms liberalised. Christian Stoffaes, in his best-seller *La Grande Menace Industrielle*, published in 1978, encapsulated this new approach.[13] His thesis holds that France risks losing its position on German markets to those third country producers (mainly developing countries) which now specialise in the goods on which French economic growth has in the past been based. He argues that France should follow the Federal Republic's example by moving to more sophisticated production in order to secure a position in West German markets in those goods where France has a 'competitive' advantage, allowing domestic markets to be penetrated by developing countries' exporters.

The Gaullist party had maintained its commitment to economic growth after the 1973–4 oil price changes. But the government objective of a 4·5 per cent growth rate for 1974–5 proved unrealistic, as world economic conditions pulled the French growth rate down to 0·3 per cent. In September 1975 the government, under Jacques Chirac, a Gaullist Prime Minister, sought a remedy in a fiscal package, combined with a budget deficit amounting to 4 per cent of GNP. Businessmen, however, proved reluctant to invest, consumption remained buoyant, and the elasticity of imports to GNP rose to over 4 per cent. The franc was once again uncoupled from the Deutsche Mark in 1976, as inflation mounted, the external balance worsened, unemployment increased and investment rates declined. Chirac's subsequent resignation symbolised that President Pompidou's implicit equation between the politics of grandeur and growth was not applicable in the post-1973 world setting. Consequently, the Gaullist party found itself without an economic policy.

The German question and the related issue of the European Community loomed largest in the dialogue between the Socialists and Communists. The Common Programme of 1972 had proposed nationalisation of the financial institutions and of nine industrial groups. A National Investment Bank combined with planning agreements between the state and corporations would enable a government of the left to subordinate the French productive system to social and redistributive priorities. However, Socialists and Communists became divided in their assessments of the experience of the 1975–6 reflation and the difficulties confronting major French industrial sectors (particularly steel, shipbuilding and textiles), as their changing electoral fortunes also began to drive them apart. In April 1977 the Communist Party demanded a revision of the terms of the Programme, but the two parties were unable to agree either on a redefinition of a common economic policy or on foreign policy, where they were divided by their attitudes to the Soviet Union and Eurocommunism, and by their assessments of the role of co-operation within the European Community.[14] Unable to overcome the incompatibility between their policies of domestic reform and continued support for the European Community, the Socialists left the way open for M. Barre to announce his version of Modell Deutschland for France in Europe.

Towards French Accommodation

A permanent feature of West European politics since 1945 has been the aspiration of both France and the Federal Republic to pursue policies of reconciliation, while preserving respective national claims on independence or reunification. Under the Fifth Republic the pursuit of national independence has provided the yardstick, while interdependence has been interpreted as joint regulation by agreed procedures among independent nation states. Where agreement proves impossible, France should make its own arrangements and resist collective decisions contrary to its interests. By contrast, the Federal Republic has eschewed a nationalist framework as the base of its policy towards the West. The American protectorate did not appear to subordinate the German people but rather to provide the security through which their economy could grow and become entwined with the rest of the Western world. The Basic Law of 1949 in its preamble urges the German people to 'complete the unity and freedom of Germany by means of self-determination', a commitment that was emphasised again throughout West Germany's efforts to seek rapprochement with the German Democratic Republic and the rest of Eastern Europe through the Ostpolitik. This has coloured Bonn's policies both towards Moscow and towards the United States and Western Europe. Any deterioration in relations between the United States and the Soviet Union, or between the East German regime and Bonn, is seen as a threat to Bonn's ability to fulfil its commitment to the German population under Pankow.

Germany's relations with Western Europe, and with France in particular, have been complicated by the differences in French and German institutions. The French Napoleonic state, reinforced by the constitution of the Fifth Republic, contrasts strongly with the 1949 constitution of the Federal Republic. These differences are evident in the approaches of the two countries to economic policy. In France decisions both public and semi-private tend to be centralised in Paris, with extensive control by the Ministry of Finance over monetary policy, the banking system and the allocation of financial resources on preferential terms to particular sectors or 'national champions'. It is precisely this system of state capitalism that was called into question by the experience of 1975–6, by the changed world economic conditions, and by the government's realisation that France could only join a 'zone of stability' with the Federal Republic in the European Community through domestic institutional reforms.

Thus, the French reaction to the crisis of 1975–6 was very different from its response in 1968–9. By 1975–6 the French government came to prefer closer alignment with German policies, whereas in 1968–9 it had opted for economic growth and an enlargement of the Community to the north so that Britain and France might counter the Federal Republic's growing economic weight in the Community.

National attitudes in the candidate countries resembled France's own preferences for a confederal type of Community. Norwegian attitudes towards the Community were coloured by fears of losing national control over North Sea oil and fishing rights, and by reluctance to jeopardise the military balance in Scandinavia. These factors influenced Norwegian citizens in their rejection of membership in the 1972 referendum. Denmark took a different path, hoping to play a bridging role between the Community and the Scandinavian countries, while retaining economic links with Britain and political ties to France to offset the overwhelming influence of its neighbour, West Germany. The French government's concern for national independence appeared a guarantee that the Community would develop as a union of independent states. Economically Danish farmers stood to benefit from the CAP, while Denmark's close links to West Germany made it an integral part of the European snake. Ireland looked to the Community as a means of reducing dependence on Britain, of assuring high food prices to Irish farmers and of providing a large market for Irish exports.

In the early 1970s the close relationship between Prime Minister Heath and President Pompidou helped shape Community politics. However, the changes in government leadership in London, Paris and Bonn in 1974 began to drive a wedge between the UK and other EC members, and paved the way to a renewed emphasis on Franco-German co-operation. As Sir Nicholas Henderson reflected in his valedictory dispatch to the British Foreign Secretary in 1979, Britain's declining standing in the Community under the Labour governments of Prime Ministers Wilson and Callaghan paralleled the tightening of links between France and West Germany.[15] British attitudes towards the Community were presented on the continent as half-hearted or even obstructive. The 1975 referendum had provided a 65 per cent majority in Britain in favour of continued membership of the Community, but Britain's minority government demanded an independent seat at the North–South conference to protect British interests as an oil producer, and sought to manipulate the exchange rate mechanisms provided by MCAs to keep down food prices for British consumers. At the same time, the British government seemed to be demanding Community protection in textiles, shipbuilding, or steel, while pressing for the principle of free trade in the Tokyo round of negotiations in GATT. Besides the repeated allusions in France to Britain's preference for 'le grand large', two arguments about British attitudes towards the Community stand out. First, French commentary on Britain's hostility to the Common Agricultural Policy has tended to emphasise industrial decline: low investment in industry, the argument runs, has led to low relative wages, and hence a continuing preoccupation with a cheap food policy.[16] Secondly, West German commentators have tended to attribute British difficulties to antiquated social structures, to the role of the pound sterling as an international currency in the postwar years and to the lack of 'concertation' between British industrial enterprises, trade unions and financial institutions.[17] By 1979 the view that de Gaulle had been correct in his appreciation of the incompatibility between British membership and a tightly knit European Community formed around Franco-German reconciliation had gained widespread acceptance in Community circles which had opposed the General in the 1960s.

Probably the most significant constitutional arrangement for Franco-German relations in the context of the European Community has been the European Council, advanced in 1974 by Giscard d'Estaing as part of his policy of placing French relations on a sounder basis with West Germany, after the débâcle of 1973. The Council may be seen, over and above the regular meetings between Bonn and Paris under the 1963 Treaty of Co-operation, as of evident Gaullian lineage, preserving the *de facto* power of each head of government to veto policies not deemed compatible with the national interest. But it may also be seen as constituting the European executive, and providing the driving force behind any progress in the Community.[18] Its innovation has tended to relegate the Council of Ministers to a subordinate role in Community decision-making, has cast a shadow over the Commission and may have further accentuated the trend in the Community for any matter, however technical, on which a government's veto may be anticipated, to float to the top of the hierarchy. Thus, the agenda of the European Council is often cluttered with matters which might have been resolved at lower levels, had the states lived up to the following observation of the heads of government on the functioning of the Community in their communiqué of December 1974: 'To improve the functioning of the Council of the Community, they consider it desirable to abandon the practice of subordinating decisions on every question to the unanimous consent of the states.'[19]

Whatever the shortcomings of the Community institutions and of the European Council, no major initiative in the Community after 1974 was possible without close co-operation between France and the Federal Republic. After Giscard d'Estaing's election to the presidency in 1974, he immediately declared his interest in closer co-operation with West Germany and improved relations with the United States over the Atlantic alliance, international monetary matters and economic policy co-ordination. France and West Germany, with the assent of the other member states, managed the Wilson government's renegotiation of Britain's entry terms, decided in 1976 to comply with the commitment in the Rome Treaty to direct elections to the European Assembly, initiated stricter control over the Community Budget and nominated Roy Jenkins as President of the Commission. The failure that year of

Franco-German efforts to co-ordinate economic policies contributed to Giscard d'Estaing's replacement of Jacques Chirac, the Gaullist leader, by Raymond Barre, as former Vice-President of the European Commission. Barre left no doubt about his intention of fashioning French economic policy on Modell Deutschland, the term the Social Democrats used in the 1976 federal elections to describe the results of their seven-year tenure of office. At the February 1977 meeting in the framework of the Franco-German Treaty of 1963, Giscard d'Estaing stated that 'we hope that the Community may renew in 1978 progress towards economic and monetary union, which we consider as a necessary passageway on the path towards the union of Europe'. In December 1977 the Commission's proposals on the European Monetary System were presented to the European Council. Nothing was done until the French general elections in March 1978, for fear of dividing further the parties of the majority over European policy. Immediately after the defeat of the Union of the Left, intense consultations between Paris and Bonn were initiated on monetary policy, and the European Monetary System (EMS) was announced at the European Council at Bremen in July 1978. In September the French government presented to the National Assembly its new macroeconomic and industrial policies overtly modelled on West Germany.[20]

Germany, France and the Development of the Community

The renewed emphasis on Franco-German co-operation after 1974 flowed from similar assessments of a deterioration in the international environment, and from a shared aspiration to preserve the Community as an island of stability in a fragmenting world.[21] The Federal Republic took three years to appreciate the international significance of the Middle East War for its traditional foreign policy priority of fidelity first and foremost to the United States, just as the French government took three years to appreciate the significance of changed world economic conditions for the conduct of economic policies. The moment of this dual realisation may be identified with the Schmidt meeting with Giscard d'Estaing in February 1977. The French President was quoted as stating that 'the Franco-German entente constitutes the cornerstone of all progress in the constitution of Europe'.[22] Chancellor Schmidt, in reply, paid tribute to the President, and to his predecessor, Charles de Gaulle, declaring that the Federal Republic desired a strong France. This mutual endorsement was prompted by shared concern about President Carter's foreign and domestic economic policies, as well as by a determination to further assert French-German leadership in Community affairs. Neither the Federal Republic nor France could escape the domestic political adjustments to the Community's development, whatever the differences in national attitudes and institutions.

German economic policy may be seen as the outcome of historical inhibitions about state control, a liberal ideology reinforced by the experience of sustained growth, and the federal political system. Three decades of success in economic policy, assuring popular support for the market economy and the country's political institutions, provide the underpinnings to the country's economic performance.[23] In Bonn, the influence of the Länder administrations lends continuity to policy. The Länder also contribute directly to the formulations of federal policy through the composition of the upper house – the Bundesrat – and their power of appointment in nominations to the Bundesbank Council. On budgetary matters, the problems of sharing fiscal receipts between states unequal in population, area and wealth have led to extremely complex budgetary processes. Given the relative weaknesses of the Chancellery as a co-ordinating mechanism in the Bonn ministries, and the symbiosis between ministries, parliament and interest groups, the Bundesbank – with its statutory independence of government – has emerged as the principal agent in setting the framework for macroeconomic policy. Its control over domestic monetary and exchange rate policies was reinforced in the 1970s with the trend to floating exchange rates. Thus German economic policy, unlike French, is characterised by delegation and decentralisation, with the onus of responsibilities firmly on management and unions. Both are committed to open markets, on which jobs and profits depend.

The German emphasis on free markets and competition contrasts sharply with France, where the language of state controls and of *dirigisme* is deeply rooted in history and experience and in the structure of the state. One of the major differences in national attitudes towards convergence or divergence between the two countries may thus be found in the ease with which the German authorities have been able to point to continuity in long-established economic policy, and the difficulties which a French government committed to economic stabilisation and market liberalisation – along German lines – has encountered in seeking to convince the French electorate that reflationary growth and full employment, as urged by the Gaullists, or a further move to state planning as proposed by the Socialists and Communists, are neither appropriate policies in the changed economic circumstances of the late 1970s, nor adequate responses to the problems of running an increasingly sophisticated and diversified economy.

One of the central debates in Western Europe over the past decade has related to the viability of Western democracies to meet the varied demands placed on them by the international environment and domestic political factors. Whatever forms the debate may have taken, the collapse of the Mediterranean dictatorships in 1974–5 confronted the Community with the immediate prospect of three new candidates for membership, and an extension of the Community from nine to twelve. Attitudes in Germany and France to the enlargement of the Community to the Mediterranean may be analysed from the viewpoint of the domestic German debate, the decision in 1976 to hold direct elections to the European Parliament, the implications of enlargement for the institutional development of the Community and the type of foreign and economic policies implicit to that development.

In the Federal Republic the various political parties and interest groups are agreed on the Community's further enlargement.[24] The Federal Republic considers that its own political and economic system has demonstrated its superiority, and forms a precedent for countries emerging from dictatorship to differing forms of parliamentary democracy. Democratic government is both a desired end in itself, and provides a guarantee for political stability, the necessary condition for a viable economic and social order. Western security and political reform in the Mediterranean countries are thus two sides of the same coin. Differences on Mediterranean enlargement between Christian Democrats and German industrialists on the one hand, and Social Democrats and trade unions on the other, focus on the relative importance attached to trade or to positive policies and resource transfers in the process of political integration. The former have tended to emphasise economic processes as leading to political inter-dependence, and have urged that discrepancies in levels of economic development between the Nine and the Mediterranean countries be overcome by the latter winding down tariff or state protectionist policies. Structural changes should be induced by giving greater play to market mechanisms as the best method of improving general economic conditions. The Confederation of German Industry looks critically at Social Democrat and trade union support for more interventionist policies in the three countries to facilitate processes of industrial adjustment. The German Labour Organisation, on the other hand, has advocated expansionary economic policies in the Federal Republic to mitigate unemployment at home, as well as a 'Southern Development Programme' to facilitate economic development in the three countries. Little has so far come of the proposal, however.

Differences between German political parties and interest groups on economic policy in the European Community and towards the Mediterranean countries reflected internal divergences over appropriate policies and priorities to deal with unemployment and inflation. Whereas the unions were critical of rising unemployment in the Federal Republic in the 1970s, Christian Democrats and industrialists were critical of the expanding deficits of the general government budget. Public sector debt might have risen more steeply but for the passage in August 1975 of the 'Law to Improve the Structure of the Budget'. The Christian Democrats, strongly entrenched in the Bundesrat, invoked the constitutional constraints on the federal government to prevent a recurrence of that year's federal deficit, amounting to 5·8 per cent of GNP. The deficit was said to stimulate inflationary expectations, discourage investment and infringe the stipulations of Article 115 of the Basic Law whereby the net borrowing requirement of federal and Land governments was not to exceed capital outlays, unless sound reasons could be quoted. The Bundesrat's influence was all the greater as the federal authorities have to refer to it for about 85 per cent of total revenues. Thus, the Modell Deutschland to which Chancellor Schmidt referred was a good deal more fiscally conservative than his party and the trade unions may have desired. Equally, the Federal Republic's ability to accede to American, French, or British requests for reflation was severely curtailed. Chancellor Schmidt's scornful attitude to Community processes reflected domestic political constraints on budgets. 'Europe', the Chancellor was quoted as saying in October 1975, 'can only be brought forward by the will of a few statesmen, and not by thousands of regulations and hundreds of ministerial councils.'[25]

In the 1970s political progress in the Community proved easier than progress in economic policy. Economic policy issues stressed cleavages between countries and within them. Political initiatives on Community institutions were broadly welcomed in most member countries. In France, their pursuit created more fluid political conditions as both the majority parties and the parties of the left could forge alliances across their national electoral divide on European matters. Gaullists and communists for different reasons opposed any moves away from the institutional status quo, as endangering national sovereignty; socialists and centrists could continue to underwrite the Rome Treaty. Thus the European Council's eventual decision in 1976 to fulfil the commitment in the Rome Treaty for direct elections to the European Parliamentary Assembly satisfied long-standing demands in the Federal Republic, as well as in Italy, Holland and Belgium, for a more democratic Community, while reinforcing the role of the President in the French political system.

The emergence of transnational party political federations in the course of the 1970s began in response to anticipations of major moves by the states towards European union by 1980. The programmes elaborated were fed by differing party political and national attitudes towards the development of the Community and by distinct approaches to economic policies. Thus, the Federation of European Social Democratic Parties moved in November 1974 towards a

Common European Socialist Programme, but soon renounced the ambition when the difficulties became clear of agreeing on basic principles between national parties, with their own traditions, structures and patterns of relations with other parties.[26] The final programme states that 'the extension of powers to European organisations must not prevent the realisation of Socialist programmes at national level'. Western European communist parties hold even more diverse national positions. The Italian Communists, who entered the indirectly elected Assembly in 1969, share the Italian attitude favouring the Community's development. The French Communists, by contrast, with their blend of nationalism, anti-Germanism and anti-Americanism, have denounced the European Community as a vehicle for German–American hegemonial ambitions in Europe. Spain's Communists support Spanish membership, partly to secure the new democracy, but also because communist voting strength is pronounced in Catalonia and Madrid, whose advanced industrial economies are closely tied into the Community's. But none of the three main communist parties aspires to set up a Federation for Western Europe that Moscow would interpret as a rival and autonomous centre of communism.

Liberal and Christian democrat parties have no such inhibitions. The Stuttgart Declaration of the liberal parties of March 1976 pointedly refers to 'the European Union' as descriptive of the present European polity, and looks to strengthening of the federal institutions. The manifesto of the European Christian democrats of February 1976 sees a European federation as the objective, capped by a European government. But the German Christian Democratic Union and the Bavarian Christian Social Union also joined the Gaullists and the British Conservatives in the European Democratic Union, initiated at Salzburg in April 1978. The party political context within which the French and German governments collaborated was thus complicated further by the establishment of new links at Community level.

The creation of these party political federations, culminating in the direct elections to the European Parliamentary Assembly in June 1979, paralleled the development of the European Council and the increasing intensity of foreign policy co-ordination in the European Community. The fall of the Mediterranean dictatorships provided an opportunity, and a demand, for Community foreign policy activity.[27] The desirability of establishing stable democratic systems in the Mediterranean countries was an objective shared throughout the Community. Member states' attitudes towards political evolution in the three candidate countries nevertheless differed in degree. The Federal Republic, like Britain, saw the Community as playing a valuable role in underpinning Western security in the Mediterranean, and in cementing the cohesion of the Atlantic alliance. This meant encouraging Portuguese resistance to the Communist Party's bid for exclusive power in 1975, and support to non-communist democratic groups in Spain during the delicate transition from General Franco's dictatorship. For France, enlargement was initially welcomed as leading to a 'new balance' in the Community towards Latin countries, which it was assumed would favour French political interests; though this was modified by uncertainties about the influence which the very different communist parties of Portugal and Spain have on the evolution of the French left.

Both Paris and Bonn have recognised that their economies may have to pay a price for the Community's southern enlargement, but domestic differences between political parties and interest groups about who would bear the cost have led only to unspecific declarations of intent. Sectoral interests in France and Italy mobilised against their governments' sympathy on political grounds for Spain's eventual membership of the Community. They have asked for the Community's price mechanisms to be applied more generously to fruit, vegetables and wine. In the Federal Republic, the trade unions are concerned that membership for the Mediterranean countries could increase the flow of immigrant labour to Germany at a time of high unemployment. None the less, the German official acceptance of the inevitable enlargement of the Community to twelve members is now shared by France. Giscard d'Estaing waited until June 1978 to declare that the entry of Spain was 'in conformity with the interest of Europe'. In December 1978 the French Foreign Minister, Jean François-Poncet, overrode Communist and Gaullist party opposition to Spanish membership on the grounds that closer economic relations, resulting from Spain's membership, would end the economic isolation of south-west France.

Neither France nor the Federal Republic appears yet to have answered the problem of how to meet the competing demands of Mediterranean countries within the existing organisation of resources in the Community. Nor have they thought through the implications of further enlargement for the Community's other Mediterranean associates, which fear the exclusion of their agricultural and industrial exports from Community markets. German industrialists, in particular, fear that the accession of three new members with an industrial base heavily dependent on sectors which directly compete with products which developing countries are trying to export to the Community will further weaken its commitment to industrial free trade. In the fields of foreign and defence policy French and German preconceptions also differ, over for example the domestic debate within Spain over the issue of eventual membership of NATO. What is however evident, given the diversity of problems to be resolved and the prospect of twelve governments struggling uncertainly to resolve them, is that no coherent Community response is likely in the absence of oligarchic leadership by the two (or three) major states in the Community.

Franco-German 'Parallel Convergence'

Part of the impulsion bringing France and the Federal Republic closer together flowed from Giscard d'Estaing's desire to prevent any repetition of the experience of 1973–4, when France and the Federal Republic fell out over relations with the United States and appropriate reactions to the crisis in the Middle East. Concomitantly, the thrust of the President's European policies has transformed the political landscape in France. On the right, the Gaullists, champions of French nationalism, maintained an increasingly uneasy alliance with the Centrists, some of whom had professed federalist views in the past; on the left, the Communists coexisted restlessly with their expanding Socialist ally. The Gaullists, after Chirac's resignation as Prime Minister in August 1976, formed the nucleus of a conservative rally against 'communism and liberalism'. But Gaullists and Communists did not break their respective alliances over ratification in the National Assembly in June 1977 of the Bill for direct elections to the European Assembly. They feared to break their ties with the Centrists or Socialists – both generally favourable to the development of the Community – in the run-up to the general elections of March 1978. The Gaullists, under Chirac, led a vigorous anti-Communist campaign on a ticket of national independence. The Communists campaigned on a nationalist platform, and were unable to agree with the Socialists on industrial policy. Communist doubts about Socialist relations with the West German Social Democrats, and Socialist convictions of the anti-Communist thrust of Communist policies, helped to undermine the confidence of the French electorate in their Union. The presidential parties, Gaullists and Centrists, thus provided the President with a narrow but adequate victory in the National Assembly.

In the months following, Giscard accentuated the European dimension of his policies. The European Monetary System was set in place; France's new economic policy was introduced; the pro-government press pointed to Germany as an example in sound labour relations, responsible management and in supportive but non-interventionist economic and industrial policies. Both Gaullists and Communists played increasingly on the theme of the President's alleged subordination of French to German interests. The Communists forcefully developed the argument that 'Europe is profitable to Germany'.[28] Simultaneously, Chirac described the

President as yielding to 'foreign interests', and later as preparing the 'subservience of France' to Germany and America. The French, he declared, should not heed the 'party of the foreigner'. He then objected to the presence of Schmidt at Guadeloupe, where, for the first time, the West Germans were represented on a footing of equality with France and Britain, in discussions with the United States on world affairs. These Communist and Gaullist campaigns constrained the centrist Union pour la Démocratie Française to trim its European sails. Prime Minister Barre, in an interview in April 1979, openly supported the UDF list in the elections to the European Parliamentary Assembly. He advanced a confederal Europe as the long-term objective, and defined a confederation as 'the most advanced form compatible with the independence of the member states of the European union'.[29] Alluding to Franco-German relations, he expressed 'the conviction of a final community of interest and destiny between the two countries'. The President argued along similar lines, condemning whoever sought to revive the old feud between France and Germany as guilty of 'culpable acts'.[30] His views were endorsed by a narrow majority of the French electorate in the European elections. The Gaullists were weakened, but the President still needed their support to win the presidential elections of 1981.

Meanwhile Franco-German rapprochement had been made easier by a major change in postwar European affairs: the Federal Republic's gradual estrangement from President Carter's America. West Germany and France thus inverted roles: whereas West German economic policy came to provide the model for French economic policy, French foreign policy towards the United States came to influence German attitudes to America. Both France and the Federal Republic developed policies of 'parallel convergence' (to use the phrase of the late Italian Prime Minister, Aldo Moro) as the precondition to preserving stability in Europe, both East and West. At the core of German–American differences lay President Carter's dollar and defence policies. The one affected West Germany's economic policies adversely, the other threatened to introduce an undesired incalculability into German–Soviet relations.

As long as the American authorities had been willing to maintain the value of the dollar internationally by restraining aggregate demand in the United States, the Bundesbank could manage to reconcile an expanding trade surplus with tight control over the monetary base, and a managed revaluation of the Deutsche Mark. But Carter's election to the White House led to a reversion of American priorities from relative restraint to expansion, at the cost of fiscal and balance-of-payments deficits and higher rates of inflation. A run on the dollar followed in mid-1977, leading to a massive demand for the Deutsche Mark as an alternative international reserve currency, to heavy inflows into the West German money supply between October 1977 and March 1978, and to a precipitate deterioration in relations between Bonn and Washington. As late as December 1977, West German authorities had expressed considerable reserve over the Commission President's proposals at Florence in late 1977 for the EMS. But a combination of union demands for stimulatory economic policies, and industrialists' fears of a sharp upward valuation of the Deutsche Mark, jeopardising foreign sales, seems to have cleared the way for the Chancellor to override banking advice and to tie the Deutsche Mark to weaker European currencies, thereby easing the stabilisation effects of previous Bundesbank policies. In April Schmidt declared in a speech at Hamburg that America was behaving 'irresponsibly' in world affairs; he launched Community negotiations with the French President for the EMS, and joined with the French, Swiss and Japanese in pressing for American monetary and fiscal restraint. The American monetary measures of 1 November 1978 came too late to prevent OPEC, in the midst of the deteriorating Iranian situation, from seeking a further increase in the dollar-denominated cost of oil products.

The year 1977 was also a turning point in German–American relations, with side-effects on German attitudes towards the Community, in matters relating to nuclear deterrence and armaments. The Soviet Union went ahead with the decision to build the SS-20s. By 1985 the Soviet Union may have 4,000–6,000 of these weapons, with a range of up to 1,000 km, and capable of delivering 'surgical' strikes on European ports, airports and bases. At the same time, Soviet parity with the United States kindled German questioning about NATO's defence philosophy, and in particular about the United States' willingness to use the nuclear threat in defence of Europe. Thus in the summer of 1977 a White House press leak on Review Memorandum 10, covering various scenarios for forward defence in Europe, was reported as betraying American willingness to abandon one-third of German territory.[31] During the subsequent discussions on the deployment of the neutron bomb, German military circles were reported as suspecting that the United States was proposing the neutron bomb, attached to a missile with short firing range, because a longer-range missile capable of reaching Warsaw Pact territory ran the risk of unleashing a central strategic exchange. Naturally, all these hypothetical battles remain in the realm of imagination and of psychology, but that is precisely the area where the Soviet Union seeks to bring pressure to bear on European, and particularly on German, opinion. In any event, German Ostpolitik, which had remained fallow since the European Conference on Security and Co-operation at Helsinki, was active in the winter and spring of 1977–8. The Federal Republic's eastern neighbours were reminded of Germany's continued interest in détente and disarmament talks, coupled with suggestions that European small and medium powers should not leave the continent's future entirely in the hands of the two great powers.[32] In May 1978, at a banquet held in President Brezhnev's honour during his state visit to the Federal Republic, Schmidt declared: 'Your innermost wish is to make détente irreversible. I assure you and the Soviet people that such is the wish of the Germans, and such is also my personal wish and aspiration.'[33]

German relations with the Soviet Union thus rest on tangible foundations. The Soviet Union is a direct military threat, in terms of both conventional arms and nuclear firepower. But at the same time, the Soviet bloc provides a significant market for West German exports, and offers ample scope for loan or investment operations by West German corporations. This dual aspect of Moscow's relations to Bonn as threat and partner is most evident in East Germany, the manipulation of which Moscow can use as a lever on Bonn either to stifle undue criticism in the Federal Republic of Soviet policies, or to encourage the Federal Republic to exert a moderating influence within the Atlantic alliance on Western policies towards the Soviet Union.

Successive French governments have long been aware of the link between their policies towards Moscow and the question of the two Germanies and Berlin. Special relations with the Soviet Union, developed by de Gaulle in the 1960s on the basis of the Franco-Soviet Treaty of 1944, were held to be necessary because of Germany – though also useful as a means of restraining the Communist Party.[34] But whereas in the early 1970s the French government had sought to counter Brandt's Eastern initiative by lifting de Gaulle's boycott on Britain's membership of the European Community, France now responded favourably to Bonn's Community initiatives, partly out of fear that a wavering American leadership in Western defence might precipitate rapprochement between Bonn and Moscow, and partly out of anticipation that a deterioration in relations between the United States and the Soviet Union on SALT II, Africa, and the Middle and Far East might leave the Federal Republic stranded in the Atlantic alliance as the only major country whose national situation left little alternative to accommodating policies towards the Soviet Union. 'The actual debate on the competence of the European Parliamentary Assembly', wrote André Fontaine, 'in fact masks another: what to do with Germany, so that she does not weigh heavily on the destiny of Europe and the world.'[35] 'France', wrote a pseudonymous civil servant in an article entitled 'German unity for when', 'is well justified in supporting the principle of the reunification of Germany.'[36] Giscard d'Estaing's visit to Berlin in 1979, and his foreign minister's visit to East Germany, may be seen in the light of this revival of French concern about 'les incertitudes allemandes'.

Moscow's growing assertiveness in Europe and the rest of the world, and the ambiguities of German foreign policy in seeking to reassure the United States of its commitment to the Atlantic alliance while at the same time hoping to maintain working relations with Moscow, have concentrated French thinking about Europe. The French government, however, has refrained from recalling de Gaulle's prophetic statement on the ineluctable decline in United States power.[37] Its silence is as much a sign of weakness as of satisfaction that de Gaulle was right. French defence expenditure is as subject as that of its partners to the painful squeeze between rising equipment costs and budgetary limitations. In the summer of 1979 some Gaullist opinion floated the idea of a German financial contribution to the French nuclear deterrent force, which would thus be enabled to extend nuclear protection to the Federal Republic. But any such attempt to extend nuclear protection would provoke bitter opposition from the French Communist Party – and would require a substantial further shift in German attitudes towards the reliability of the American guarantee. The Federal Republic's determination to maintain that guarantee was demonstrated in its advocacy of theatre nuclear force modernisation, and in its acceptance of the largest share of the proposed missiles on German soil. In a crisis as acute as that which followed the Soviet invasion of Afghanistan, the French government was as careful as its German ally to avoid giving offence to the United States – reflecting an awareness of military weakness *vis-à-vis* the superpowers which paralleled the underlying consciousness of French economic weakness *vis-à-vis* Germany.

In a deteriorating international environment, in which the French drive to créate an economy capable of competing on equal terms with Germany must be matched by a reassertion of political solidarity, France can no longer afford to block German aspirations for progress in Community affairs. Like Bonn, Paris has sought to keep alive established relations with Moscow. The President's domestic political task has been both eased and made more complicated. It has been eased by the Communist Party's reversion to a Moscow-line policy, in particular since the Afghanistan invasion: the gulf between the Communists and their former allies in the Union of the Left is wider than ever. It has been complicated by the continued importance of the Gaullist party in the majority, and that party's identification with foreign policies which changes in the international constellation of forces have rendered increasingly difficult to maintain. Furthermore, the Gaullist party forms a crucial bastion of the Common Agricultural Policy in the Community. Both Giscard d'Estaing and Chirac have so far avoided rupture through political acrobatics and intransigence in defending the *acquis communautaire* on the European stage. Thus Schmidt in the December 1978 European Council defended the agricultural status quo on the Common Agricultural Policy to satisfy his Free Democrat coalition partners, while Giscard d'Estaing demanded reform of the agricultural subsidy schemes to satisfy the Gaullist party, which in 1969 had been instrumental in setting them in place. Furthermore the President did so to acquire their acquiescence in the European Monetary System, which both Gaullists and Communists were branding for different reasons as evidence of France's subordination to the Federal Republic. The French President appeared equally unyielding in the face of Prime Minister Thatcher's demands at the European Councils at Dublin in December 1979 and at Luxembourg in April 1980 for a reduction in Britain's contribution to the Budget, and hence to the Common Agricultural Policy to which British opinion is opposed in its present form.

Conclusions

Giscard d'Estaing's remark in February 1977 that the Franco-German entente constitutes 'the cornerstone of all progress in the construction of Europe' thus calls for some qualification. First, the argument frequently deployed in France and elsewhere in the Community during the 1970s that the Federal Republic is the leading power in the European Community suffers by oversimplification. Such an assertion derives from too direct an equation between the Federal Republic's economic performance and the national situation. The economic indicators may all have been relatively favourable, though the shift to high rates of inflation and current account deficits may circumscribe German economic policy with more severe constraints in the 1980s. But the national situation hardly provides cause for rejoicing. Germany is divided; Bonn may preach but may not impose economic virtue on other governments in the European Community; the Federal Republic lacks raw materials and oil; it depends on Western European markets; it is greatly affected by, but may exert little influence over, events in the Gulf; its domestic economic and monetary policies are vulnerable to the vagaries of the dollar; its citizens have been the object of repeated psychological campaigns by the Soviet Union. The Federal Republic, in short, is a European country with modest means in need of allies, and has found one in the France of Giscard d'Estaing.

Secondly, Giscard d'Estaing's statement on the Franco-German entente conceals a paradox which lies at the root of European difficulties in adjusting to new political and economic conditions in the world. France and the Federal Republic are huddling together to preserve a 'zone of stability' in Western Europe. This interest appears sufficiently overriding for the French President to have taken considerable risks on domestic and Community policies to bring domestic French arrangements closer to the Federal Republic's, while Schmidt has accepted that reunification is a very distant goal. Interest in European stability is also evident in the efforts in Bonn and Paris to preserve the vestiges of détente, and to develop a distinctly European position on events in Afghanistan and Iran, at the risk of further damaging European relations with the United States and of failing to dissuade the Soviet Union in its ambitions. Similar conservatism underlies the French willingness to quote the international situation in 1980 in support of continuation of the Common Agricultural Policy. Yet the Community's political stability is threatened by continuity, as much as by any major modification to that policy.

Thirdly, the Franco-German entente remains a delicate web of interests and alliances vulnerable to the evolution of national and European politics. Paris and Bonn have manipulated the web to their mutual advantage most of the time, but whenever national considerations have dictated – on agriculture, Britain, the Mediterranean enlargement, or relations with the United States and the Soviet Union – differences have come to the fore. As long as neither side has sought, or been forced, to exaggerate them, both have been satisfied with compromising. Neither partner has proved willing to support policies considered damaging to the relationship. But Mrs Thatcher's determined campaign to reduce Britain's budgetary contribution has revealed the limits of the entente in opposing a member state, willing to use the veto power to block Community business. Nor is there any way for either to exclude Britain from membership, while both may only delay the entry of the Mediterranean candidates. Thus, the agenda, content and institutional development of the Franco-German entente are conditioned at least as much by third parties as by the priorities and preferences of Paris and Bonn.

Fourthly, the politics of compromise and bargaining, that have informed Community affairs over the past decades, reflect the extraordinary complexity of Western Europe. Many member states have experienced similar problems of inflation, unemployment and lower growth. Their representatives may have been able even to agree on diagnosis and cure. But the diversity of political institutions, ideologies and situations impedes the subordination of political action to any blueprint, or timetable, as implied in the Rome Treaty. Equally, European complexities imply a different logic to the simple dialectics of a return to the Cold War, or to market-formed as opposed to state-defined economies. Western Europe contains not one, but a multiplicity of contradictions, assimilable neither to the Marxist-Leninist nor to a capitalist textbook. Seen in this light, the conservative policies of the European Community, both internal and foreign, are an emanation of the Community's condition. Political and institutional diversity, rather than diverging or converging economic performances, lies at the root of the Community's failure to live up to Article 2 of the Rome Treaty.

Notes: Chapter 9

1 Suzanne Berger, 'Politics and anti-politics in Western Europe in the 1970s', *Daedalus*, 'Looking for Europe', Winter 1979, pp. 27–50.
2 *Bulletin des Communautés Européennes*, no. 11, 1979, p. 28 (author's translation).
3 Edward J. Kolodziej, *French International Policy under de Gaulle and Pompidou, The Politics of Grandeur* (Cornell University Press, Ithaca, NY, 1974), pp. 235–91.
4 R. Rummel and W. Wessels, *Die Europäische Politische Zusammenarbeit, Leistungsvermögen und Struktur der EPZ* (Europa Union Verlag, Bonn, 1978).
5 'The tough German', *The Economist*, 23 February 1974.
6 OECD, *Economic Survey*, Statistical Annex, 1979.
7 Brendan Brown, *The Dollar-DM Axis: On Currency Power* (Macmillan, London, 1979).
8 Peter J. Katzenstein, 'Die Stellung der Bundesrepublik Deutschland in der Amerikanischen Aussenpolitik, Anker oder Makler?', *Europa Archiv*, 6 June 1976, pp. 347–56.
9 For a sophisticated analysis, see Roger Morgan, *The United States and West Germany 1945–1973* (Oxford University Press for Royal Institute of International Affairs, London, 1974).
10 See Helmut Schmidt, 'The struggle for the world product', *Foreign Affairs*, April 1974, pp. 437–51.
11 Jonathan Story, 'Le printemps de Madrid', *Politique Etrangère*, no. 1, 1978, pp. 21–58.
12 Anne-Marie Le Gloannec, 'La RDA et l'EuroCommunisme', *Revue Française de Science Politique*, no. 1, February 1979, pp. 19–32.
13 Christian Stoffaes, *La Grande Menace Industrielle* (Calmann Lévy, Paris, 1978).
14 Fernando Claudin, *L'EuroCommunisme* (François Maspero, Paris, 1977).
15 'Sir Nicholas Henderson's valedictory dispatch', *The Economist*, 2 June 1979.
16 Alain Giraudo, 'Cinq ans d'Europe verte, déception sur toute la ligne', *Le Monde*, 1 July 1977.
17 'Das Kranke England', *Der Spiegel*, 22, 29 January, 5 February 1979.
18 Maurice Duverger, 'Le présidium de la Communauté', *Le Monde*, 7 December 1978.
19 'Le communiqué des "Neuf"', *Le Monde*, 12 December 1974.
20 *Rapport Economique et Financier: Comptes Prévisionnels pour l'année 1978* (Ministère de l'Economie, Paris, July–August 1978).
21 David P. Calleo, 'The European coalition in a fragmenting world', *Foreign Affairs*, vol. 54, no. 1, October 1975, pp. 98–112.
22 Maurice Delarue, 'Paris et Bonn resserrent leur coopération', *Le Monde*, 5 February 1977.
23 H. Kreile, 'West Germany: the dynamics of expansion', *International Organization*, vol. 31, no. 4, Autumn 1977, pp. 775–808.
24 The succeeding paragraphs follow the argument in Beate Kohler, 'Germany and the further enlargement of the European Community', *The World Economy*, vol. 2, May 1979, pp. 199–212.
25 *Frankfurter Allgemeine Zeitung*, 30 October 1975.
26 See Rudolf Hrbek, 'Der Europäische Gemeinschaft auf dem Weg zu

Programmatischen Profil', *Europa Archiv*, vol. 10, 15–30 May 1978, pp. 299–310.

27 N. van Praag, 'Krisenmanagement im Süden Europas', in Rummel and Wessels, op. cit., pp. 189–220.
28 Jean-Pierre Godard, 'L'Europe profite à l'Allemagne Fédérale', *L'Humanité*, 20 February 1979.
29 'Entretien de Raymond Barre avec André Fontaine', *Le Monde*, 23 April 1979.
30 Valéry Giscard d'Estaing, conférence de presse du 10 février 1979, *Le Monde*, 12 February 1979.
31 Alex A. Vardamis, 'German-American military fissures', *Foreign Policy*, no. 14, Spring 1979, pp. 87–106.
32 Chancellor Schmidt's speech to the Polish Institute for International Affairs, *Europa Archiv*, 25 January 1978, pp. 24–32.
33 Quoted in *International Affairs*, Moscow, July 1978.
34 See Pierre Hassner, 'Western European perspectives of the USSR', *Daedalus*, 'Looking for Europe', Winter 1979, pp. 113–50.
35 André Fontaine, 'Que faire de l'Allemagne', *Le Monde*, 22 November 1978.
36 *Le Monde*, 16 August 1979.
37 Pierre Lelouche, 'La France, les SALT et la sécurité de l'Europe', *Politique Etrangère*, vol. 2, 1979, pp. 249–71.

10

Integrating Divergent Economies: The Extranational Method

John Pinder

Whether the yardstick be inflation, external balances, or growth rates, the behaviour of European economies in the 1970s has been divergent in the extreme. In reaction, the discussion of integration has concentrated on the need for convergence. But the effect has been the opposite of the intention: integration has been prevented because attention has been diverted from the practicable to the impossible.

Although hopes have been raised once more by the launching of the European Monetary System, they are only too likely to be dashed again unless the reasons why the earlier scheme for economic and monetary union failed are properly understood. For the EMS could be driven into the same cul-de-sac as the EMU if its development is based on the same insistence on convergence as a precondition of further integration.

The Goal of Parity-Locking and the Reality of Divergence

This urgent insistence on convergence arose only because the permanent locking of parities was chosen as the Community's central medium-term aim. Convergence in some sense is doubtless helpful to integration in various forms: similar growth and productivity trends allow long-term equilibrium in conditions of free trade; similar economic structures make it easier for the costs and benefits of membership to be fairly distributed; similar economic weight can be a condition for a balance of political power. But it is only the fixity of exchange rates that requires the convergence of economic trends in the short term; for if price trends differ substantially among the member countries, payments disequilibria quickly require their governments to apply deflationary or inflationary policies to an extent that they do not wish to accept. Ironically, the aim of parity-locking was adopted a decade ago at the same time as economic divergence was beginning to put quite new pressures on the exchange rates. Price trends differed widely, so the snake was quickly broken and the goal of parity-locking receded into the distance. Those who saw it as central to the Community's progress therefore pressed for convergence as the basis on which integration could recommence.

Unfortunately for this concept, the contemporary economies proved remarkably resistant to efforts to make them converge. Whether the approach to economics is monetarist or Keynesian, whether the remedy for price divergence is monetary or incomes policy or both, the structure of the modern economy makes it hard to combine price stability with full employment and growth. Imperfect markets breed cost and price push whose strength depends on a country's social behaviour and economic institutions. Even in Germany, where behaviour and institutions are more favourable than in most other countries, the price of controlling inflation has been, so far, half a decade with a million unemployed despite the employment-creating trade surplus and the return home of many migrant workers. Elsewhere, the trade-offs between inflation and unemployment (which may perhaps be called, for short, propensities to stagflation)[1] are worse. There is a strong adverse current against which policy has to push; and if policy pushes hard enough to keep inflation down to German rates, other countries will suffer worse, or much worse, unemployment and growth than the Germans do. If the purer monetarists are right, all can return to a paradise of price stability and growth after a purgatory of severe monetary discipline. But the time in purgatory could be long; and those of lesser faith will fear that paradise may not follow.

It is against such intractable economic facts that the Community has sought convergence through the co-ordination of member governments' economic policies. But inflation rates continue to diverge by margins which keep the goal of irrevocable parity-locking as distant as ever. If the imperfection of markets in advanced economies has reached a point where new methods of economic management, such as incomes policies, must be developed in order to combine price stability with full employment and growth, a convergence on compatible economic performances may take a very long time to bring about. But whether new methods must be developed, or the orthodox monetary medicine can suffice, it will be some years before the inflation rates of member countries are similar enough for parity-locking to be sustained. This brings into the foreground a second conclusion, political rather than economic, which can be derived from the experience of recent years: that the co-ordination of the Community member governments' policies through the use of member states' own policy instruments is not enough to secure effective common action towards an aim as important and difficult as the achievement of compatible economic policies.

Co-ordination of National Policies: an Ineffectual Method

This ineffectiveness of policy co-ordination has not been caused by any tendency on the part of the member states to defy their legal obligations under the treaties when these are subject to judgement by the Community's court. With few exceptions, they have been legally punctilious. The problem arises when their Community obligations are not of the kind that can be regulated by precise legal texts. Compared with the eighteenth and nineteenth centuries, from which many of our ideas about federal and confederal systems are derived, so much of modern government involves policies that require political and executive judgements more than precise decisions in the courts. General economic and monetary policies are essentially of this type. It is hard to envisage a law fixing the inflation rate at 0·5 per cent or a prime minister being impeached for failure to carry it out. The objectives cannot reasonably be defined in terms that are amenable to judgements in law; except in the most rigidly controlled or the most *laissez-faire* economies, the methods cannot be defined exactly in advance; and changing circumstances impose constant revision of both objectives and methods. Co-ordination of economic policies requires, therefore, a constant Community influence on the interpretation of objectives and the use of instruments by the member states.

Since economic policies are at the centre of politics in modern parliamentary democracies, this means that the Community must influence the central political process in the member countries, in a matter where the detail of what has been agreed can be subject to continually changing interpretation. Common sense indicates that, in such circumstances, the interpretation will respond to the stronger political pressures; and given the existing political structure of the Community, these come from inside the member states. So, however genuine the intentions to co-ordinate may be, actions based on national policy instruments are inherently centrifugal in any matter that is important enough to be an issue in national politics and imprecise enough to escape decision in the Community courts.

The Need for Common Instruments

We should not be surprised, then, that attempts to co-ordinate have achieved little of political importance where the Community lacks its own policy instruments, whereas the Community's outstanding achievements are firmly based on such instruments. The common external tariff has made the Community equal to the United States, or perhaps even the world's greatest power in international trade negotiations; the achievements of foreign policy co-operation among the Nine have not been remotely comparable. The Common Agricultural Policy, whatever one may think of its present impact on British interests, has been enormously more effective than Community energy policy where the common instruments are relatively slight. By the same token, the commercial policy and the agricultural policy stand in a different class from Community monetary policy, where efforts at co-ordination without substantial common instruments have resulted in the exchange of information rather than in real influence on national monetary policies. The exchange rate mechanism of the EMS will have a decisive effect on monetary policies if it leads to the permanent locking of parities or, in effect, a common currency as the central economic instrument for the Community. But until this happens, the EMS exchange rate mechanism is more like the former adjustable peg system in the IMF than a common instrument for a more closely integrated monetary union. Even if the adjustments are to be agreed through a Community procedure, it is hard to believe that member governments, which will themselves wish to retain the right to adjust, will prevent their partner governments from doing so.

Without a policy instrument brought to bear from beyond the nation state, then, the co-ordination of policies in a politically important matter is not likely to be effective. Where there is a hegemonial power, such as the United States in NATO or the Soviet Union in Comecon, the weight of its own instruments may be sufficient to influence and if necessary coerce its partners, although the relationship of France with NATO shows that among democratic countries such influence may be limited. Within the Community, where there is no hegemonial member, the examples of commercial and agricultural policy have shown that common Community instruments may be required.

Anarchy, Autarky or Centralisation: an Awkward Trilemma?

Does it follow that the permanent locking of parities, leading to a single Community currency, is the only way to give the Community real influence in the conduct of member countries' economic policies? Without an unlikely degree of convergence in the differing propensities to stagflation the single currency is not likely to be adopted, for it could force very high levels of unemployment and perhaps inflation on different member countries. Even if they were to accept this risk, the likely consequences would hardly be a favourable context for such a massive transfer of sovereignty to institutions that may still be too weak to bear such heavy political responsibility. Yet the indefinite continuation of what amounts to anarchy in international economic and monetary policy is not an encouraging prospect. Over a fifth of the gross products of the member countries enters into international trade, half within the Community and half outside; international flows of money and of people and the multinational organisation of production further erode the governments' control over their national economies; and this erosion is a continuing process with the secular internationalisation of the economy. It surely follows that a capacity to manage the European and international economies must be established, if we are to regain and retain adequate control over money, the conjuncture of the economy, the externalities of specialised or large-scale industries, the development of advanced technology, and security of supply for energy and other materials. For it is hard to conceive as a serious alternative a return to autarky, reducing our levels of technology and living standards and endangering international co-operation.

The argument up to now confronts us, then, with a most awkward trilemma: a single currency which could cause high unemployment and inflation in different countries at the same time as there is a sharp transfer of sovereignty to weak institutions; a scarcely conceivable return to autarky; or a continuation of international anarchy, which will do increasing damage to our national economies as they become more and more internationalised. The hopes that convergence may lead to a single currency, or that an adjustable peg system with co-ordination of national policies can bring the anarchic international economy under control, merely obscure the failure to envisage an alternative that is both palatable and effective.

Parallel Instruments

The most successful of Community policies, dealing with external trade relations, is based on the common external tariff, which has replaced the former tariffs of each member country. Likewise the generally accepted concept of integration, reflected in the use of the word supranational, is of a Community that is, in the fields of integration, above and superior to the member states. It is not surprising, then, that the model for monetary integration should have been a single currency which would replace the member states' several national currencies, or the irrevocable locking of parities and freeing of movement of money within the Community, which amounts to the same thing with only a cosmetic difference.

In fact, however, most of the Community's instruments do not suppress and replace the instruments of the member states. The regional, social and development funds do not suppress the member countries' own regional, social and aid budgets. The guidance part of the Community's agricultural fund does not preclude the member governments from providing more money to help their farmers make structural adjustments. The Investment Bank does not stand in the way of the numerous public bodies that supply finance for investment in the member countries. Euratom's research centres such as Ispra work in parallel with the atomic research centres established by individual member governments. The Community's share of up to 1 per cent of value-added tax (unlike the customs duties and agricultural levies, which are exclusive to the Community) leaves the member governments free to raise any further percentage of VAT that they may wish. The Community's anti-trust laws, while they take precedence over national legislation where cases affecting intra-Community trade are concerned, leave the national legislation intact for all other cases. Since the change of policy following 1973 under Commissioner Gundelach, common Community specifications often define a product whose sale all member countries agree to accept in their territory, while leaving them free to allow in their own markets the sale of products that meet their own existing specifications.

Each of these Community funds, enterprises, taxes, laws and regulations operates, then, in parallel with member countries' funds, enterprises, taxes, laws and regulations. It has not been found necessary to pre-empt the exclusive right to legislate or possess policy instruments, in order for the Community to do something useful for the member countries. It is the contention of this chapter that such parallel instruments are enough to enable the Community to embody many of the common interests of the member countries; and that parallel monetary instruments in particular could do much to satisfy the needs for economic and monetary co-ordination, without requiring a degree of convergence that is at present out of reach for the member countries' economies.

A Parallel Currency

The concept of parallel instruments was introduced into the discussion of European monetary integration by Williamson and Magnifico,[2] and has been carried further by a number of other sources, including the All Saints' Day group of economists,[3] the Community's Optica group of experts[4] and the Commission's contribution towards the Tindemans Report.[5] Now, in the context of the EMS, there is for the first time an opportunity for parallel monetary instruments to be developed on a major scale. What is needed is to recognise the importance of this opportunity for Europe's political economy and to ensure that, instead of losing it by default, the Community goes on to realise its full potential.

The greatest potential in the EMS lies in the depositing of 20 per cent of the participating states' gold and dollar reserves in the European Monetary Co-operation Fund in exchange for European

Currency Units (ECUs) to regulate central bank interventions. The EMCF is now a good deal more than 'a plate on a door in Luxembourg';[6] and by 1981 a European Monetary Fund is in principle to be created, in which the reserves held by the EMCF are to be placed, thus becoming Community reserves in parallel with the member states' national reserves. Provided the decision-taking process for the use of these Community reserves is sufficiently effective, the ECU can then become a genuine parallel currency, with the roles of a reserve and an instrument of settlement.

Outside the scope of the ECU's official reserve functions, the Community is also developing its financial instruments in the capital markets. The Investment Bank has, since the foundation of the EEC, been such an instrument, and now that its annual lending amounts to more than a billion EUAs, it has some weight in the international capital market and in the field of public investment. The Ortoli facility, whereby Community bonds of up to a billion UAs are being floated, is a further instrument that operates in the international money markets, with the proceeds to be used for Community purposes.

Such parallel instruments should begin to give the Community weight in its dealings both with member governments and with external monetary authorities such as the US Treasury and Federal Reserve system. The governments will continue to make their own monetary policies with their own currencies, reserves and monetary institutions, and the national economies will not be forced prematurely into a common monetary straitjacket. But the common Community interest, when defined in the Community institutions, will have behind it the means to influence national policies, in the form of reserves equivalent to the reserves of a major member state, plus other funds that can be used as an incentive for co-operative behaviour. The Community could similarly intervene massively with its common reserves in the market for dollars or other non-Community currencies. It would thus be better able to influence the policies of the United States and other countries, as well as the IMF. This influence both within and without the Community would, moreover, be multiplied in so far as the strength of its own monetary resources can induce the member states to align their national policies on a Community policy more readily than before.

The idea of the ECU as a European equivalent of the dollar in its international roles will remain only very partially realised, however, until the Community parallel currency is more fully developed for commercial use. Following the original contribution by Williamson and Magnifico,[7] a number of proposals for this have been made. What has been lacking is the political decision to implement them. Some of the proposals[8] have raised fears that the parallel currency would in fact replace the weaker national currencies in the Community, thus presenting for them the same risks as an exclusive single Community currency. But exchange controls on the movement of the parallel currency could, in principle, be similar to those on the movement of member countries' currencies within the Community and of the dollar across its frontiers. The essential aim of the parallel currency would be to meet the need now met by the dollar in its international roles, both official and commercial. In this way it should, without awaiting a degree of convergence that will be a long time coming, enable the Community to gain the sort of influence that the United States has had on both national and international monetary policies.

A Parallel Community

The parallel currency is the most important of the parallel instruments so far established or proposed in the Community. At the same time it symbolises an idea of more general application.

Much of the political debate about Europe presents the crude alternatives of a Community which is above the member states, dictating to them on central political issues, or a Community below the member states, subject in all its actions to the several wills of each of the member parliaments and governments. The parallel instrument embodies a different concept, of a Community alongside the member states, possessing its own instruments with which to act in matters of common interest, in particular those international matters which a single member country can no longer itself control, while leaving the member countries in possession of their own instruments to implement their own national policies.

In a pure form, this concept of a parallel Community could imply that all the Community's instruments would be parallel ones, like the Regional, Social and Development Funds, the Investment Bank and the elements of European currency so far established. But this would unduly restrict the potential for common action.

The parallel specifications, for example, are perfectly suited to such products as bread and beer, where cultural diversity demands differing definitions in different countries, while there is enough common taste to justify an additional common definition that will encourage international trade. Differing specifications for machinery may be less justifiable and more detrimental to economic efficiency, and here common specifications can with advantage replace the national ones, rather than be introduced alongside them.

The application of national anti-trust laws to international transactions creates obvious conflicts, as European reactions to the long arm of American anti-trust have shown; and if national anti-trust is not applied to them, the vast and growing international sector of the economy escapes any such legal control – unless anti-trust laws are introduced at the international level. This is the logic behind the Community's anti-trust activity, which has been among its most successful policies. Here, the Community law necessarily takes precedence over the member states' laws where transactions affecting intra-Community trade are concerned. To this extent, the Community law is supranational rather than parallel. Yet the national jurisdictions remain for cases that do not involve intra-Community trade; and the national courts administer the Community law, while the Community court is available for appeals. So the national laws and courts continue to apply; and the national and the Community systems operate in parallel, even if for some purposes they have been unified.

This suggests that the concept of parallel instruments can be used at a certain level of aggregation. Despite the precedence for Community anti-trust law where intra-Community transactions are concerned, the Community and the national laws and courts are certainly operating in parallel if we consider the application of anti-trust laws to business in the Community as a whole. Perhaps, with the growth of intra-Community transactions, the Community share in this field of law will become the more important. But if we aggregate it with other fields of commercial law, the concept of parallel Community and national systems, rather than of supranationalism and subordination, will surely remain valid for a very long time.

If one aggregates the several branches of external economic policy, one finds that the unification of the external tariff is still balanced by the national retention of currencies, with overseas aid, contributions to commodity schemes and various other instruments shared between Community and member states; so the Community and member states still act in parallel in external economic policy taken as a whole. The justification for common action in this field by the Community members, as small and medium powers in a harsh world economy, is rather strong, however; and if the parallel currency realises its full potential, external economic policy will become mainly a Community function. But if we extend the aggregation either to external relations or to economic policy in general, we will still find that the Community's activity, taken as a whole, is parallel, not superior, to that of the member states.

Generalising the concept to the limit, we could say that a Community whose whole set of instruments, fully aggregated, was equivalent to that of one of the major member states would be a parallel Community, neither superior nor subordinate to the member states but an equal alongside them. If this is not the usual view of what a well-developed Community would be like, the centralising concept propagated by many Europeanists may be to blame. The common market itself, if reduced to a witch-hunt against any 'distortion of competitive conditions', can become the enemy of diversity and autonomy; and some neo-liberal purists together with Jacobin centralisers have combined to give it more than an element of this. Those with a centralist view of political organisation may, conversely, prefer to retain their national capital as the exclusive centre; and it is no accident that Britain and France, as the most centralised states in the Community, contain so many last-ditch defenders of national sovereignty, who believe that the development of the Community can lead only to a tightly centralised superstate.

Neo-functionalists have reflected the centralist view, with the idea that spill-over would continue until all important functions had been transferred from the member states to the Community.[9] But the economic pressure towards the transference of all major functions to the same level was less than those neo-functionalists thought. Since the member states retained the preponderance of policy instruments and political power, moreover, they would almost certainly have clawed functions back from the Community if the separation of functions between Community and states had been found untenable. As it was, the governments have quite easily resisted any seeping away of power to the Community. So long, indeed, as political and bureaucratic elites in major member countries see the exercise of new functions by the Community as leading to a centralised superstate, they are likely to resist proposals to increase the Community's capacity for action. This harms the interests of all the member countries, for their mutual economic interdependence, and their common economic and political insecurity as small and middle powers in an uncertain world, demand greater capacity for common action than the Community now has; and the need is continuing to increase.

Decentralised Federalism?

If the Community is to develop, then, we need a less centralist idea for its development. The parallel Community, itself disposing of resources of the order of those of a major member state, could be such an idea. Various names may be given to it, such as extranational (rather than supranational) Europe, or Europe as a middle power.[10] Although the monolingual federations such as Australia, the German Federal Republic, or the United States are much more heavily centralised, it is not so different from federalism as seen by the Swiss. But what is suggested here differs in three respects from the concept of federalism to be found in many writers on the subject.[11]

First, policy instruments have been stressed rather than functions or powers. This may reflect a way in which the character of government in the modern state differs from that of the eighteenth or nineteenth century. It certainly does reflect the observation that the Community is ineffectual when it tries to act in a given field solely through member states' policy instruments, even if it has formally been given a function in that field.

Secondly, the political weight of the Community as such is introduced as a concept, with the aim of making it equivalent to that of a major member state; and this weight is related to the importance of the sum total of instruments given to the Community, which would likewise be equivalent, in some senses, to that of a major member state. The correlation between the instrumentarium and the political weight will be very far from perfect; instruments will not necessarily confer legitimacy or be used effectively. But adequate instruments are one of the conditions of political weight, alongside legitimacy and effective institutions.

Thirdly, most of the literature on federalism has laid more stress than this chapter on the form of the political and legal institutions. It is, again, a matter of observation that the Community, despite the political weakness of its constitution, has succeeded in acting when it has a common instrument such as the external tariff. The governments have reached agreement when the need to deploy the common instrument required them to do so. Yet the largely intergovernmental method is slow and indecisive, gives formidable blocking power to a recalcitrant defender of the status quo, and is undemocratic in reaching decisions by the method of a diplomatic conference rather than a parliamentary democracy. If the Community gains new responsibilities as well as new members, overload on the already creaking system would make these problems worse; and the intergovernmental method might prove unable to deliver the decisions that the Community and its member countries need. A move towards parliamentary democracy at the Community level is the obvious solution for a group of states which are all parliamentary democracies. Perhaps the idea of an extranational Community, which does not greatly reduce the sum of instruments in the hands of member states or acquire preponderant political weight, would allay much of the resistance to giving the Community a more democratic and efficient system, based on a greater role and powers for its elected Parliament alongside the Council of Ministers.

From the Parallel Currency to Extranational Europe

Although the idea of the parallel instrument was introduced in this chapter as a way of ensuring monetary co-operation without requiring an impracticable degree of convergence, it can be seen to have a wide application to the development of the Community. The parallel currency is certainly one of the most important examples, for which the European Monetary System provides a promising springboard. If the European Monetary Fund and the reserve role of the ECU evolve as foreseen, and a start is made in promoting the ECU's commercial use, a parallel instrument will become central to the conduct of economic policy in the Community.

There should also be much scope for the use of parallel instruments in other fields of policy. It is suggested that a thorough study of these possibilities should be made in the Community institutions and by member governments, particularly in fields such as energy policy, industrial policy, foreign policy and security, where the need for common action may be particularly strong. This could be expected to result in a set of proposals for new instruments, whether legal and regulatory or financial and budgetary, to be established alongside both the monetary ones and those others which already exist.

Although there is severe resistance to the increase of budgetary expenditure in the Community, the MacDougall Report[12] suggested that the Community Budget could usefully be expanded from less than 1 per cent to 2½ per cent of gross Community product. As this expansion at the Community level would be paid for partly by savings from national budgets, this does not seem an impossible order of increase during, say, the 1980s, provided that governments are persuaded that the common action which the expenditure makes possible will be sufficiently useful to the member countries.

With a parallel currency and a substantial parallel budget, together with a set of parallel legal instruments, the Community as a collective entity would possess the resources of a middle power, at least in the economic field. Extranational Europe would have become a major reality. The member countries might then conclude that this parallel Community meets their needs for common action. If they do, there would certainly be no automatic spill-over to the accretion of more functions to the Community. The political weight of the member states would remain too important for that. Thus the Community on this scale could remain for a long time in equilibrium with the member states. If on the other hand the member countries found the time was ripe to lock their parities irrevocably to the ECU and thus in effect replace the national currencies by the common currency, or if for other reasons they found it desirable to tilt the balance towards the European or federal institutions, they would be well placed to carry out their political decisions to do so. Meanwhile, extranationalism and a medium-power parallel Community might provide the concept that is needed if we are to move towards a new and more dynamic phase of Community development, compatible with both the needs for common action and the facts of economic divergence.

Notes: Chapter 10

1 Following Magnifico's original coining of the term 'propensity to inflation', in his *European Monetary Unification* (Macmillan, London, 1973), p. 13.

2 J. Williamson and G. Magnifico, *European Monetary Integration* (Federal Trust, London, 1972).

3 *The Economist*, 1 November 1975.

4 *Towards Economic Equilibrium and Monetary Unification in Europe*, Optica Report 1975, Commission of the European Communities, II/909/75-E final, 16 January 1976.

5 'The European Union', *Bulletin of the European Communities*, Supplement 5/75, Brussels, 1975.

6 L. Tsoukalis, *The Politics and Economics of European Monetary Integration* (Allen & Unwin, London, 1977), p. 151.

7 Williamson and Magnifico, op. cit.

8 For example the All Saints' Day statement (note 3).

9 See, for example, Leon Lindberg and Stuart Scheingold, *Europe's Would-Be Polity* (Prentice-Hall, Englewood Cliffs, NJ, 1970), p. 68.

10 Some have been tried out in John Pinder, 'Europe as a tenth member of the Community', *Government and Opposition*, London, Autumn 1975; and 'Das Extranationale Europa', *Integration* 1/78, Bonn, 1978.

11 For example, W. Ivor Jennings, *A Federation for Western Europe* (Cambridge University Press, Cambridge, 1940); Patrick Ransome (ed.), *Studies in Federal Planning* (Macmillan, London, 1943); K. C. Wheare, *Federal Government*, 2nd edn (Oxford University Press, London, 1951).

12 *Report of the Study Group on the Role of Public Finance in European Integration* (Commission of the European Communities, Brussels, April 1977).

11

Conclusions

William Wallace

The problem of economic divergence came to preoccupy the Community at the end of the 1970s, in the wake of the economic, monetary and energy crises which coincided with the first enlargement, and in anticipation of the difficulties which the second round of enlargement was likely to pose. Yet — as previous chapters have argued — the underlying issues have a much longer history, and a much longer-term significance. The analysis of Daniel Jones's chapter makes it clear that the underlying trends of divergence in structure and performance are secular phenomena. In the case of Britain and Germany, it is possible to trace the divergence in performance and the distinctive strengths and weaknesses which underlay this to the early years of the twentieth century; though the pattern for France and Italy is less unilinear. The Community may have failed to reverse these trends, but it can in no way be held responsible for bringing them about. The crises of 1973–5 and the consequent sharpened divergence in monetary parities, inflation rates and patterns of economic recovery re-emphasised these differences, perhaps even exaggerated them; but, again, they cannot be said to have created the problem.

It should also be clear that the convergence issue carries echoes of arguments about the Community's objectives and proper role which go back through the 1960s to the Treaty of Rome and before. Some members of the Spaak Committee were well aware of the awkward questions of economic policy co-ordination and of regional imbalance which lay beyond the initial stages of the removal of barriers and the establishment of the customs union; but they recognised that this was a political minefield, and prudently left it for later resolution within a Community which they hoped would by then have become sufficiently integrated to withstand the strains which open debate of these issues would impose. It is hardly surprising, therefore, that Article 2 of the Rome Treaty is open to different interpretations, and that the only specific reference to 'reducing the differences existing between the various regions and the backwardness of the less favoured regions' is in the Preamble. To have confronted the differences between French and German conceptions of economic policy, or to have considered directly how far the Community should assume the responsibility for assisting the development of the Italian Mezzogiorno, would have threatened the successful conclusion of the negotiations.

The Treaty was very thin on the objectives and instruments of economic policy. Article 103 commits member states to 'regard their conjunctural [short-term economic] policies as a matter of common concern'; Article 105 states that member states 'shall co-ordinate their economic policies', but only in pursuit of the objectives of maintaining balance-of-payments equilibrium and 'confidence' in their currencies. As so often repeated in later debates and proposals, it was easier to agree on monetary collaboration than on the other dimensions of economic policy. The Treaty therefore established a Monetary Committee, and indicated its objectives, but postponed for later discussion the institutions and objectives of other aspects of economic co-operation.

There were, it is true, some limited attempts to broach these difficult issues during the Community's first decade. A Conjunctural Policy Committee was set up in March 1960, in pursuance of Article 103. In April and May 1964 the Council of Ministers agreed to establish three further committees of national officials to promote the co-ordination of economic policies – a Medium-Term Policy Committee, a Budgetary Policy Committee and a Committee of Central Bank Governors to strengthen co-operation in monetary policy and in managing the exchanges (this last reflecting the extent to which the Monetary Committee had already come to concentrate on the co-ordination of policies towards international monetary co-operation). The Commission's Proposals of 31 March 1965 on financing the Common Agricultural Policy and on independent revenue for the Community included (in Article 5) the requirement that 'If . . . the Commission provides for payments to the Member States, it shall take into account the economic and social situation in the different regions of the Community and the need to ensure that burdens are equitably shared within the Community'; the accompanying explanatory memorandum dared even to refer to 'redistribution'.[1] But other parts of these ambitious proposals sparked off the dispute which culminated in the Luxembourg Compromise, in which such advanced ideas were put on one side.

In spite of this check to the too easily assumed momentum of economic integration, 'the extremely favourable conditions for the creation of the customs union in the 1960s created an erroneous impression about the role of unconstrained choice of objectives and of political will exercised in pursuit of them by the Community'.[2] Thus, in the aftermath of the retirement of President de Gaulle and the devaluation of the French franc in 1969, the Commission and national governments chose to ignore the increasingly unsettled international environment and to use as the vehicle for launching the second stage of economic integration the 'technicians' scheme' put forward by the Werner Committee. The hope, again, was that early experience of successful collaboration in the monetary sphere would provide sufficient momentum to carry the Six on towards Economic Union over the hard choices about conflicting priorities in economic policy, about the distribution of resources, and above all about the transfer of authority away from national governments, which the Werner Committee had lightly touched on and left for later decision. The politicians and experts who participated in the whole attempt to launch Economic and Monetary Union were, of course, distantly aware of the strains which progress might impose upon the Community's weaker economies. But it was easy to accept the monetarist prescription as the way forward, to assume that convergence of policies would bring about convergence of performance, and to trust in the apparent dynamism of the Italian economy – and to conclude that such problems as would occur would be temporary and minor.

The problem of divergence similarly loomed in the background of the negotiations for the first enlargement, without ever fully emerging into the light. The British government chose not to complicate the difficulties of entry by raising fundamental issues; the Irish government put its faith in the likely benefits of the CAP. The issue of the Regional Development Fund was thus played tactically, as the *quid pro quo* for Britain's contribution to the CAP, rather than as an essential part of the Community's commitment to 'strengthen the unity' of its member states' economies 'and to ensure their harmonious development' – the phrase in the Treaty Preamble which its negotiators took to quoting six years later.[3] The Commission, as guardian of the Community interest, registered its concern about the imbalance in the pace of expansion between the richer and the poorer regions, and bluntly stated that 'rapid progress towards Economic and Monetary Union would be arrested if . . . excessive divergencies between the economies of Member States' were not avoided by positive measures of policy.[4] But the Commission was only a minor actor in the bargaining between Britain, Germany and France over the size and shape of the RDF.

The impact of the 1973 Middle East War and its aftermath, however, transformed the discussion of economic policies and priorities within the Community, and brought the issue of divergence – or, at least, some aspects of the issue of divergence – to the fore. Movements in exchange rates were worrying in themselves, reflecting and reinforcing widening differences in inflation rates as member states struggled with varying success to absorb the increased cost of imported energy and to pay for that energy through increasing exports. The stronger European economies were thus immediately concerned with the threat of imported inflation, and with the implications of continuing divergence in exchange rates for the CAP and for the Community as a whole. Less immediately apparent were the fundamental strains which the necessity for more rapid economic and industrial adjustment placed on the Community's weaker economies, as the pressures of international recession, increased raw material prices and heightened competition for international markets weighed down the sluggish British and Italian economies with problems which the established dynamism of the German economy was sufficient to overcome.

The sober and gloomy conclusions of the Marjolin Report, from a study group commissioned to examine progress towards 'Economic and Monetary Union 1980' in the adverse conditions of 1974, explicitly pulled together for the first time most of the central themes of the convergence/divergence debate. It sharply criticised 'the centrifugal movement which characterises national policies' – and which had come to characterise national policies in response to increasing international economic and monetary turbulence even before the shocks of 1973. It noted the absence of 'Community solidarity' in the aftermath of the 1973 shocks, as undermining the political assumptions on which the commitment to economic union had been made. It noted also the progressive 'concentration of wealth to the detriment of certain peripheral regions', accepting the arguments of regional policy exponents that the workings of a common market tend to reinforce existing imbalances rather than to spread benefits equally or promote convergence. Though it laid much stress on the reassertion of 'political will' as the key to overcoming this succession of setbacks, it listed among the 'necessary decisions to bring nearer the time when the creation of an Economic and Monetary Union might be seriously envisaged . . . the establishment of a Community budget on such a scale that the important transfers which the maintenance of Economic and Monetary Union will require can take place and be financed out of Community taxation'. 'The need for a large-scale regional policy', it added, 'is urgent'; venturing beyond a simple regional fund to consider investment incentives for disadvantaged regions and to touch on such delicate and difficult issues as Community support for unemployment benefits and social security transfers.[5] These arguments have since been taken further, in the MacDougall Report on *The Role of Public Finance in European Integration*,[6] and in the series of published and unpublished papers which accompanied the formulation of the European Monetary System – though the evident absence of sufficient political will within the member states to support anything more than modest additional burdens in conditions of economic recession has led to increased preoccupation within successive Commission proposals with minimalist schemes which might somehow combine acceptability with effectiveness.

The arguments of 1978–80, in the context of the establishment of the EMS and the Budget controversy, have however helped to clarify the terms of the debate and to force all member governments to consider the underlying problems. A report from the European Parliament's Economic and Monetary Affairs Committee on progress with the EMS (the Ruffolo Report), in April 1980, still found it necessary to criticise 'the ambiguity as to the real meaning of "convergence"' and of 'parallel measures'; noting that the weaker economies had allowed the issue to be reduced to a struggle over the reallocation of Budget contributions and receipts, while the wealthier member states still identified convergence with economic stabilisation and the reduction of inflation.[7] But the 'Conclusions' of successive European Councils from Bremen on reflect a gradual acceptance of a wider definition. The carefully negotiated language of the Conclusions of the Paris European Council of March 1979, in phrases hard-fought between the British and German delegations, commit the Community explicitly to a concern with 'increased convergence of the economic policies *and performances* of the Member States' (my italics), and charge the Council of Ministers (Economic and Financial Affairs) and the Commission 'to examine in depth how the Community could make a greater contribution, by means of all its policies taken as a whole, to achieving greater convergence of the economies of the Member States *and to reduce the disparities between them*'. The Conclusions of the Dublin Council of November 1979 'expressed its determination ... to reinforce those policies most likely to favour the harmonious growth of the economies of the Member States and to reduce the disparities between these economies. They further declared the need, particularly with a view to the enlargement of the Community and necessary provisions for Mediterranean agriculture, to strengthen Community action in the *structural field*.'

What Lies Behind the Convergence Debate?

The debate about convergence and divergence has, of course, been for many of its participants fundamentally about the necessary conditions for economic union. Divergences in economic policy and performance derailed the first, ill-thought-out, attempt at Economic and Monetary Union. Successive Commission study groups were therefore detailed to diagnose the problem more deeply and to prescribe more subtle remedies. The Community remains in principle and in rhetoric committed to European Union, a concept less precise even than that of convergence but which necessarily implies economic union as an integral aim. Explicitly to abandon that aim would be to throw into question the whole ideological underpinning of the Community. The Commission, as institutionally charged with the promotion and protection of the Community interest, must therefore address itself to the removal of obstacles to economic union, and strive to persuade member governments to agree to the actions necessary. In so far as the EMS may be seen as a cautious step forward towards EMU – which was certainly the Commission's perspective – the arguments over parallel measures were thus a direct continuation of the discussions in 1970 about the economic dimensions of the Werner Plan and the controversy in 1972–4 over regional policy.

Commitment to the eventual aim of economic union overlapped with the much more immediate concern, both within the Commission and within many member governments, that the Community's established common policies, the *acquis communautaire*, would be put at risk if trends within different national economies remained so disparate. Part of the impetus for the initial attempt at Economic and Monetary Union, after all, lay in the fears of the French government and others that divergence in exchange rates would threaten the CAP. By the late 1970s, there were understandable fears – as Stephen Woolcock notes – that the difficulties of the weaker economies and the increasing imbalance between the strong and the weak would progressively undermine the common market itself. Anthony Crosland, in his 'presidential' speech to the European Parliament on 12 January 1977, remarked that divergences in economic performance had now increased 'to an extent that in practice rules out major measures of integration'. His successor as Foreign Secretary and President of the Council of Ministers, David Owen, asserted more strongly that 'were the present trends of economic divergence to become firmly established, they would present a serious threat to the cohesion of the Community'.[8] Few in other governments disputed his analysis – even though they resisted the British proposals to alleviate the problem. The debate has thus in another sense been about preventing the Community's disintegration, and about considering what changes in national and Community policies might be necessary to prevent the re-erection of barriers to trade.

From another perspective, the debate of 1978–80 was about the Community Budget and its distribution of costs and benefits. Since of the three 'weaker economies' Britain was by far the most disadvantaged in terms of receipts, this appeared to be primarily a British problem – all the more so because the British defined it in those terms, and thus failed to create and sustain an alliance with their less prosperous partners. During much of the discussion over the EMS in 1978 Ireland and Italy worked in informal alliance, successfully gaining some useful concessions on interest rates and EIB loans as a compensation for joining the scheme, with Britain offering only wavering support. Thereafter the Irish government, as a massive beneficiary from the CAP, was satisfied, though the Italians continued to maintain their concern with the broad issues of convergence – as they had in related negotiations ever since the drafting of the Rome Treaty. The British government rested its case for adjustment of its budgetary receipts and contributions primarily on grounds of equity, using the Treaty's commitment to promote harmonious and balanced development as a supporting argument. But in so doing it reduced the scope of the debate about convergence and divergence into a battle over figures and financial transactions, instead of a wider concern with the impact of Community policies as a whole. The dominance of the Budget issue in arguments over convergence in this period is demonstrated by the repeated appearance, in agendas for European Councils and official drafts, of the combined heading 'Convergence and Budgetary Questions'.

For the French, as Jonathan Story points out, and less directly for other member states, the problem of convergence and divergence is also the problem of Germany. The rapidity of the German adjustment to the changes in energy costs in 1973–4, its success in containing the inflationary surge which followed, the continuing strength of its exports through repeated revaluations of the Deutsche Mark (which in themselves posed problems of balance for the other member states), all impressed and concerned Germany's less buoyant partners. A report from a 'Group of Experts' to the Commission in 1979 on 'Changes in industrial structure in the European economies since the oil crisis, 1973–8' (the Maldague Report) spelt out the extent to which the German economy had now distanced itself from the rest of the Community. 'The Federal Republic of Germany's industry is well ahead of that of its main Community partners', partly because it had become 'highly specialised . . . and . . . concentrated on products with a high technology input, requiring highly-qualified labour'. 'The Federal Republic of Germany is the only European Community country in as favourable a position as the United States and Japan' in terms of high skill and capital input into goods traded, and adjustments out of sectors in which the newly industrialising countries were becoming competitive; 'overall it is clearly a case apart from its EEC partners'. 'The position of France is less certain', while both Italy and Britain were clearly highly vulnerable to competition from faster-growing countries, and ill-supplied with new products to replace declining industries.[9] As Daniel Jones argues in his chapter, these all represent the continuation of trends established well before the shocks of 1973–5; but the effect of those shocks was to increase the pressures upon the Community's economies, and thus to increase the pace of divergence.

Divergence is not therefore a simple picture of a Community developing into two separate tiers, but of a range of divergent developments, in which only Germany (and to an extent also the Netherlands, as its closest economic associate) could afford to be concerned more about problems in other members' economies than in its own. The picture is complicated further when Greece, Spain and Portugal are included. Loukas Tsoukalis and Geoffrey Denton note the scale of the challenges which the second round of enlargement poses for the Community. The Commission's approach to enlargement, from its controversial *Opinion* on the Greek application (in January 1976) on, has been to emphasise the difficulties which it would pose for the existing balance of Community policies, and the consequent need for the Council to face up to the need for some major changes in that balance. This was, for example, the theme of Roy Jenkins's speech to the first Council of Ministers discussion on the implications of enlargement, in October 1977, which specifically raised the issues of reducing disparities and promoting convergence – arguing that 'the problem of the economic gap, which has long weakened the process of integration, is exacerbated by and central to the question of enlargement'.[10]

Initial reactions within the German SPD to the need to reinforce newly democratic governments with economic assistance led to discussions about a 'European Solidarity Fund', a Marshall Aid type of programme for the three applicants, to be financed by the more prosperous European countries. This emerged as a budget authorisation of DM500m., authorised by the Bundestag Finance Committee in January 1978; but it was blocked by the Finance Ministry, and the proposal lost in the gathering arguments over the Community Budget and more specific demands for economic assistance to Turkey. In 1979–80 the argument over the Budget and convergence paid remarkably little attention to the linked problems raised by Greek entry in January 1981 and by the progress of the Spanish and Portuguese negotiations; the agreement on Britain's contributions to the Budget for 1980–2, finally reached at the end of May 1980, appeared not to have taken into account that Greece would be a member of the Community for two of the three years covered. But the complications of enlargement were at the back of the minds of most of those involved in the whole convergence debate from 1977 onwards.

The Implications for the Community

As we have seen, the Treaty of Rome committed its signatories to the principle of economic convergence, but refrained from spelling out any of the implications of such a commitment. The economies of four of the original six members – the Benelux and Federal Germany – were already closely linked; the French were prepared, in the end, to stake their hopes on a successful trade-off between agricultural and industrial free trade. The problem of the sixth member, Italy, was recognised and alleviated by the inclusion of the European Social Fund and the European Investment Bank. But the general expectation that the Community would generate more rapid growth, and its realisation under favourable international circumstances in the early 1960s, pushed the issue of how balanced that growth might be into the background. The assumptions of economic integration theory that market integration brought benefits for all – in effect, brought about an automatic process of complementarity – were thus easy to accept. They enabled governments to avoid acrimonious argument on issues of economic and budgetary policy which would have sharply divided them.[11] The absence of any substantial economic critique of the assumptions of market integration also made it easier to accept such an optimistic approach; with few exceptions, economic studies of regional imbalance and of the possibility that market integration reinforces imbalance did not emerge until after the common market had been created.

By 1980 most of these favourable conditions had ceased to apply. The end of the long period of rapid economic growth and its replacement by prolonged international recession unavoidably redirected attention away from the size of the cake and how fast it was rising to the distribution of the slices. The evident dynamism of the German economy in contrast to those of Britain and Italy (and south-western France), the phenomenon of the 'Golden Triangle' with its concentration of industry and services, have undermined the faith of all but the most dedicated free traders in the equitable effects of untrammelled market integration. The French government has proved itself much more successful than most had expected in 1958 at competing in industrial goods; but by the end of the 1970s it was becoming much less certain that the CAP operated to its advantage, rather than to that of Germany.[12] A Community of Nine was already notably different in the balance of economic interests from the original Six. A Community of Twelve, stretching from Salonika to Lisbon and from the Straits of Gibraltar to the Skaggerak, would be fundamentally different in the spread and diversity of economic interests from the original grouping, of which all but Italy shared a common heartland in the Rhine valley and delta and northern France.

Increased concern about the problem of divergence and the role which Community policies play – and could play – in exacerbating or alleviating it is therefore understandable. Unfortunately, it is equally understandable that opinions on the appropriate Community response are diverse. Economists of different schools and in different member states are further away from consensus on the instruments and objectives of economic policy than they were twenty years ago; the advice available to the Commission and to member governments is therefore various, at times even contradictory. Important national and sectional interests are at stake: that of German industry in preventing its dynamism being inhibited by restrictive measures to aid industrial development in the weaker countries, those of the national finance ministries which would be asked to contribute more to an expanded budget and of those other finance ministries who would hope to receive more, regional interests both in the less prosperous and the more prosperous states, and so on.

Since the Community is clearly not primarily responsible for the problem of divergence, it is open to argument how far it should now assume the responsibility for its correction – or how far it *can* assume that responsibility. The Conclusions of the Paris European Council in March 1979 emphasise, in language which owes much to the efforts and arguments of the German government, that 'achievement of the convergence of economic performances requires *measures for which the Member States concerned are primarily responsible*'; the Italian and British governments were largely responsible for the balancing phrase 'but in respect of which *Community policies can and must play a supporting role* within the framework of increased solidarity' (my italics). Self-evidently, the social, political and economic contexts within which British and Italian policies are framed are important factors in their long-term tendency towards economic weakness. These, their more successful partners have argued in private, require national action to alter, to bring down the rate of inflation and to raise the level of investment, to change the attitudes of management and labour. To ask the more prosperous countries to burden their own economies and possibly to restrict their own industrial and economic growth, through financial transfers, crisis cartels and industrial location policies, without requiring the less prosperous to look to their own failings, would result in wasted resources and a general lowering of the Community's economic capacities. Politicians and economists from the stronger economies have therefore naturally tended to hold to the benign view of market integration, to emphasise the importance of political action to deal with structural problems by the less prosperous states themselves, and to insist that Community action must be ancillary to this.[13] Theirs is an argument with much plausibility when the subject is Italy or Britain – but hardly applicable to the situation of Greece, Portugal, or Spain when they enter the Community.

A further and major conceptual problem in considering the

appropriate Community response is the scepticism of economists and the uncertainty of politicians about how best to correct regional imbalances and promote convergence. The record of regional policies within the member states is mixed, in spite of a range of instruments and a scale of financial transfers far more extensive than the Community could hope to aspire to. Financial transfers to disadvantaged regions may simply enable the postponement of economic adjustments which are needed, instead of encouraging change. Automatic inter-regional transfers through social security systems, pension payments and fiscal equalisation schemes are characteristics of unified states and of developed federations with large federal budgets, extremely difficult to envisage on a Community basis within the foreseeable future. Radical solutions such as a Community input into long-term subsidies for employment costs in disadvantaged regions, to encourage inward investment and discourage outward migration, are faced with formidable barriers in economic and financial orthodoxy.[14]

Yet the Community cannot avoid some sort of response. Leaving aside the exact interpretation of the opening phrases of the Rome Treaty, there are three reasons why the Community has to be concerned to reduce divergence and promote convergence: the distributive and redistributive effects of its current Budget and common policies, the expectations of its weaker members and the renewed commitment to make the Community 'an area of monetary stability' (in the words of the Presidency Conclusions from the Strasbourg European Council in June 1979) through the establishment and further development of the EMS.

In the course of the controversy over the British contribution to the Budget, in 1978–80, a great deal of evidence was collected on the distributive effects of the Community Budget and on the impact of common policies on the terms of intra-Community trade. Their incontestable conclusions were that the Community was already redistributing resources, primarily through the CAP, in a perverse manner. The effects of agricultural trade and transfers were strongly to the advantage of the Netherlands and Denmark, two of the most prosperous members of the Community, and to the disadvantage of Britain – and would be as strongly to the disadvantage of Portugal, as a substantial agricultural exporter, on its accession. The CAP's effects were also regressive *within* member states, raising the income of prosperous as well as marginal farmers at the expense of consumers. The redistributive effects of Community policies were therefore to reinforce divergence rather than reduce it: at once at odds with the Community's declared objectives and politically unaccept-able to the disadvantaged states. Those who benefited from the current *acquis* still maintained the argument that this was simply a secondary effect of the Community's common policies, and that deliberate redistribution of resources was not an objective of the Treaty; but this was an increasingly difficult position to maintain in the face of the evidence and the protests of the disadvantaged.[15]

Whether or not the promotion of convergence was an aim of the Community on its establishment, the expectation that membership would have 'dynamic effects' on their economies has been shared by all applicants – except perhaps for Denmark, which was already heavily dependent on its economic ties with Britain and Germany. The anticipation of direct and indirect economic benefits from entry was fulfilled in the case of Ireland, largely because of the operations of the CAP. It was disappointed in Britain, partly because successive British governments had underestimated the severity of the weaknesses of their domestic economy, partly because Britain's entry coincided with international economic crisis and the end of the era of fast growth. An understandable sense of grievance and disappointment therefore adversely affected Britain's political relations with its partners in the Community. Greece, Spain and Portugal in their turn all approached the Community in the expectation of gaining direct and indirect economic benefits from membership – expectations not necessarily any better founded than those of Britain. If the other member states attach political importance to their adhesion and satisfied membership – and the commitment to enlargement, in both the first and the second rounds, was fundamentally political – the predictable outcome if these hopes were disappointed would be to undermine, perhaps even destroy, the political objectives of entry.

The close link between convergence and moves towards economic union has been noted above. What needs to be questioned further is how seriously the Community and its members – above all its more prosperous members – are committed to economic union. This in turn takes us back to the underlying question of the Community's objectives and its member governments' perceptions of the purpose of membership. If the Community was fundamentally a political creation, of which the economic expression was a convenient symbol and path forward, then the continued reality of shared political aims and interests might be sufficient to hold it together despite economic divergence and imbalance. The rhetoric of economic union might still be rehearsed, in obeisance to the stated objectives of the founders; but the unwillingness of member governments to breathe life into the concept of economic union, while demonstrating their commitment to co-operation in other fields, would point to the underlying realities of a limited but valued political community.

The argument can be advanced further along these lines that divergence is thus not a vital problem for the future of the Community. The European Community has, after all, survived a considerable period of economic divergence without collapse and without more than temporary checks to its political progress. Certainly, it is important that the workings of the Community should help rather than hinder the economic prospects of its weaker members; the British problem (and potentially the problems presented by the new Mediterranean members) did therefore present real difficulties. But the Community was held together by sets of expectations and interests other than simply economic advantage. Shared political commitments, to democratic governments within Western Europe and to an open and stable international order outside, shared concerns about the Atlantic alliance and American leadership and about the Soviet threat, shared advantages in acting as a caucus in international negotiations both on economic and on security issues, now provided the real cement of European co-operation.

This argument cannot be dismissed lightly. The motives which led the original Six to negotiate and accept the Treaties of Paris and Rome were at least as much political as economic; so were those which led Britain and Ireland (though not Denmark) to apply, and which led in their turn Greece, Portugal and Spain to follow. The political dimension of European co-operation seemed all the more important in 1980, in an international environment dominated by an uncertain United States and an expansionist Soviet Union, and all the more firmly established with the democratic authority of the directly elected European Parliament and the regular and close relations between governments from the European Council downwards. But it ignores the close and mutually dependent relationship between political and economic factors, which has been a central characteristic of the European Community since the creation of the ECSC. For the German public and their political and industrial leaders, the Community has been the framework through which they have regained international acceptance and influence. But it has also been the framework for the sustained expansion of their economy – and it is the coincidence of these which has made the German commitment to the Community so strong. For successive British governments, the strongest arguments for joining and remaining in the Community were political; the economic case was always doubtful. Dissatisfaction with the perceived economic disadvantages, however, spilled over into political attitudes to the Community, among both leaders and public. Whether the Community is at bottom primarily a political or an economic undertaking is in this sense immaterial; it has to be *both*, to provide demonstrable benefits for its members both in the economic and the political sphere if it is to maintain its cohesion.

The relationship between political influence and economic strength is extraordinarily difficult to describe; but that there is a relationship, that governments see such a relationship, is clear. The French government's preoccupation with the German economy and its attempts to keep abreast of it were at once political and economic, fearing that to fall behind a dominant German economy would force it also to accept German political influence. The hostility of the British government, in particular, to suggestions about a 'two-tier' Community owed much to the fear that acceptance of a second-class status in economic terms would unavoidably carry political implications. The growing German self-confidence in foreign policy and in political relations with its partners during the 1970s owed much to the consciousness of economic success, just as the increasing British hesitation owed much to the consciousness of economic failure.

The most direct link between political and economic influence is of course provided by the leverage economic instruments supply for political ends. European aid to Turkey, in response to Turkish pleas and American pressure in conditions of rising East–West tension in 1979–80, meant above all German aid; the British, Irish and Italian governments contributed far less, and accepted that their influence was thus also lessened. It is not only in external policy, however, that economic leverage carries political implications. Within the Community, as within the IMF, creditor nations expect to exert influence over the policies of debtor nations, and resist attempts to influence their own policies in return. The issue at stake in the argument among member governments over a parity grid or a currency basket basis for the European Monetary System was about whether the weaker economies could avoid being forced to take the full strain of policy adjustment within a fixed rate or crawling peg system. Their demand for 'symmetrical rights and obligations' was essentially political: an attempt to frame the rules of the EMS so that strong economies (most of all Germany) would also have to accept the obligation to adjust domestic policies when their currency diverged from those of their partners. It was a measure of the political advantage which economic strength provides that the 'divergence indicator' which resulted bound the German government to respect the 'obligations' of a strong economy to its weaker partners much less than the majority of member governments had initially desired. The issue of conditionality in Community loans and funding is of similar character, reflecting the understandable attitude of those who provided the largest contributions to such transfers that they should have some say in the way such funds are used and the policies they support.[16] But such a claim to 'Mitspracherrecht' is naturally less welcome to the recipient countries, who see in such economic leverage an interference in their domestic policy-making which has no counterpart for them in their efforts to influence the policies of the more prosperous.

We are thus talking about an essentially political process, in which the different member governments (and the parties, groups and lobbies which influence them) pursue economic interest and advantage, using the political and economic instruments available to them. The rules, policies and stated objectives of the Community are a significant resource for the actors in this political process. Thus arguments over the intentions of the founding fathers, attempts to define – and redefine – the objectives of economic co-operation, appeals to 'Community solidarity' or the *acquis communautaire*, are part and parcel of the process of political bargaining among the member states. Motives and concerns are almost always mixed, for all governments; bending the objectives and rules of the Community to support immediate interests, but at the same time bearing in mind their commitment to maintaining the Community, and the necessity therefore of playing the game within the rules. It is characteristic of this process that the Luxembourg European Council in April 1980 found itself debating a draft on the 'fundamental principles' of the Community as an integral part of its efforts to reach a compromise on the budgetary dispute. It is characteristic, too, that the French representatives attempted to substitute for the Presidency's draft a longer statement which included commitments to exports of food and the maintenance of family farming concerns among this list of principles.[17]

The Treaty is sufficiently explicit about the economic aims of European co-operation to support the arguments of the less prosperous countries – half the membership in a Community of Twelve, accepting the definition of 'less prosperous' hammered out by the Economic Policy Committee in the context of the EMS negotiations – that positive action is required to reduce divergence. Their case that Community policies and financial transfers should, at the least, not have the effect of promoting divergence is particularly difficult for the more prosperous to resist. A minimalist interpretation of what response is required of the Community would thus be that the structural reform of the Budget, agreed in principle in the settlement of the dispute over Britian's contribution in May 1980 but left for later definition in detail, should lead to a pattern of contributions and receipts which bore some relation to the capacities and needs of member states; that regional policies should be further developed; and that the Community should pay more attention in its competition policies, rules on state aids and industrial adjustment measures, and in its trade policy, to the needs of its less prosperous members. Such a response could be accommodated within the current framework of Community co-operation, without raising major issues of institutional change and the transfer of authority.

A more ambitious interpretation of the response needed would however raise major political issues. If, for example, a recognition among the more prosperous that the advantages of monetary stability, or the preservation of the common market, justified financial and policy concessions were combined with a concerted effort by the less prosperous to promote more integrated policies, then the promotion of convergence might become a more operational objective. The issues skirted and suppressed during the Spaak Committee, the Werner Committee and the whole debate over Economic and Monetary Union would then come to the surface: effective co-ordination of economic policies, as required by the more prosperous, a larger financial and policy-making role for the Community, industrial policies broadly defined, and − if the demands of the less prosperous were to be met − acceptance of a degree of discrimination in Community policies to redress the balance of advantages which an open market offers to the centrally situated and already successful. All of these presuppose a substantial degree of consensus on the objectives and priorities of economic policy and on the political values which they serve. To spell them out is to require a much closer definition of the 'decision-taking centre' which the Werner Report warned would be needed, 'the creation or transformation of a certain number of Community organs to which powers until then exercised by the national authorities will have to be transferred'.[18] Closer integration of economic policies thus implies closer political integration; the two go together.

Economics and Politics, Theory and Practice

In the confident years of the 1950s and 1960s economists claimed to be able to predict the consequences of pursuing different combinations of economic policies. Political scientists aimed to emulate them by careful examination of trends and the construction of theoretical frameworks within which they might be interpreted. The corpus of integration theories built up during the early years of European co-operation aspired to prediction, postulating a cumulative process through economic integration, sector by sector, towards a gradual transfer of political loyalties, and thus eventual political union. A degree of initial political commitment was of course necessary; but once an economic entity was established, it could be argued that 'the progression from politically inspired common market to an economic union to a political union amongst states is automatic'.[19] Economic causes, political consequences; political integration followed from economic integration. As with many economic theories, this perspective carried with it implicit political assumptions; and, again as with many economic theories, it became embedded in the rhetoric of several governments, though without being fully accepted or understood.

After the shocks and disappointments of the early 1970s, 'the idea which has been the basis for the past twenty years of the views of many Europeans, namely, that European political unity, particularly in the economic and monetary field, will come about in an almost imperceptible way', came to be widely questioned. 'It is clear that experience up to now shows nothing that supports the validity of this idea. One may legitimately wonder today if what may be required in order to create the conditions for an economic and monetary union is not perhaps on the contrary a radical and almost instantaneous transformation... giving rise at a precise point in time to European political institutions.'[20] What was needed, according to this alternative approach, was the reassertion of 'political will', rather than the accumulation of economic interests. It was a political commitment which had created the European Communities, overcoming a number of economic hesitations and obstacles; a political commitment to over-ride immediate economic concerns was the necessary condition for the transformation of European co-operation into union. From this perspective, economics follows politics: first the commitment, then the discovery of mutual economic benefit.

Looking at the process of European co-operation in 1980, one is struck far more by the number and variety of different forces at work. Some economic interests pull the Community members together, while others pull them apart. External threats and uncertainties provide powerful incentives for closer collaboration; but they also impose considerable strains on the uncompleted structure, leading to near-disintegration in conditions of crisis. Domestic constraints in the different states vary, as governments and elections come and go and the political context changes, but provide continuing limits to Community co-operation. Political leadership can in exceptional circumstances over-ride these limits, building new coalitions of interests, redefining priorities, easing the path to consensus; but changing political leadership can also make co-operation more difficult, as politicians pay domestic electoral debts and as they bring non-consensual attitudes into the intimate atmosphere of inter-governmental consultation.

The Community has made some significant political advances during the late 1970s, in the further development of Political Co-operation, in the move to a directly elected European Parliament, in the closer interlinking of its member governments through the whole network of meetings of which the European Councils provide the summit. It has made some significant economic advances as well, most notably in the establishment of the European Monetary System. But there have also been failures, both in economic and in political collaboration; it has proved extraordinarily difficult to adjust Community policies, except under crisis conditions, and the pace of collaboration has been painfully slow. It is hard to discern steady trends, either in the development of a political community or in the Community's capacities to manage economic integration. It is arguable that the strength provided by the close and extensive network of political consultation and by the commitment of the more prosperous countries to the maintenance of the Community's cohesion is now sufficient to offset the strains exerted by economic divergence. But it is evident from the preceding chapters that economic divergence *does* exert considerable strains on the political cohesion of the Community, which might well prove more than the limited achievements of political integration can bear.

There is no way the political scientist can predict how the Community will respond to the political problems posed by economic divergence. This should not be a matter for despair; in the uncertain conditions of the late 1970s, most economists too became less confident of their predictive powers, more cautious about the relationship between different trends. Politics is an intricate process, with a very large number of variables. All one can say with confidence is that the problem has now been placed firmly on the Community's political agenda; and that the prospect of enlargement will make it all the more sensitive an issue for a Community of twelve.

Notes: Chapter 11

1 Supplement no. 5 to *Bulletin of the EEC*, 1965.
2 Andrew Shonfield, 'The aims of the Community in the 1970s', *Report of the Study Group 'Economic and Monetary Union 1980'*, Vol. II (Commission of the European Communities, Brussels, 1975).
3 Helen Wallace, 'The establishment of the Regional Development Fund: common policy or pork barrel?', in Helen Wallace *et al.* (eds.), *Policy-Making in the European Communities* (Wiley, Chichester, 1977).
4 'Regional Problems in the Enlarged Community', *Bulletin of the European Communities*, Supplement 8/73.
5 *Report of the Study Group 'Economic and Monetary Union 1980'*, Vol. I (Commission of the European Communities, Brussels, 1975), pp. 2, 6, 15 and 34.
6 *Report of the Study Group on the Role of Public Finance in European Integration* (Commission of the European Communities, Brussels, 1977).
7 *The EMS as an Aspect of the International Monetary System*, Report of the Economic and Monetary Affairs Committee of the European Parliament (Ruffolo Report), Working Document No. 1/63/80, 1980.
8 House of Commons, 1 March 1977.
9 This report appeared as a special issue of *European Economy*, Commission of the European Communities, November 1979; the quotations are from pp. 43 and 79.
10 *Agence Europe*, 28 October 1977.
11 Jacques Pelkmans, 'Economic theories of integration revisited', *Journal of Common Market Studies*, June 1980, pp. 333.
12 Yao-Su Hu, 'German agricultural power: the impact on France and Britain', *The World Today*, November 1979; *L'Europe: les vingt prochaines années* (Commissariat Général du Plan, Paris, 1980).
13 See, for example, Carsten Thoroe, 'The transfer of resources: comment', in

William Wallace (ed.), *Britain in Europe* (Heinemann, London, 1980), pp. 153–7.

14 Wynne Godley, 'The United Kingdom and the Community Budget', in Wallace, op. cit., pp. 83–4, argues for such a Community 'Regional Employment Premium'.

15 See Geoffrey Denton's contribution on the Budget issue, above, Wynne Godley's chapter in Wallace, op. cit., and Helen Wallace, *Budgetary Politics: The Finances of the European Communities* (Allen & Unwin, London, 1980), particularly ch. 2.

16 Helen Wallace, op. cit., pp. 47–8.

17 *Agence Europe*, 28–29 April 1980.

18 Supplement no. 11 *Bulletin of the EEC*, 1970, p. 24. See also William Wallace, 'The administrative implications of Economic and Monetary Union within the European Community', *Journal of Common Market Studies*, 1974, pp. 410–45.

19 Ernst Haas, ' "The Uniting of Europe" and "The Uniting of Latin America" ', *Journal of Common Market Studies*, June 1967, p. 315.

20 Marjolin Report (note 5), p. 5.

Index